T0296148

Praise for *Indecent Advances*

"To shed light on these killings, the social conditions and psychological conflicts that gave rise to them, and the manipulative and sensationalist coverage that they often received in the press, the cultural historian James Polchin has written *Indecent Advances*, a grisly, sobering, comprehensively researched new history. The subject matter doesn't make for light reading; Polchin admits to feeling 'haunted' by what he discovered in archives. But it's impossible to understand gay life in twentieth-century America without reckoning with the dark stories. Gay men were unable to shake free of them until they figured out how to tell the stories themselves, in a new way." —CALEB CAIN, *The New Yorker*

"Important . . . A compelling account." —BILL BURTON, *Provincetown Banner*

"[A] fascinating new book on the treatment of gay men in true crime and crime fiction [that] reexamines the violence that people at the Stonewall Inn had faced every day, and the rage crackling up underneath . . . What makes Polchin's readings stand out is the way he pursues an underlying story across several seemingly separate crimes." —ALEXANDER CHEE, *The New Republic*

"*Indecent Advances* collects and rescues significant gay history and goes a long way toward clarifying why we fight, what we fight for and how prejudice is an historically institutional force." —TOM CARDAMONE, *Lambda Literary*

"Formidably researched . . . A significant contribution to queer history and to understanding the forces that shape contemporary queer identity . . . *Indecent Advances* is an important book not least of all because, as the Stonewall celebrations begin, it reminds us that queer identity has been shaped as much by trauma as by courage." —MICHAEL NAVA, *Los Angeles Review of Books*

"Polchin (liberal studies, New York Univ.) presents a reflective, thoughtful first book that perfectly blends true crime and the history of discrimination against gay men in the 20th century . . . His insightful history of crimes perpetrated against gay men is essential for social history fans. Readers who enjoy well-researched, deliberate social commentary will appreciate Polchin's enlightening and descriptive style."
—*Library Journal* (starred review)

"For readers searching for a fast-paced, meticulously researched, thoroughly engaging (and often infuriating) look-see into the systematic criminalization of gay men and widespread condemnation of homosexuality post–World War I, cultural historian James Polchin's first book, *Indecent Advances: A Hidden History of True Crime and Prejudice Before Stonewall*, is a smart bet."   —ALEXIS BURLING,
San Francisco Chronicle

"Beginning in the years before the Stonewall Riots, *Indecent Advances: A Hidden History of True Crime and Prejudice Before Stonewall* by James Polchin takes a look at the crimes committed against gay men, long before equality and rights were a notion, let alone even being on the table. Murder, of course, lines the pages of this book but you'll also read stories of harassment, assault and minor crimes that were embellished so that they could be charged as more serious. Polchin also looks at how criminal acts committed by and aimed at LGBT people came under controversy when attention was paid to one minority group's safety and not to that of another group. This, the embedded presence of many (in)famous criminals, and other stories lightly linked to Stonewall make it an interesting book."
—*Washington Blade*

"James Polchin has written an important book about a critical chapter of LGBT history, carefully documenting the victimization and discrimination that gay men suffered before Stonewall. Much has changed, but discrimination and hate crimes still go on, and there are still many battles left to fight and win. The stories in this book are often heartbreaking and brutal, but the larger story of oppression needed to be told."   —BILL BURTON, *The Gay & Lesbian Review/Worldwide*

"Polchin recounts the cases as a series of short thrillers organized by decade through the 20th century. These true stories remain suspenseful episodes of surprising brutality and sensationalized press. Polchin pays scholarly attention to the politics of each era, and tales that were once grisly exploitation of murder victims become tense examinations of journalism and detective work."

—DEVLYN CAMP, *Chicago Reader*

"Polchin's harrowing account of the history of violence against queer men hits shelves on the eve of the 50th anniversary of the Stonewall riots. It's perfect timing for a book that dives deep into these never-before-told true crimes, and looks at the power mainstream messaging had on both the violence and the mounting resistance. Resurrecting a forgotten era of queer history, Polchin masterfully weaves brutal true crime research with critical analysis of the social history, exploring the way the media and nascent psychological theories were weaponizing prejudice and perpetuating a deviant stereotype of gay men." —CAMILLE LeBLANC,
Literary Hub, One of the Most Anticipated Books of the Season

"Polchin's book illuminates the dark side of true crime reporting . . . Full of specific, brutal tales, this is a captivating and troubling read." —NICK YEAGER,
The Austin Chronicle

"A unique and interesting book." —*South Florida Gay News*

"There's seemingly no one better than Polchin to unearth and make sense of these stories . . . Both a social history and a true crime page-turner . . . *Indecent Advances* opened my eyes to a history I didn't know and pained me to learn . . . With *Indecent Advances* now in the world, a bit more honor has been restored to the lives of these men."
—CAMILLE LeBLANC, *CrimeReads*

"One book I have found indispensable this summer has been *Indecent Advances: A Hidden History of True Crime and Prejudice Before Stonewall* . . . The history of social (in)justice runs deep . . . [A] tremendous addition to that legacy."
—DAVE WHEELER, *Shelf Awareness*

"Polchin's deep dive into the history leading up to the riots underscores the difficulty of telling a story that's so bound up in myth—and the importance of doing it anyway . . . Polchin pulls the lives out of the archives with relentless precision in his book. The particularity of Polchin's accounts restores some honor to the memory of the men whose brutal stories tell." —JASON TOUGAW, *Electric Literature*

"James Polchin wants us to have the specifics. His book *Indecent Advances*, published this month by Counterpoint, collects and analyzes news reports of gay-related crime from the 1920s to the 1960s. The result is an act of witnessing that will reconfigure anyone who came of age after Stonewall. Once we know all this, we have to reckon differently with our country . . . It's almost unbearable to see this pattern of shame and violence so clearly laid out. How do we cope with these victims, who were only guilty of trying to exist? How do we accept that many of these murderers seem to have been gay men themselves, warped by self-loathing until they massacred their own? It's beyond weeping. To his credit, Polchin never commands us to weep. His writing is unvarnished and unsentimental as he takes us chronologically through these decades of crime, and when the facts need context, he clearly explains how scientific, religious, and political forces of the time helped endorse these murders. And while there are moments when he allows himself some tart editorializing, he doesn't linger over his own outrage. Instead, he trusts the details will make us angry on their own. In his wallop of a conclusion, though, Polchin does describe being haunted by his own research, as well as being deeply moved." —MARK BLANKENSHIP, *The Blotter*

"Insightful . . . Will likely delight true crime fans and satisfy academics." —*Publishers Weekly*

"Thoughtful, accessible and well-researched, Polchin's book offers useful insight into some of the lesser-known cultural currents that gave rise to the gay rights movement. An enlightening provocative cultural history." —*Kirkus Reviews*

"Polchin's extraordinarily well-researched account offers a valuable contribution to both social and previously neglected gay history." —*Booklist*

"Excerpts from sources as stylistically disparate as tabloids, texts, novels, and the *Physicians' Desk Reference* . . . enrich the scope of the book's analysis to an extent otherwise impossible . . . Whether large or small, many of these stories function like mirrors, reflecting light onto one another or reflecting nearly identical images from today. James Polchin's *Indecent Advances* inspires further exploration into the hidden histories of marginalized populations and how the violence they suffer might be the result of a system that excludes some people from its protections, exiling them to places where they are made more vulnerable." —LINDA THORKALSON, *Foreword Reviews*

"Useful history resource for public and undergraduate level libraries; extensive footnotes cite a host of primary resources useful for a graduate level researcher." —A. B. JOHNSON, *Choice Connect*

"Compact and powerful, Polchin's social history of crimes against queer men in the first half of the 20th century coincides with the 50th anniversary of the Stonewall Riots in New York City. An important book for an important anniversary . . . Required reading. Highly recommended." —SARAH HENDESS, Historical Novel Society

"*Indecent Advances* is a chilling, relentless catalog of murders of gay men in the decades of repression, when their killers could get off by alleging the titular phrase. James Polchin has done remarkable work in extracting their stories from the newspapers where they lay hidden in plain sight." —LUC SANTE, author of *Low Life: Lures and Snares of Old New York*

"It is tempting to think of James Polchin's *Indecent Advances* as the first noir queer history of the twentieth century. Its fascinating, vivid, case-by-case survey of violent crimes committed against gay men reads like a page-turning clash of tabloid headlines and pulp fiction. Yet, beneath this shocking, unfolding narrative is a beautifully written, deeply researched examination of how this violence has been institutionalized, accepted, and excused. Polchin's detective work on the crimes is thrilling—news stories, police reports, trial excerpts—and his decade-by-decade contextualization is astute and compelling. This is a history that has been waiting to be written, a splendid narrative that grips the reader as it illuminates its subject."
—MICHAEL BRONSKI, author of *A Queer History of the United States*

"In his revelatory and meticulously researched book, James Polchin has discovered a forgotten chapter of queer history hiding in plain sight: in sensationalistic newspaper articles documenting decades of antigay violence, often in coded terms. Looking at gay life through this novel lens offers an entirely fresh take on what previous generations endured. Like the best true crime stories, *Indecent Advances* is both brutal to read and impossible to put down." —WAYNE HOFFMAN, author of *An Older Man*

"*Indecent Advances* is fascinating rediscovered history that reads like the best true crime murder mysteries. But, in fact, the stories it tells reveal a community under siege, a brutal era of violence against queer men in which society and the law often looked the other way." —WILLIAM J. MANN, professor of LGBT history at Central Connecticut State University and author of *Tinseltown: Murder, Morphine, and Madness at the Dawn of Hollywood*

"James Polchin has written a vital, masterful corrective on American sex crime that redefines who the criminal was. In *Indecent Advances*, it was often the arresting agents and biased reporters who conspired to abuse the rule of law. Polchin skewers the triumphalist narrative of LGBT+ rights—the notion of a long march to freedom—by excavating a lost record of atrocities. Ray Bradbury would call this 'the terrible tyranny of the majority' against a minority group. This book reveals, existentially, why queer Americans had to rise up."   —ROBERT W. FIESELER, author of *Tinderbox*

"Breathtaking and compelling, *Indecent Advances* is a history book that reads like a novel written by a historian who uncovers evidence like a detective. James Polchin rediscovers the heartbreaking stories of how gay men's sexual desire often left them dead in empty hotel rooms. For too long, these harrowing accounts have appeared as fragments set against the backdrop of larger narratives of progress. *Indecent Advances* dares to say their names and to tell their stories, and refuses for them to be left dead and alone."   —JIM DOWNS, author of *Stand by Me: The Forgotten History of Gay Liberation*

Indecent Advances

INDECENT ADVANCES

A Hidden History of True Crime
and Prejudice Before Stonewall

JAMES POLCHIN

COUNTERPOINT
Berkeley, California

For Greg

The Library of Congress has cataloged the hardcover as follows:
Names: Polchin, James, author.
Title: Indecent advances : a hidden history of true crime and prejudice
  before Stonewall / James Polchin.
Description: First hardcover edition. | Berkeley, California : Counterpoint,
  2019.
Identifiers: LCCN 2018058382 | ISBN 9781640091894
Subjects: LCSH: Crime and the press—United States—History—20th century. |
  Gays—Press coverage—United States. | Criminals—Press coverage—United
  States.
Classification: LCC HV6168 .P65 2019 | DDC 070.4/493643—dc23
LC record available at https://lccn.loc.gov/2018058382

Paperback ISBN: 978-1-64009-387-4

Cover design by Donna Cheng
Book design by Jordan Koluch

COUNTERPOINT
2560 Ninth Street, Suite 318
Berkeley, CA 94710
www.counterpointpress.com

Printed in the United States of America

Contents

Indecent Advances

Introduction

Criminalizing Queer Men

n January 1943, the thirty-one-year-old playwright Tennessee Williams
wrote in his journal about the first time he was physically struck by another man:

> Unhappily I can't go into details. It was a case of guilt and shame in which
> I was relatively the innocent party, since I merely offered entertainment,
> which was accepted with apparent gratitude until the untimely entrance
> of other parties. Feel a little sorrowful about it. So unnecessary. The sort
> of behavior pattern imposed by the conventional falsehoods . . . Why do
> they strike us? What is our offense? We offer them a truth which they
> cannot bear to confess except in privacy and the dark—a truth which
> is inherently as bright as the morning sun. He struck me because he did
> what I did and his friends discovered it. Yes, it hurt—inside. I do not
> know if I will be able to sleep. But tomorrow I suppose the swollen face
> will be normal again and I will pick up the usual thread of life.[1]

Today we might describe his companion's response as "homosexual
panic," that dubious psychological condition that had its origins among

sailors and soldiers returning from World War I. If Williams's attacker had been arrested for the assault, he might have claimed that Williams provoked the attack through a sexual solicitation; sodomy was then a felony punishable with prison sentences in every state in the country. In the press, editors would have reported that Williams's bruised and swollen face was a result of his "indecent advance," a euphemistic term that resonated with sexual deviancy and violence, and would have reminded readers of the specific kinds of criminal threats queer men posed to society. While the term was used to describe all manner of violent sexual assaults, editors were reticent to offer details given the journalistic standards of the day, which allowed for such references only through suggestion and innuendo.

Like many queer men of the era, Williams risked police arrests or attacks by would-be robbers while he went in search of sexual and social encounters on the margins of the city—along the docks, parks, and street corners where such encounters could be had. A few weeks after that initial violent incident, Williams would have another encounter that verged on the edge of violence. This time, it was not a case of homosexual panic, but rather one of intended intimidation and robbery. The man he brought back to his room began insulting and bullying Williams, threatening him with physical violence as he rummaged through his things. The experience "carried on for about an hour," Williams wrote, and while he remained calm, he was fearful that his abuser would steal or destroy his manuscripts. Williams wrote: "He finally despaired of finding any portable property of value and left, with the threat that any time he saw me he would kill me. I felt sick and disgusted. I think that is the end of my traffic with such characters." While this encounter lacked the physical violence of the earlier incident, it clearly had a stronger effect on Williams emotionally. The man's threats of future violence, and even murder, stiffened him to the dangers of such encounters. Williams did not report either incident to the police, for to do so in 1943 would risk his own arrest for sodomy, disorderly conduct, or some other criminal offense. The next day in his journal, he described the night as "the most shocking experience I've ever had with another human being."[2]

Williams's two encounters, which left him with physical and emotional injuries, were fueled as much by the era's social prejudices as by a long history of criminalizing queer men, making them vulnerable targets for violence and abuse. "The history of Western representation is littered with the corpses of gender and sexual deviants," writes the critic Heather Love. Queer history has often focused on narratives of progress in which sexual minorities prosper despite the social injuries done to them. This progressive and affirmative narrative has made injury and violence historical realities we often write against, through an emphasis on community building, cultural expressions, and political activism. Sexual minorities survived and flourished, the story goes, despite all they had to endure. But there is another story of queer experience, one that tries to recover encounters much deadlier than the ones Williams recorded in his journal. "Modern homosexual identity is formed out of and in relation to the experience of social damage," Love argues, adding, "paying attention to what was difficult in the past may tell us how far we have come, but that is not all it will tell us; it also makes visible the damage that we live with in the present."[3]

This book offers one way into this record of such damage by recovering a lost history of queer true crime stories published in the press between World War I and the Stonewall protests of 1969. Most of these stories have never been read since their original publication; their documentation of injustices and discrimination has been buried for decades. In these stories, we encounter men found stabbed, shot, or strangled in hotel rooms, apartments, public parks, and subway bathrooms. We witness accounts of brutal violence between roommates, sailors and civilians, young men and older men, working-class men and wealthy companions. Many of the victims were married men, living their sexual lives in secret rendezvous, under false names to hide their identities. Others were clearly living as homosexual men, single or partnered, participating in the queer worlds that were emerging in many cities across the country with increasing visibility. Not surprisingly, such crime reports were mostly stories about encounters between white men. When men of color were present in the mainstream press, they were usually, if not always, the killers of the white men they met, reflecting how the crime pages embodied the broader racial segregation of the times.

In returning to these long-forgotten stories, we see how newspaper editors and writers shaped the human dramas with sensational appeal and cautionary concerns, furthering the era's focus on the salacious and entertaining elements of crime. Not only did the press educate readers about the nature of crime and violence, giving insights into police investigations and the courtroom battles, it also reflected and shaped ideas of morality and immorality, particularly as homosexuality was increasingly a subject of public concern. In an era when queers were understood as despised criminals, the press did much to fan the fears about sexual deviancy with sensational headlines, suggestive details, and shocking accounts of crime scenes. Such fears were acutely evident in numerous sex crime panics, frenzied moments where violent crimes that simmered with a sexual undertone became front-page news, pointing readers to the problems of sexual deviants and often targeting homosexuals for increased arrests, vigilante violence, and new efforts to criminalize harmless sexual behaviors. While queer true crime stories reflected and amplified social prejudices and state-sanctioned discriminations, they also show us how queer men were forced to navigate such dangers in their search for sexual adventure and social life.

While readers encountered queer true crime stories in scandalous front-page headlines, they also found them in smaller, more mysterious accounts. Just a few months after Williams recorded his violent encounters in his journal, *The New York Times* published this account in its evening edition about the mysterious and fatal incident between two men in a rooming house on Manhattan's west side:

> A slightly built middle-aged man who registered yesterday afternoon at a rooming house on 608 Eighth Avenue with a sailor as a companion, was found dead in his room there an hour later, with his skull shattered. He had been stripped of his suit by the sailor who disappeared.
>
> The civilian had registered at the rooming house as Harry Bowen of New York City, and his companion, about 19 years old, who was in

the naval uniform, as C. E. Bowen. Shortly after they had gone to their room the sailor reappeared, carrying the older man's suit, and left the house. Mrs. Rebecca Seligsohn, the housekeeper, decided to investigate and found the sailor's roommate dead.

Buried on the bottom half of page thirty-eight, this was the entire article about the crime. The next day, the paper revealed "the elderly man found beaten to death Saturday afternoon" had used a false name. The murder victim was not Harry Bowen, but rather Charles Patterson, a sixty-nine-year-old postal worker who lived in the leafy suburban town of Summit, New Jersey, with his wife, Adelaide, in a large nineteenth-century Dutch colonial in the center of town.[4]

Patterson had taken the train into Manhattan to buy theater tickets to celebrate his upcoming forty-seventh wedding anniversary the following week.[5] At some point he met a sailor—or a man dressed in a sailor uniform—and found his way to the rooming house just a few blocks from Bryant Park, an area known for its vagrants and queer cruising in the 1930s and 1940s. There the two men registered with oddly similar names, suggesting they might have pretended to be related to avoid problems with the manager. The mysterious details of the encounter were central to press reports as they circulated through the Associated Press wire service to newspapers in New Jersey and Delaware. Readers learned that Patterson was found "half-clothed," and that police were searching for a "young, blond sailor."[6] But after the few initial stories, and, apparently no real leads in the case, the crime disappeared from the newspapers.

Many readers in the 1940s would have understood the sexual undertones of the crime that seem so apparent to us today. While a married man meeting a younger man in public and renting a hotel room together under assumed names may not easily fit into the history of queer experience, it is undeniably a part of that history. The press found in Patterson's murder a familiar tragedy of urban crime, with a thinly veiled subtext of sexual deviance that coupled homosexuality with criminality. Although Patterson's murder is horrific to us today, not only for its brutality but also for how the queer victim was targeted for robbery by the younger assailant, in 1943 Patterson's harmless search for a sexual encounter with another man would have been considered a felony, punishable with harsh sentencing. While his murder was shocking, what led him into that hotel room with the younger man would have been equally appalling and criminal.

Even when they suffered such violence, queer men in the courts and the press were not always understood as victims. How the press defined these queer true crime stories—who were the victims and who were the criminals—was set within a constellation of cultural values, journalistic ethics, and political trends. In this sense, queer true crime stories give us much more than compelling headlines of dramatic and horrifying tales of murder and assaults. They also show us how violence and prejudice can take hold when you criminalize a group of people, harness the expertise of the medical and legal professions, and circulate these ideas through the press.

The true crime story was an invention of the nineteenth century, when the press increasingly offered frightful tales to eager audiences. Weaving intricate accounts of violent murders that were populated by unscrupulous men and defenseless women, the true crime genre in Victorian America offered both the pleasure of a murder mystery and the shock of a morality tale. Circulated through a growing tabloid press such as the *National Police Gazette*, a publication that appealed to its male readers with crime stories and burlesque images, or later the scandal-hungry newspapers of the Hearst empire, these stories of real-life violence were increasingly popular in the era, sitting alongside the new genre of horror stories and the other recently invented literary form: murder mysteries. From their origins, true crime stories in the press have never simply been about the crimes themselves. Rather, they take the shape of their era, embodying and educating readers on the nature of justice, the meaning of morality, the lines between rationality and insanity, and, most acutely, normality and abnormality.[7] "By dismantling various narratives of murder," historian Sara Knox reminds us, it becomes possible "to expose the cultural meanings given to murder, that irreplaceable taken-for-granted quality of a murder that, when narrated, says so much about *what a culture knows* and *what it will not let itself know*."[8]

While the nineteenth century gave us true crime and murder mysteries, it also gave us scientific theories about the nature of deviant human behaviors. Central to these new theories was the notion that deviancy was a somatic condition, an inherited trait that could, if you looked closely enough, be easily read on one's body. The French doctor Jean-Martin Charcot, known as the father of neurology, famously photographed most of his female patients who were suffering from the newly defined condition of female hysteria in the 1880s. Such visual evidence was meant not only to confirm the dire nature of the illness as evidenced on the body, but also to form part of the treatment itself.

It was in the field of criminology that such theories were actively explored. Cesare Lombroso, a well-respected Italian criminologist, pioneered an approach to crime that shifted older notions of punishment from a focus on the nature of the crime to a concern with the nature of the criminal. In his book *Criminal Man*, published in 1876, Lombroso proposed the radical idea that criminals were born, not made, arguing that some people were more prone to criminality than others. You could predict such criminal propensities, his theory went, by examining certain bodily features. As Lombroso was theorizing the nature of the criminal man, French criminologist Alphonse Bertillon used the relatively new technology of the camera to photograph Parisians arrested on all manner of crimes, and recorded specific physical details of each on standardized forms, creating the first mug shots that could be easily shared with police across the city or the nation. At the same time, the English sociologist and eugenicist Francis Galton was also interested in the camera's power to capture the criminal type, but he went even further, convinced that fingerprints could not only uniquely identify individuals, but might also reveal racial markings and criminal propensities, adding to his systematic categorization of racial types.[9] While such approaches to crime had their detractors, their impact on modern criminology would be felt for decades to come.[10]

The nature of the criminal led also to the nature of the sexual deviant.

Lombroso claimed that homosexuals were a class of moral criminals who should be committed to insane asylums, their sexual proclivities an inherent part of their being. As criminology developed new theories about the nature of the criminal, a newly formed field of sexology in Europe and the United States was investigating and theorizing about the nature of abnormal sexual desires. Like crime, sexual desire was increasingly understood as an inherent, biological propensity, offering a radical shift in the centuries-long understanding of homosexuality as a behavior.

Since the Middle Ages, much of Western history held to religious and legal dictates against the practice of sodomy. Enacted through church inquisitors, royal tribunals, or, later, parliamentary decrees, proscriptions against sodomy defined sexual and social impurities. While charges of sodomy were directed at sexual immoralities, they were also used as a vital weapon against anyone deemed a threat to social order or religious doctrines, such as foreigners, heretics, or political foes. By the Renaissance, the act of sodomy gave birth to the sodomite, and with it increasingly harsher penalties and tortures were imagined and enacted to control him. In the English colonies of North America, sodomy was punishable by death, a reality that did not change until after the Revolution. But charges of sodomy, like other notions of sin, had their own social order. Lower-class men were more likely to be charged with sodomy than their upper-class neighbors.[11]

The idea that same-sex desires were a biological fact of the person was most acutely defined in the radical new figure of the "homosexual." Whereas the sodomite was a victim of sinful behaviors including such activities as masturbation or lustful desires, the figure of the homosexual was born with his sexual desires. First coined in the 1860s in a German-language pamphlet decrying a Prussian antisodomy law, the term "homosexual" was from its birth a defense against the criminalization of same-sex desires.[12] In 1886, the German doctor Richard von Krafft-Ebing published *Psychopathia Sexualis*, a large collection of first-person accounts of sexual deviances from a wide variety of men from different social classes. The accounts ranged from same-sex eroticism to transvestism and bestiality. These accounts made evident how sexual desires were inherent from an early age, however outside the social norms they may have been. Among the many terms he offered to categorize the various accounts of sexual activities were two recently coined words that for the first time entered Western medicine: "homosexual" and "heterosexual." A decade later Havelock Ellis, an English physician, would draw on Krafft-Ebing's work but define same-sex desire as a kind of "inversion" from normal heterosexuality, thus coining the term "sexual invert." It was this idea that would buttress a number of English writers and artists of the era, who found in sexual inversion an empowering term against the social stigma and legal offense of sodomy. For Ellis, inversion was also aligned with another new term—"sexual perversion." The two increasingly would be used interchangeably.

The idea that homosexuals were born and not made fostered all kinds of theories and opinions about who exactly was more prone to such sexual deviancy. One American doctor in the 1890s described how homosexuality was mostly practiced among "the lower classes and particularly Negroes," while another expert pointed to foreigners and especially those "among the low and degraded" classes as the likely culprits of such vice. Few embodied these ideas more acutely than the infamous Anthony Comstock, who as a postal inspector and president of the Society for the Suppression of Vice wielded great power and influence in New York City at the turn of the century as he pushed his brand of Victorian moralism. Along with his crusades against books and magazines he found unseemly, Comstock also targeted sexual deviancy. "These inverts," he intoned, "are not fit to live with the rest of mankind. They ought to have branded on their foreheads the word 'Unclean,'" adding, "Their lives ought to be so intolerable as to drive them to abandon their vices."[13]

The word "unclean" was a choice one, for it underscored how Comstock and other moral reformers of the era pushed a social purity in an antivice crusade that targeted sexual deviancy, prostitution, pornography, and other practices it deemed impure. These campaigns were happening amid a rapidly growing urban population in the late nineteenth and early twentieth centuries hastened by a huge influx of immigrants from eastern and southern Europe, who some believed threatened the racial purity of the country.

At the same time, industrialization transplanted large numbers of single men and women to diverse cities and well beyond the social and sexual conventions of their small towns, allowing for anonymous experimentation with older codes of sexual and gender norms. Antivice committees were a common response to these social changes, as police and social reformers attempted to control the social and sexual deviancies that many viewed as a pervasive problem, especially among the working class. The Chicago Vice Commission, for example, reported in 1911 that homosexuality was among the worst problems the city faced.[14]

Within these social changes, a paradox about sexuality in the years leading up to World War I became clear: at the very moment that science and medicine were offering new theories of same-sex desire and new categories that proscribed sexual identities, sexual deviancy was increasingly viewed as a dire social and criminal threat.

Drawing on his experiences in Europe during the Great War and his studies of the work by German sexologists, Henry Gerber established the Society for Human Rights in Chicago in the early 1920s, a group that promoted the idea of homosexual rights. Gerber dared to imagine a world where homosexuals were not targeted by police arrests or harassment by vice wardens. While his organization was quickly suppressed by the police, Gerber continued to promote his radical ideas. In the early 1930s he wrote, "Homosexuals live in happy, blissful unions, especially in Europe, where homosexuals are unmolested as long as they mind their own business, and are not, as in England and in the United States, driven to the underworld of perversions and crime for satisfaction of their very real craving for love."[15]

While Gerber's words point to the prejudices directed toward homosexuals, they also underscore the central tension between public control and private freedom that defined homosexuality in the decades before Stonewall—and after. Nowhere did these tensions play out more acutely than in the crime pages of the press. This book argues, in part, that these long-forgotten crime stories were a vital way that the competing and contradictory theories of homosexuality circulated to the broad reading public in the years between World War I and Stonewall—making homosexuality a dire public concern. World War I marked a watershed for interest in sexual deviancy within the growing fields of criminology and psychology in the United States. At the same time, an expanding tabloid press and popular magazine industry offered true stories of sex and crime with unprecedented salacious and shocking details, giving shape to a compelling genre of the modern era. The image of the queer criminal came to define homosexuality in these decades, harnessing all manner of state and medical responses. By the 1950s, queer true crime stories illustrated for early gay activists how homosexuals suffered amid the injustices of random violence, courtroom arguments, and press biases.

We see in the crime pages an evolution of queer criminality. The Depression-era 1930s gave us the sex criminal, a vague character that included a big net of suspects, from child molesters and rapists to queer men. The FBI was active in promoting the problem of sex crimes, both in the 1930s and in the postwar years. Under its long-serving director J. Edgar Hoover, the agency expanded its private files of political subversives to include a new category called "sex deviants," which included all manner of sex offenses and made homosexuality a national policing concern. The sex criminal would play a central role in the constant ebb and flow of sex panics in the press from the 1930s to the 1950s. In such fevered moments, queer men were often the targets of police surveillance and vigilante violence.

Another way that queer men were made targets of abuse was in the homosexual panic defense, which was increasingly used by defendants in the 1930s and would be a compelling argument for attacks and murders of queer men for decades. Crime stories of men killing their queer companions because of their "indecent advances" embodied the perceived threats that queer men posed to the sexual and social order. But homosexual panic was also part of the post–World War II psychologizing of homosexuality, in which sexual desire was not, as the nineteenth-century sexologists had deemed, an inherent biological imperative, but rather a factor of one's environment and childhood sexual development. If homosexuality was not biological but developmental, so these ideas proposed, it could in fact be changed, giving rise to all manner of forced treatments and therapies to cure the condition.

The Cold War also gave us Alfred Kinsey's famous study *Sexual Behavior in the Human Male*, published in 1948. The study was groundbreaking in what it revealed—occurrences of sexual experiences between men were much more common across different ages of men's lives than had been previously acknowledged. The sexual practices that Kinsey and his researchers recorded confirmed the pervasiveness of private same-sex experiences. But the importance of the study also lay in what it made uncertain: that homosexuality was not an easily identifiable or a marginal characteristic that marked abnormal men.

Kinsey's ideas went beyond the descriptive, as he also advocated against the imprisonment and institutionalization of homosexuals—seeing homosexual practices as causing little harm to society. One impact of Kinsey's study was the idea that homosexuality should be viewed as a private concern rather than a social problem. That sexual experiences between two consenting adults should be a private right was a concept that was growing in the postwar years among the early homosexual rights advocates, who increasingly argued the radical concept that homosexuals constituted a distinct social minority. Critiques of the crime pages offered civil rights groups such as the Mattachine Society explicit examples of the prejudice and injuries homosexuals endured. These critiques fostered a growing collective awareness of how homosexuals were criminalized in the press, in the courtroom, and on the streets. This awareness would grow with ever-increasing urgency and confrontation in the sexual liberation movements in the late 1960s, exploding with determined force on a warm summer night in June 1969 when patrons resisted the violence forced on them by police raids at the Stonewall bar in New York.

Queer true crime stories show us this movement from criminalization to social protest in the history of modern homosexuality. In the process, these forgotten stories demonstrate how queer men navigated the prejudices around them when there was no recognition of the dangers they faced, nor much compassion for the violence they endured.

When the Men Came Home

Sailors, Scandals, and Mysteries in the 1920s

"MURDERED IN HOTEL ROOM"

On November 4, 1920, the front page of the New York *Daily News* announced in large block letters a disturbing milestone in the city: the one hundredth murder of the year. The accompanying article detailed the fatal beating of Leeds Vaughn Waters in a room at the Plymouth Hotel on West Thirty-Eighth Street. The tabloid reported that police had found Waters slumped on the floor with "a fractured jaw and skull and a deep wound over his left eye, which was apparently inflicted by a blunt instrument." Waters was the scion of a wealthy New England family who had made its fortune in piano manufacturing. Since his graduation from Columbia College in 1896, he had lived much of his life in London, England. The *Daily News* described the forty-eight-year-old victim's life as "a series of kaleidoscopic glimpses of social activities in North and South America, in England, and on the continent."

As there was no apparent robbery, New York City detectives were baffled by the motive for the crime. The editors, however, speculated about the murder by casting doubts on the character of the victim himself. "According to friends," the newspaper reported, Waters "has never been engaged in industry and has never been known to exert himself to labor," adding "riches and idleness are shown as powerful influences toward his tragic end." The term "idleness" was often used in the press in the 1920s to hint at moral and criminal duplicities. "How he was lured from his usual haunts along the rosy path of luxury," the newspaper asked, "to hostelry of the character of that in which he was slain is a point of mystery which no one has been able to solve."[1]

In the coming days, newspapers in New York and across the country would pursue this question, with articles that detailed the last hours of Waters's life. Readers learned he spent the evening at the Delta Kappa Epsilon Club, a thirteen-story, private gentlemen's club on East Forty-Fourth Street, where he had been a member since his college days. News accounts referring to Waters as a "clubman" signaled his social standing. Inside the brick and stone building, DKE men enjoyed a gymnasium with squash courts, a mahogany-paneled taproom, a rooftop café, and five floors of guest rooms. Waters spent most of the evening playing cards, indulging his love of gambling. Around one in the morning he told his friends he was leaving to return to Bronxville, a suburb north of the city where he was staying with his mother at her hotel.

Instead of going north, however, Waters instructed the taxi driver to take him a few blocks west to Times Square, where, as *The New York Times* conjectured, he met a "swarthy," "dark-skinned man, who was believed to be the one who shared the hotel room." In 1920, Times Square still had the reputation of a genteel theater district, though queer encounters were common in the area. Its seedier nightlife would emerge in the 1930s during the Great Depression. A few blocks west of Times Square was the more notorious Tenderloin neighborhood, known for its overcrowded tenements, crime, and vice. The Tenderloin was also known for its queer men, particularly in the West Forties and Fifties, many of whom worked in the theaters. It was in the Tenderloin, at Ninth Avenue and Forty-Fourth Street, that Waters and his companion allegedly dined at a restaurant in the early morning hours.

Witnesses reported that Waters bought a meal for his companion and an apple for himself.[2]

Eventually they arrived at the Plymouth Hotel at six in the morning as the yellow light of dawn filled the sky. John Carney, the night clerk at the Plymouth Hotel, would tell police that the two men made a strange sight as they entered the lobby. While Waters was "expensively dressed," his companion "wore shabby clothes and seemed to be of a much inferior social standing." In a front-page article headlined "Murdered in Hotel Room," the *New York Tribune*, never shy in promoting a good crime or a good scandal, gave readers a more detailed image of the contrast between the two men. While Waters wore a "light overcoat, a fashionably cut blue suit, patent leather shoes, and carried a silver-headed walking stick," his companion "wore a cheap cap which he kept well pulled down over his eyes."[3]

At the front desk, both men registered under aliases. Waters claimed to be J. Talbot from Milwaukee, Wisconsin. His companion signed his name James Dunn, also from Milwaukee. Carney assigned the men to room 805 on the top floor of the hotel with a view of West Thirty-Eighth Street. They didn't need the service of a bellhop because neither man had luggage. But at the Plymouth Hotel, this was not unusual.

Within an hour, guests in an adjoining room called the front desk to complain about the shouting and loud noises coming from room 805. Carney and a bellhop took the elevator to investigate. When Carney knocked on the door, Waters's companion opened it with a sudden rush and Carney asked if everything was all right. As one account described it, both men were then "bowled over by a man who dashed out and disappeared down the stairway." Carney and the bellhop ran after him down eight flights of stairs and out the side entrance, chasing him eastward toward Seventh Avenue, where the assailant disappeared amid the early morning crowds.[4]

A doctor arrived minutes before the police and declared Waters dead. From letters and personal items found in the room, detectives learned his real identity. "Robbery was not the motive for the crime," the New York *Daily News* declared, "as money and jewelry including a massive gold ring" were found in the room. The newspaper also noted that a friend of Waters claimed that he "knew of no acquaintance of Waters by the name of Dunn."[5]

Lacking a clear motive, the mystery of Waters's murder hinged precisely on the relationship between the two men. The press offered up a number of clues and speculations about why a shabbily dressed man and his well-dressed, wealthy friend ended up in room 805 at the Plymouth Hotel that day. "Silk Underwear Clew to Slayer" ran a front-page headline in *The Washington Post*, which related that a pair of underwear with the initials "W. H. A." were traced "to a laundry in Fifty-ninth street, where it was recently cleaned."[6] Such a detail pointed to the fact that the companion must have been naked at some point in the early morning hours. "There are mysteries all around the crime," the *St. Louis Post-Dispatch* declared, hinting at the sexual subtexts of the encounter. "The act," the article concluded, "was clearly the work of a person with an abnormal mind."[7]

But as news accounts made clear, it was not only the killer who had an "abnormal mind." The victim's own normality was also put into doubt. Reporters had learned that Waters had been secretly married over twenty years earlier to a woman named Baroness Blanc. Born Elizabeth Nicholson in Philadelphia, Baroness Blanc was, by one account, a "woman who streaks across society once in a generation." The press described her as charming and beautiful, an actress who had performed on stage in opera and vaudeville. In the late nineteenth century she had entertained in "unconventional sections of metropolitan society," as one article noted, adding that she moved between bohemian circles and European royalty with ease. She also had a succession of failed marriages that began at the age of sixteen. Her second marriage, which conveyed with it the unofficial title of baroness—a title that most news reports placed in quotation marks—lasted only as long as the honeymoon in Europe. Her third marriage, to Waters, nearly a decade her junior, would also end abruptly. The two had wed secretly in 1896, the year Waters graduated from college. A Philadelphia newspaper reported that the two had "lived together thirty-one days. Mrs. Waters then went to France, returning to this country later. She obtained a divorce in Chicago."[8] Waters's mother, either forgetting or deliberately ignoring the Baroness

Blanc, told police and reporters that her son had never been married and lived as a bachelor.

One interpretation of the crime the press offered up concerned Waters's love of gambling. The wealthy cosmopolitan bachelor might have been "lured to the scene of his death by the promise of a game of chance," noted the New York *Daily News*. *The Washington Post* described Waters as having "suffered from heavy gambling losses."[9] The assistant district attorney furthered this explanation in a convoluted statement to the press, where he claimed that the murder was most likely not premeditated. Rather, he suggested, Waters, "who is said to have been a gambler and who might have been in a habit of picking up strangers, took the man who registered under the name of 'James Dunn' to the Plymouth Hotel; that this man became infuriated when he discovered Waters only had the change from a ten dollar bill and the fight which ended in murder followed." As the *Daily News* speculated, Waters's killer surely inhabited a "morass of gambling, thieving, and murder, the haunts of sin and crime." Such speculations hinged on the image of the assailant as a working-class thief and killer. One report declared detectives were working on the theory the killer was a "notorious character of the Tenderloin district," adding that he most likely was one of a gang of "leeches" who worked the "White Light district and are known to prey on wealthy idlers."[10]

Two weeks after Waters's body was found in the Plymouth Hotel, another violent murder made headlines in the New York press when a forty-eight-year-old chauffeur named Frank Barbor was shot and killed in Central Park near the West Seventy-Second Street entrance. Barbor visited the park nightly because of his "poor health," wrote the *Daily News*, and on the night of his murder, he had been walking along a pathway with a sailor from the USS *Arizona* named Charles Becker when three men with "caps pulled down over their faces" approached them and one asked Barbor for a match. According to the newspaper, as Becker offered a match, "the tallest of the three drew the revolver" and shot Barbor. Becker added that he didn't see any of the three men physically strike Barbor—a detail that would soon be questionable.[11]

Since Becker was the only eyewitness to the murder, his story would be central to the news reports of the crime, which varied in different publications. The *New York Tribune* reported that Barbor was not strolling along the pathway with the sailor, but rather Becker was walking by himself when he spied "Barbor sitting on a park bench and asked him for a match. He then walked toward the Central Park entrance, he said, and heard somebody yell 'Hands Up!'" Becker turned back and "saw Barbor surrounded by three men. When Barbor shouted for help, Becker said, the three men ran and one of them fired a shot."[12]

On the front page of *The New York Times*, Becker claimed he was leaving, not entering, the park when he saw three men approach Barbor. One of them asked him for a match. Barbor "began to fumble in his clothes," Becker told the police, and he then intervened. "Never mind buddy; I'll give them a match," he claimed to have said. He explained how at that point one of the three pulled out a pistol and pointed it at Barbor's head. Barbor, according to Becker, exclaimed, "I won't let you rob me." Becker saw a "flash from the pistol" and the man fall on the ground. After the shooting, the three men fled east into Central Park, and Becker ran to a nearby hotel to alert police.

The New York Times also reported that Dr. George Homan, the assistant medical examiner, determined that Barbor had "depressed fractures of the forehead and a compound fracture of the skull." From such facts, Homan concluded that he died from a severe blunt force to the head. The shooting was after the fact. Any mention of the blunt force was absent in Becker's account of events, presenting a contradiction in the news articles that was not resolved. Such discrepancies may have resulted from the reporting, or they may have reflected the different stories that Becker told the press. Either way, the facts of how Barbor was murdered were decidedly inconsistent in these accounts.

In early December, police arrested four men for the murders of Leeds Vaughn Waters and Frank Barbor. John Reidy, a twenty-four-year-old navy seaman, confessed to killing Waters. Twenty-five-year-old Charles Benner, who lived in the Tenderloin, was charged in the shooting death of Barbor. Two other men were held as material witnesses. The New York *Daily News* echoed its earlier description, calling the men "members of a gang of 'leeches' who prey upon rich men under the influence of liquor, robbing and often killing them." The article included mug shots of Reidy and Benner, both wearing large, tweed newsboy caps. Another photograph depicted detectives standing near the spot in Central Park where Barbor was murdered. Edward Kohn, an ex-soldier and one of the men arrested as a material witness, stood next to the detectives pointing toward the pavement where the shooting occurred. All three men gazed at the ground with dramatic intention.[13]

To corroborate the confession, detectives took Reidy to the Plymouth Hotel, where the clerk identified him as Waters's companion. There he wrote the name "James Dunn" to compare the handwriting with that of his hotel registration. Reidy told the detectives that he had met Waters at a Times Square subway station at four o'clock in the morning. Waters invited him to the hotel, where the two drank from Waters's flask of whiskey. "After both had been drinking," *The Boston Globe* reported, Reidy said he and Waters "had a quarrel and he hit the clubman with his fist and then struck him over the head with Waters's cane. Waters fell to the floor, striking his head against the bed railing."[14] The nature of the quarrel remained unexplained.

Originally from Milwaukee, Reidy had served on the USS *Arizona*, the battleship which had led the flotilla that brought President Woodrow Wilson to France for peace talks at the end of World War I. In August 1920, Reidy deserted the ship at the Brooklyn Navy Yard. *The New York Times* noted that Charles Becker, the sailor who claimed to have witnessed the killing of Barbor, had also been stationed on the *Arizona*, where he was now "confined to the naval brig." He was charged with fraudulent enlistment for not informing the navy that he was an ex-convict.[15] His role in the murders, if any, was left uncertain.

At his murder trial in the spring of 1921, Reidy wore his naval uniform to court, presenting the image of military wholesomeness. The judge cleared the courtroom of spectators as he "did not consider the evidence in the case proper for public consumption." According to *The New York Times*, Reidy testified he did not intend to kill his wealthier companion, but Waters "had insulted him, and he struck him." The press never detailed the nature of the insult, leaving readers to speculate all manner of possibilities. In Reidy's home state, the *Wisconsin State Journal* offered a dire scene of the hotel encounter, describing how Reidy had defended himself after "Waters had attacked him."[16] Reidy's defense proved persuasive. After two days of testimony, the jury found the sailor not guilty of second-degree murder.

Three weeks later Benner would stand trial for the murder of Frank Barbor. In contrast to the extensive coverage of Waters's case, the press proved less interested in Benner's trial. A small article in the *New York Herald* on page four reported that Benner, "a member of a band which operated during the crime wave last winter," was found "guilty of murder in the second degree in the killing of Frank Barber." The *Herald*'s editors misspelled the victim's last name. Readers learned nothing more about the trial or Benner's defense, and no other New York newspaper even reported on his conviction.[17] This contrast to Reidy's trial coverage most likely reflected the differences in social status between the two victims. As was often the case in the era, Waters's wealth made his death more newsworthy, and the salacious subtext of the hotel room encounter more scandalous.

"RETURN TO NORMALCY"

The press coverage of the murders of Waters and Barbor was set within a moment of deep political and social change in the country. The same night that Waters met his killer, the nation was enthralled by the presidential election. It was the first time that election returns were broadcast through the strange and exciting means of radio transmission, relaying vote counts to listeners almost as they were being cast—though the listening audience was small in 1920. It was also the first time that women had the right to vote in the United States.[18] The Republican Party candidate, Warren G. Harding, intoned in a campaign speech that "America's present need is not to heroics but healing; not nostrums but normalcy; not revolution but restoration." "Return to Normalcy" would become his campaign slogan.[19] The neologism was a symptom of Harding's well-known limits with the English language. It also conjured a political nostalgia that included a halt to immigration, controlling socialists and anarchist radicals, curtailing the spread of labor unions, restricting government regulations on the marketplace, and adopting an isolationist foreign policy that kept the United States free from European entanglements, specifically President Wilson's internationalist vision embodied in the newly conceived League of Nations.

Harding was an unlikely candidate for the Republicans. His love of bootleg liquor just as Prohibition became the law of the land was well-known, as was his dubious circle of business friends, a group that would eventually be enmeshed in scandal. His extramarital affairs were an open secret, as was his disinterest in big ideas. One editor at the time characterized Harding as "almost unbelievably ill-informed" about most matters.[20] Harding's biographer termed it more generously: "Harding had a good mind but he simply made little use of it."[21] But as the son of an Ohio farmer and editor of a small-town newspaper, Harding embodied a rural wholesomeness that included good looks, modest three-piece suits, and an affable character.

Harding won in a landslide, beating the progressive Democratic candidate James Cox and his running mate Franklin Delano Roosevelt. The Republican Party also won both houses of Congress and a slew of state legislatures. *The New York Times* called the win a "startling electoral avalanche" that "astonished even the most sanguine Republican leaders."[22] In pointing to the deepening economic recession of 1920 and signaling a restored social order, the tabloid New York *Daily News* editorialized Harding's victory with the headline: "Now Let's Get Back to Work." The editors' opinion reflected the era's rising spirit of nationalism, characterizing the election as "a win" for the country. Harding, the editors declared, was "elected because he believed in America first and Europe afterward."[23]

Such nationalist rhetoric had been boiling since the end of World War I. Newspaper headlines about violent labor strikes, protests between radicals and self-described patriots, a virulent and active Ku Klux Klan in the South, and a rising tide of anti-immigrant sentiment were common. In the popular press, the image of the political radical was often that of an eastern European or Mediterranean immigrant, particularly Jews and Catholics. Descriptions of Waters's killer as a "swarthy," "dark-skinned," and "slovenly dressed man" would have resonated with readers, interlacing the dangers of working-class and immigrant radicals with criminality and urban vice.

In the summer of 1919, several mail bombs targeting politicians and businessmen made headlines. The Washington, D.C., home of Attorney General A. Mitchell Palmer was bombed twice in as many months. Some in Washington feared that a Communist revolution, not unlike the upheaval taking place in Russia, was looming. The government took unprecedented action. Enlisting local police forces, officials from the Justice Department executed raids across the country, targeting Communist Party members and others deemed progressives and political radicals. Known later as the Palmer raids, the actions threw out a wide net, searching businesses, private homes, and political and community organizations. Files and records were confiscated, all without search warrants. Thousands were arrested. Many who were arrested were immigrants, over five hundred of whom were deported.

The Palmer raids were immediately criticized by journalists and congressmen for the broad overreach of government powers and an assault on individual rights. "America," wrote a columnist in *Harper's Magazine*, "is no longer a free country," adding "liberty is a mere rhetorical figure."[24] Most of the men and women hauled up in the raids were eventually released for lack of evidence.[25] But Attorney General Palmer remained steadfast in his actions, claiming that "alien filth" who professed "unclean doctrines" needed to be suppressed and deported.[26]

Two months before the 1920 presidential election, a bomb hidden in a horse carriage exploded in front of the headquarters of the J. P. Morgan bank on Wall Street, killing thirty-eight people and injuring hundreds of others. The bombing dominated headlines across the country. Newspapers described windows shattered and body parts strewn around the street, and many tabloids were eager for photographs that would complement the most sensational front-page stories. *The New York Times* dedicated seventeen pages to the event, giving readers lurid details of the evidence and offering all manner of speculation about the culprits of the attack. While some newspapers called the bombing "an act of diabolism unparalleled in the annals of terrorism," others were less shocked, noting the political and social tensions that had been simmering even before the war. "It is not surprising that the massacre was accomplished in New York," *The Washington Post* editorialized, adding, "it would have been surprising if this festering sore had not come to its horrid head."[27]

Officials in neither New York nor Washington were prepared for the investigation required into an attack of this magnitude. The work of finding those responsible would fall to a young J. Edgar Hoover at the Bureau of Investigation, the predecessor to the Federal Bureau of Investigation. Uncovering the radical roots of the bombing would shape Hoover's ideas about law enforcement and social order. Unlike the government's response in the Palmer raids, which roped in thousands of innocent citizens and trampled on civil liberties, Hoover took a more directed approach. He began building a file of suspected radicals and subversives—and, in the 1930s, of sex deviants and homosexuals. It was a file he would continue to compile for the next fifty years.[28]

"CHARGES OF GROSS IMMORALITY"

At the same time that the Justice Department was rounding up suspected political subversives, another investigation was ratcheting up in Washington, this one focused on sexual perversion. In the press reports about the arrests of Reidy and Benner, there was a curious but noteworthy detail. The two men had been arrested, the article explained, in "a general roundup of idle ex-service men who have been seen loitering around Times Square and Columbus Circle," adding, "about fifty men, including deserters from the navy and former sailors, were included in the roundup."[29] The two detectives involved in the investigation were Detective James Finn of the New York City Police Department and Detective Thomas Sheehan of the Naval Intelligence Bureau.

Such a detail also appeared in a small article in the *New York Tribune* from December 1920, citing the arrest of Frank C. Ciance, an ex-sailor, for the murder of John Rice. Known as "Big Frank" for his size and sturdy stature, Ciance had been dishonorably discharged from the navy and caught up in what the newspaper described as a "joint crusade of the Police Department and the naval intelligence bureau against ex-service men alleged to be preying upon habitués of the Times Sq area and Central Park district." Ciance's hair, readers learned, "which is naturally dark brown, had been dyed yellow."[30] The article not only suggested the active queer cruising geography of midtown Manhattan in the years after World War I, it also pointed to how such activities had caught the attention of officials well beyond the borders of New York.

The involvement of naval intelligence in these strange cases of murder would soon erupt in a major national scandal. "Paint Newport as Vice Hotbed" blared the headline of an article in *The Washington Herald* in the winter of 1920, detailing the findings and methods of the government's investigation into "charges of gross immorality in the navy" in Newport, Rhode Island.[31] Known as the summer playground for America's richest families, Newport was also the home to the Naval War College, which housed a population of almost two thousand sailors. With war mobilization, the summer resort community swelled to include nearly twenty thousand sailors, mostly enlisted men. But it was not until the spring of 1919 that the sexual habits of some of these sailors became a concern for the navy. Officials had heard rumors of sailors engaging in "perversions" with local citizens, both in private and public places around the city. Nowhere was this more evident, the investigation revealed, than in the Sailors and Soldiers YMCA in the center of Newport, where queer locals often socialized with officers and enlisted men, sometimes renting a private room together for the night.[32]

That summer, officers at the training base had initiated a covert investigation called "Section A" that was approved by Secretary of the Navy Josephus Daniels and his assistant secretary, Franklin Roosevelt. It was just one of many such investigations that the navy was conducting at its bases along the East Coast designed to weed out sexual perversion. One of the officials in charge of the investigation prided himself on his skills at identifying "fairies"—a talent he acquired as a police detective in Connecticut in the years before the war when, in his own words, he "ran down perverts." In Newport, the navy employed its own sailors as decoys to seek out and entrap local citizens. They were instructed to do anything they could in their detective work, even encouraged to have sex with the men they snared as that might produce more substantial evidence. "You will have to use your own judgment," investigating officials told their sailor decoys, "whether or not a full act is completed. If that being the fact, it might lead to something greater."[33]

Whatever results the dragnet had achieved, the Newport operation blew up when the navy arrested Reverend Samuel Kent, a well-respected local pastor, in July 1919. The reverend's arrest, based on limited evidence, provoked several religious leaders to call for Congress and the navy to start an inquiry into the navy's investigative practices, which, they claimed, were making "perverts by official order" out of the sailors involved in the entrapment schemes.[34] The editor of *The Providence Journal*, John Rathom, a feisty Republican eager to point to the moral failings of the Democratic Wilson administration in the months before the next presidential election, published scathing letters about the investigation. *The New York Times* reported on the scandal in early 1920, reprising Rathom's own unvarnished criticism: "Many seamen in the navy," Rathom wrote, "have been used in the most vile and nameless practices in order to entrap innocent men."[35] Rathom's outrage lingered for months. When Roosevelt was nominated for vice president on the Democratic ticket in the summer of 1920, *The New York Times* lauded him for his "frankness and manliness." In response, Rathom reminded readers of *The Providence Journal* of the assistant secretary's role in the Newport investigations and, in a jab at Roosevelt's own masculinity, sarcastically declared that he was anything but a "fine-fibered young man in public office."[36]

The naval inquiry into the entrapment scheme dragged on through 1920, and included testimony by some of the sailors who had participated as decoys. Their accounts were often explicit about their encounters with Newport civilians, though the details never made the press. One of the more striking revelations was how the sailors were encouraged to engage in sex acts. One sailor testified that he was instructed "to get through" with an encounter, meaning to have an "erection and an emission." In response, one lawyer asked, "And up to the time of your instructions, you were a perfectly clean boy?" To which the sailor responded, "Yes, sir."[37] As the inquiry continued and more salacious details emerged, many sailors refused to answer pointed questions about their detective work, fearing they would put themselves in legal jeopardy. Accusations of sodomy could get a sailor dishonorably discharged from the military and felony charges in civilian court. But even the suggestive descriptions of their encounters with queer men underscored a troubling reality about the investigation: the complexities of defining homosexuality itself.

Since the late nineteenth century, many in the American medical profession subscribed to the idea of homosexuality as a form of degeneracy, a diseased human state, often viewed as a problem particularly prevalent among the working class. Others argued that homosexuality was less a defect than a variant of human sexuality common across all strata of society, exemplifying the diversity of human biology.[38] While the problem of homosexuality had been a concern for doctors and moral reformers for a number of years, World War I marked a watershed in both the understanding of homosexuality and the policing of it, as the legal and medical professions increasingly focused on sexual deviancy as a dire social problem. Ironically, the more attention doctors, social reformers, and the state dedicated to the understanding of the nature of homosexuality, the more murky it became. Despite the navy official's skills at identifying "fairies"—which usually relied on bodily expressions of feminine features—the Newport investigation revealed a troubling reality: that even seemingly normal men could engage in same-sex encounters.

Among its other revelations, the inquiry illustrated the different ways that sexuality was understood across classes. For many of the working-class enlisted men, sexual activities were viewed through gender roles, such that a homosexual encounter was acceptable if the man played the "masculine" role during sex. However, middle-class officers tended to view same-sex sexual contacts within the language of the era's social reformers—a troubling, unhealthy vice and a threat to sexual purity, regardless of the sexual position. As the historian George Chauncey notes, the Newport scandal "brought so many groups of people—working-, middle-class gay and straight-identified enlisted men, middle-class naval officers, ministers, and town officials—into conflict, it revealed how differently those groups interpreted sexuality."[39]

In his testimony defending the sexual sting operation, Secretary Daniels declared that he had "exhausted every one of the regular channels" of investigation, adding that using the sailor decoys was necessary to "clean up conditions that could not possibly be allowed to exist."[40] Exposure to sexual perversion among civilians in Newport, like exposure to any contaminating disease, was a compelling argument because it deflected any concerns about same-sex practices among sailors themselves toward problems that existed outside of the navy. The war was also a useful pretext for the perceived rise of sexual deviancy on the home front. As one social reformer put it, "American boys undoubtedly became familiar with perverse practices while in France or while at sea."[41] Europe as bastion of all manner of sexual perversity was a dubious but compelling notion. More tellingly, the suggestion that homosexuality was something foreign reflected other intolerances of the age concerning political radicals and immigrants as outside forces contaminating American life.

For Newport, the contention that it was a town overrun with homosexuals was an image it actively combated. Continuing on a theme, Newport's chief of police declared that Newport was "the cleanest city in America." Similarly, the mayor told *The New York Times*: "I prided myself that Newport was as clean as any city in the United States, North, South, East, or West."[42]

As with their concerns about the Palmer raids in 1919, congressional leaders were even more disturbed by government overreach and abuse in the Newport investigations. In the spring of 1921, just as John Reidy and Charles Benner went on trial for murder, a Senate subcommittee led by Republicans issued a scathing report on the Newport operation. The committee criticized the navy for recruiting and compelling sailors to "commit vile and nameless acts." The fact that any government official would allow "immoral acts to be performed" by sailors for the "purpose of running down and trapping certain specified alleged sexual perverts" was "indefensible." The idea that any sailor in the U.S. Navy might actually be homosexual was never considered in such arguments, furthering a contrast between homosexuality and military service that would only intensify in the coming decades. The subcommittee specifically pointed to Secretary Daniels and Assistant Secretary Roosevelt for their lack of moral leadership, describing the use of entrapment as a "great injustice" that caused "inhuman" treatment of the sailors involved in the investigation. Such harsh criticism was of course directed to the practices of using the sailors in the sting and not the goal of removing the contaminating forces of sexual perverts who threatened naval sexual purity. The "moral code of the American citizen" had been trampled on, the report concluded, adding that the navy's methods violated "the rights of every American boy who enlisted in the Navy to fight for his country."[43]

"THE SAILOR'S CONFESSION IN ITSELF WAS INSUFFICIENT"

Although the Newport scandal faded from the headlines, the effects of the episode continued to be felt on the crime pages. Editors offered details about the violent and mysterious encounters between servicemen and their civilian companions to an eager reading public increasingly fascinated by scandals in the press. When a soldier was found murdered at the fashionable McAlpin Hotel on New York's Herald Square in August 1919, reports described how the victim had been "beaten to death and robbed." *The New York Times* reported that two men had registered for the room, "both in civilian attire," though detectives found underclothing of "military issue." The men registered as "C. E. Landon" and "P. J. Powerer." The victim was described as "30 years old, 5 feet 7 inches in height, and weighing about 140 pounds with black hair and blue eyes." The only description of his companion, the article noted, was that he was "well dressed." The police theory, the press offered, was that "the soldier had met a chance acquaintance in his companion, and the latter, having discovered that the soldier had money, had accompanied him to the hotel for purpose of robbery."[44]

A few days later, the press revealed the identity of the victim as Cecil E. Landon, a twenty-one-year-old soldier who had served in Europe with the army's quartermaster corps. The New York *Daily News* reported that Landon had arrived back from France a few days before he entered the McAlpin with his mysterious companion. A military colleague offered that he "had no idea who it was who accompanied Landon to his room" at the hotel. The report also noted that an autopsy confirmed the soldier had died from a fractured skull. The editors speculated that Landon may have been drugged before he was killed, as "folded papers such as heroin is sold in, were found lying near the body."[45]

News of Landon's murder circulated throughout the country via the United Press wire service, appearing on the front page of *The Oregon Daily Journal* in Portland, Landon's hometown. In its detailed article, readers learned that "police believe Landon, who had $300 in back pay with him, was lured to the hotel by a Broadway 'floater,' who killed him to get the money." The article related that police found the murder weapon, "a bloody candelabra," hidden under the bed. While the motive of robbery was likely, the article pointed to a lingering mystery: "No explanation can be given, however, of the reason for the removal of the man's collar, tie, and socks."

Readers also learned that Landon had written his parents from New York about his impending return: "Don't tell anyone I am coming home. Let it be a surprise." The article ended on a poignant note: "Happy that their boy had arrived safely from France, they were expecting a letter with specific plans for his homecoming. They were prostrated by the news of the murder."[46]

Such stories of urban vice and violent criminality played on readers' contradictory impulses of moral outrage and fascination with the grotesque details of the crime scene. In April 1923, Alfred Lafee, a twenty-two-year-old rabbi, was found beaten unconscious in a San Francisco hotel room. Newspapers described his "mysterious assailant" as a "strongly built man" who "wore the uniform of a seaman in the United States Navy." Around eight o'clock in the evening, the rabbi and his companion had registered at the Gates Hotel in the Fillmore neighborhood, an area populated with Jewish and Japanese immigrants. At the front desk, the rabbi signed his name as "A. Layne" and his companion registered as "H.B. Hickman." Early the next morning, hotel staff found the rabbi lying in bed. "His skull was battered, and an attempt had been made to strangle him," *The New York Times* reported.[47]

Three weeks later Lafee's attacker, Gladwell Richardson, a nineteen-year-old navy deserter, was arrested in Phoenix, Arizona. Richardson had been stationed on the USS *Vigilante* and jumped ship in San Francisco weeks before the crime. Police found a diary in Richardson's possession that, as *The Arizona Republic* reported, "vividly describes the assault on Rabbi Lafee."[48] In the diary Richard refers to Lafee as "the Jew" and recounts how in the hotel room "he struck 'the Jew' with a cuspidor in defending himself from assault and then washing the blood from his hands, went out through the hotel lobby, asking the clerk 'something about the weather.'"[49] Later, Richardson stated that the diary was simply a "figment of his imagination," a claim that he would subsequently recant. "Rabbi Slayer Arrives Here, Admits Guilt," the *San Francisco Chronicle* declared, relating how the young sailor met Lafee in Golden Gate Park, and then the two went to the New Fillmore Theater before registering at the hotel. In the room, Richardson claimed he was "defending himself" after he "was attacked by Lafee at about 3 o'clock in the morning." Detectives compared Richardson's handwriting in his diary with that of his hotel registration and concluded that "there is no longer any doubt that Richardson is the slayer."[50]

Such evidence would seem to have assured Richardson's conviction. But by late June it was announced that the judge had dismissed the case on the request of the prosecution. The *San Francisco Chronicle* reported that the prosecuting attorney "declared that the sailor's confession in itself was insufficient and that police investigation had failed to substantiate it." The specific faults in the investigation were not made public in the press, but the article added that Richardson was "requested to report to the naval authorities at Goat Island from which station he is alleged to have deserted."[51] What brought the two men together in Golden Gate Park, what they did over the course of the evening, who might have seen them together, and why Richardson agreed to spend the night with Lafee in the hotel room were puzzles left unexplained. But the image of a rabbi engaged in a violent and perverse encounter with a young sailor in a hotel would have resonated in a number of ways within the larger nationalist rhetoric of the period and its tones of anti-immigrant and anti-Semitism.

In a depressingly similar incident, in June 1926 Francis Milton Bloom, an "18-year-old Navy Apprentice," was found dead in the Wilson Hotel in San Diego, according to the *Los Angeles Times*, "naked except for shoes and socks." Bloom's clothing was found in the bathroom in a "disheveled state and some of his underclothing badly torn." While initial reports conjectured the death may have been a suicide, Bloom, it was reported, registered at the hotel with another man "dressed like a sailor."[52]

A few weeks later three sailors were arrested for Bloom's murder. W. H. McAfee, John Despirito, and Irving Miller had all served with Bloom on the USS *McCauley*. The *Los Angeles Times* reported that the three confessed to police that after meeting with Bloom, they "all went to the room in the Wilson Hotel, which had been rented under the name of 'W. H. Smith.'" There, they claimed, "Bloom was struck a heavy blow on the chin and another blow on the back of the head." All three denied that Bloom was dead when they left the hotel room, and, the newspaper added, "none of them will say who struck the blows."[53]

In October, Miller pleaded guilty to manslaughter in exchange for testimony, while a jury convicted McAfee of first-degree murder and Despirito of manslaughter. The Associated Press reported on the case in a short, three-paragraph article, which simply noted Bloom died of "injuries inflicted on him by the two defendants and by Irving Miller." What prompted the three men to join the navy apprentice in the hotel room was never reported. Did the men lure Bloom to the room with the intention of assaulting and murdering him? Was their rage prompted by something Bloom did? Was it, perhaps, an expression of remorse and guilt after a sexual encounter between the men? The motives and meaning of Bloom's death would remain a mystery. While the initial accounts of Bloom's body found in the hotel room made headlines beyond Southern California, few newspapers reported on the confession of the three sailors or their eventual conviction. In this, and other reports of similar unexplained deaths, readers learned nothing about the victims themselves. Journalists rarely reported on the life or character of the queer victims beyond what was learned through the confessions of their killers, which were not entirely reliable.

"ACUTE HOMOSEXUAL PANIC"

While the navy was actively investigating the threat of sexual perverts in Newport, at St. Elizabeths Hospital in Washington, D.C., Dr. Edward J. Kempf was studying soldiers and sailors hospitalized for mental illness in his research on male sexuality. At the time, St. Elizabeths was the only publicly funded hospital dedicated to mental health in the United States. It had a reputation as a humane facility for the treatment of mental illness, in contrast to the awful conditions common in many mental asylums. Toward the end of World War I, the hospital expanded its campus to accommodate the growing demand to treat the mental disorders of returning servicemen.

Kempf arrived at St. Elizabeths in 1914, after short-term tenures at

Johns Hopkins University and the Central Hospital for the Insane in Indianapolis. Raised in Indiana, Kempf followed a family tradition of studying medicine. But his interests would soon shift to theories of psychoanalysis and their uses in neurological and physiological disorders—an unorthodox approach to mental illness at the time. Colleagues described Kempf as an intelligent doctor with a difficult temperament.[54] One observer described him more bluntly: "he had a driving single-mindedness of a zealot. He never acknowledged the slightest doubt that others might have a point of view worth considering or that he might not be absolutely right."[55] Later in his career, Kempf recalled his motivation for the study of psychology: "My present interest in the problem of *how* nature makes life and life makes mind began, it seems, in the curiosities of childhood. When I was six years old, my older sister was given a doll that had eyes that would close when it was laid down and open when held erect. I cut the head open with a hatchet to see how the eyes worked."[56] At St. Elizabeths, Kempf enjoyed relative freedom to explore his experiments and unorthodox practices, but his temperament often brought him in conflict with colleagues who took issue with his methods and his conclusions.

In 1921, Kempf published *Psychopathology*, an exhaustive 762-page study that detailed a range of psychological conditions and treatments, including anxieties, neuroses, and personality disorders, to name a few. Chapter 10 of the study outlined Kempf's theory of "acute homosexual panic." Based primarily on his work with nineteen young soldiers and sailors who suffered a number of mental traumas resulting from their experiences in World War I, the theory pointed to a tension between sexual desires and social interaction. "The mechanism of the homosexual panic (panic due to the pressure of uncontrollable perverse sexual cravings)," wrote Kempf, "is of the utmost importance in psychopathology, because of the frequency of its occurrence wherever men or women must be grouped alone for prolonged periods, as in army camps, aboard ships, on exploration expeditions, in prisons, monasteries, schools, and asylums."[57] For Kempf, the problem of homosexual panic threatened the functioning of highly gendered spaces, particularly those where masculinity and U.S. empire building converged, such as the military and exploration. In this sense, acute homosexual panic was as much about national readiness as it was about individual psychology. Crucial to this readiness was a sense of control. As a student of Freud, Kempf embraced the view that humans were bisexual in nature and homosexuality was a natural form of human sexuality, but, as psychoanalysis instructs, one that needed to be controlled through proper upbringing so that such desires were directed toward heterosexual impulses in adulthood. Homosexual panic was a symptom of an individual's inability to contain the latent, "perverse," and childlike homosexual cravings that threatened to overcome the more "normal" heterosexual expressions of desire. Such a state of panic could, according to Kempf, last from "a few hours to several months" and resulted in mental breakdown, passivity, antisocial behavior, or violence.[58]

Kempf's theories were groundbreaking in the United States since they combined psychoanalysis with older theories of biological degeneracy in the study and treatment of sexual perversion. Although he did not discount older ideas of homosexuality as a result of hereditary or mental defect, he brought to such ideas a developmental understanding of sexuality—one that would increasingly shape the clinical and public conceptions of sexual deviancy in years to come.

The theory of "acute homosexual panic" was, in fact, a mash-up of many ideas about homosexuality circulating in the early twentieth century to explain homosexual desires. Drawing on both biological and environmental factors, Kempf echoed the approach advocated and popularized by the Swiss-born Adolf Meyer, an influential neurological physician at Johns Hopkins University.[59] Meyer's work in the new field of psychobiology combined principles from psychoanalysis, behavioral sciences, and biology to explain homosexuality. A longtime member of the National Committee for Mental Hygiene, which sought to reform the treatment of the mentally ill, Meyer found the ego was much more important than the id in understanding human behavior. Crucial to his theories was the dynamic between a person's psychological development and the social environment the person is exposed to. Meyer believed homosexuality was a problem rooted in a person's emotional state and how it was shaped by the difficulties of the social environment. The problem of homosexuality was, for Meyer, a problem of modern life, from urbanization and technological changes to the shifting definitions of gender roles in the early twentieth century.[60] Kempf too had more pragmatic views of sexuality, rejecting psychoanalysis's sole focus on the unconscious as a key to individual behaviors. Instead, environmental factors and evolutionary theory were crucial in understanding and treating sexual perversion. In this way, Kempf forged his own, often controversial understanding of psychobiology.

Central to the theory of acute homosexual panic was a loss of emotional control over sexual desires—a loss often prompted by factors in the environment itself. Many of Kempf's patients expressed feelings of being manipulated or lied to by those around them, as well as fears of persecution and violence by others. Kempf interpreted such symptoms as indicative of a "loss of control of [one's] sexual cravings," which forced the patient to see himself "as a sexual object." He added, when a patient feels he is being manipulated or persecuted, "it may be accepted that in some manner this particular person is either sexually attracted to him or is very intimately associated with someone who is sexually attracted."[61] When an individual comes into contact with someone who stimulates such homosexual desires, Kempf argued, "[o]ften such men and women attack the innocent person or yield to the hallucinated assault; or even both."[62] While he acknowledged that he never actually encountered such "aggressive homosexual panic," he concluded that such violence was possible because the individual was in a state of psychotic fear anchored to "a persistent vigorous, pernicious counter-attack of hatred ... directed against the conventions of society." Following the logic of evolutionary theory, this violence stemmed from the patient's "loss of social adaptability," marked by a struggle between individual desires and sexual and social norms.[63] Homosexual panic was, in this sense, understood as a defense of human evolution itself—a psychological mechanism meant to protect against extinction.

In defense of his theories, Kempf included in his book photographs of men suffering from sexual disorders he termed "perverse erotic cravings."

Posed sitting for the hospital's cameraman, the men look despondent and uncertain, their faces revealing a number of possible emotions. The captions pointed readers to the "tension of facial muscles" as evidence of "anal or phallic eroticism," suggesting that perversity could be easily read on a man's face.[64] Kempf's use of photographic evidence was not new in medical studies of mental illness or sexuality. During World War I, the military used photographs of naked recruits to weed out possible sexual abnormalities. In one photograph, an unsuitable individual was described by an army official as having a "feminine pelvis and waistline, feminine distribution of pubic hair, and great muscular weakness."[65] Even as late as the 1930s, researchers in New York City photographed participants' naked bodies in different poses as part of an extensive study of homosexuality, which also included family case studies. The researchers ultimately found little consistency among their subjects, confounding the efforts to systematize sexual deviance.

But it was the case studies of his young soldiers and sailors that proved the most useful for Kempf's study. In *Psychopathology*, Kempf described many of the patients' desperate actions in response to their illnesses. He noted how men pleaded with doctors to save them, or wrapped their arms around nurses or attendants, begging for help. While Kempf viewed such gestures as further evidence of each patient's lack of self-control, they also suggested the helplessness and resistance such men felt at the treatment they endured. Many of them expressed the urge to self-harm or had attempted suicide. It is hard to say what Kempf's nineteen servicemen suffered from: shell shock, traumas of war, or fears of their own homosexual desires. Reading the case studies, it is easy to imagine they might have suffered from all of these conditions. Poignantly, Kempf's theory of acute homosexual panic may have drawn as much upon the deeply devastating traumas of the Great War as upon any sexual and social anxieties the servicemen experienced.

While *Psychopathology* was met with a mixture of criticism and praise when it was first published, Kempf's theory of acute homosexual panic found its way into clinical practices for the next several decades and would, in the coming years, become a common defense in the murder of queer men in the crime pages and in courtrooms.

"THIRD SEX PLAGUE SPREADS ANEW!"

As the horrors of war receded, the expanding and ever-popular tabloid press provided Americans a new set of concerns. Writing in the 1930s, historian Frederick Lewis Allen pointed to one important impact of the booming press in the era: "There was more than coincidence in the fact that as they rose, radicalism fell." He added, the tabloids "presented American life not as a political and economic struggle, but as a three-ring circus of sport, crime, and sex, and in varying degrees the other papers followed their lead under the pressure of competition."[66]

While the "sex" was mostly heterosexual, the press, like the widely popular detective stories and true crime and true confession magazines, offered readers an intimate view of vice and helped shape public sentiment about the problem of sexual deviancy in all of its many forms. But it wasn't only the tabloids. The press in general found in crime stories a new urban reality of vice and shocking sexual perversions that it promoted and circulated as a public scandal and entertainment. A small article in *The New York Times* in February 1923 detailed a police raid of a number of cafés and bars in "Hobo-Hemia," its mocking term for Greenwich Village. "The police continue to pay special attention to Greenwich Village," the article reported. "Every tea-room and cabaret in the village was visited yesterday morning by Deputy Inspector Joseph A. Howard and Captain Edward J. Dempsey . . . and a party of ten detectives." There, the detectives arrested "what they thought were five women and eight men. It developed later, however, that one of the 'women' was a man." Harry Bernhammer, the article explained, was "familiarly known in the village as 'Ruby,'" adding that police charged him with "disorderly conduct for giving what police termed an indecent dance."[67]

With their emphasis on urban vice and police authority, queer crime stories like this reflected a new reality of American life: for the first time more Americans lived in cities than in rural areas. During World War I, African Americans moved north in large numbers to work in factories that supported the war effort—a migration that would increase through the 1920s. For over three decades, cities had been bulging with an influx of immigrants, creating diverse and often overcrowded neighborhoods. Bohemian neighborhoods of artists and writers were also expanding and becoming more visible in the 1920s, not only for speakeasies and a rising popularity of cabarets and jazz clubs, but also as spaces where young men and women, independent and unfettered by the social and moral values of family and rural communities, found new expressions of social and sexual life.

Such social changes provoked increasing concern for the contamination of sexual perversions. In New York City, arrests for homosexual solicitation increased from 238 in 1918 to over 750 in 1920, and continued to average around 500 a year throughout the ensuing decade.[68] As if such arrest numbers were insufficient, in 1923 the New York State Legislature revised the disorderly conduct statute to criminalize "degenerate disorderly conduct"—a vague phrasing that police and courts would use for all manner of queer associations. But the statute would have a more powerful use in the years to come. As historian George Chauncey notes, the law "became one of the underpinnings of new state regulations after the repeal of Prohibition in 1933 that, for the first time, specifically and formally banned the assembly of gay people in a public space."[69]

A changing urban demographic also provided for a greater variety in the nature of crime stories. The mysterious murder of Clinton DeForest in Central Park in September 1926 made front-page headlines in the African American newspaper *New York Amsterdam News*. Described as a female impersonator, DeForest had entered the park Tuesday evening to "pay tribute at the bier of Rudolph Valentino." At some point he encountered patrolman Joseph Higgins, who ordered DeForest to leave the park. "An altercation ensued in which Higgins admits using his fists," the newspaper reported, adding "no reason seems to be given for not having made an arrest." The beating was so severe that DeForest's mother could identify her son only by his hands, as "his face was too badly mutilated to be recognizable." Mysteriously, while the confrontation with the police happened on the west side of the park, DeForest's body was found on the east side, a discrepancy that was never explained.

Unlike the front-page attention it received in the *Amsterdam News*, *The New York Times* reported on the arrest and trial of Patrolman Higgins in a series of short articles buried deep in the body of the paper. On the stand, the newspaper reported, Higgins admitted striking DeForest "when the latter fought desperately and kicked him in an effort to avoid arrest." The article added, "The witness said he suspected De Forrest [sic] and another man of having committed a felony . . . The other man got away." The next day the paper reported the jury convicted Higgins of manslaughter; he was the second policeman to be convicted of manslaughter that week. (The other conviction was for the murder of "Arthur Bright, the alleged proprietor of a 'speakeasy' in Eleventh Avenue near Twenty-third Street."[70]) Higgins was sentenced to three to seven years in prison. But two years after his conviction, New York Governor Franklin Delano Roosevelt commuted his sentence. News of Higgins's release was reported on the front page of the *Amsterdam News*, where the editors declared: "Police brutality scored a point on Sunday."[71]

The stark differences in the ways each of the newspapers reported the crime reflected more broadly the differences in an understanding of crime itself. *The New York Times*, with its emphasis on Higgins's testimony in which DeForest had committed a suspicious crime with another man and resisted arrest, told a tale of law and order. For the editors of the *Amsterdam News*, DeForest's murder was another blatant and enraging example of police brutality against African Americans in the city. While many would have read the *New York Times* articles, few beyond the African American community were exposed to the *Amsterdam News* recounting of the crime.

In November 1931, the New York gossip and scandal tabloid *Brevities* proclaimed on its front page, "Third Sex Plague Spreads Anew!" The story reported on the "fairy round-ups of recent months" in Manhattan and Brooklyn, including in such places as Bryant Park and the Brooklyn Navy Yard. At a bar in Brooklyn, the article noted, "the average citizen would scarcely believe his eyes had he been transported there as recently as the late spring, when the 'fleet was in.'" Conjuring a tone of shock with a hint of camp, the article detailed how "night after night anywhere from fifty to seventy-five sailors were there, and anywhere from fifty to a hundred men and boys, with painted faces and dyed tresses, singing and dancing."[72]

Amid such sensational accounts of working-class vice were also stories of upper-class tragedies. A few months earlier, the murder of Edward Humbert had captured front-page headlines in the Boston and New York press. "Decorator Slain; Companion Sought," declared *The New York Times*, detailing how the twenty-three-year-old Humbert, described as an interior decorator, former dancer, and chorus man, was found "with his skull crushed in a Summer bungalow" on Bell Island, a wealthy summer retreat in Connecticut.[73] The cottage showed signs of a struggle including a "mop handle nearly broken." Police were searching for Humbert's companion, Charles Chapman, described as a wealthy antique dealer who had rented the cottage. Two days later Chapman was found dead in the posh Copley Plaza Hotel in Boston, having committed suicide by overdosing on six bottles of Veronal, a widely popular sleeping drug. A maid found Chapman's body lying in the bathtub; "a laundry basket, inverted so as to form a sort of table, was placed within arm's length of the bathtub, and on it was the picture of Humbert," *The New York Times* reported. "On the back of the picture," the article added, with heavy innuendo, "was written a memorandum describing it as a photograph of 'My Pal, Teddy,' and indicated that Chapman had intended taking a sea voyage with 'Teddy,' but that the death of the latter had prevented."[74]

In Boston, the *Globe* reported that the police were questioning twenty-three-year-old Alfred Aarhus, who had called the hotel inquiring about Chapman the day after his suicide, in connection with the mysterious death. The article related how Aarhus had met Chapman "by chance at Boylston and Tremont streets" when he asked Chapman for a match. "He said he got to talking with Chapman, and when the traffic light changed, he went one way and Chapman another." Aarhus was eventually released by the police.[75] In its coverage, *The Hartford Courant* included a photograph of Chapman and Humbert, both clad in bathing suits, sitting along a stone wall on a bright summer day, smiling at the camera. The article described how the wealthy Chapman had suffered from a heart ailment, and willed his estate, which included property and land in England and was estimated at $500,000, to Humbert. Quoting an unnamed friend, the article noted that "Chapman's health had improved and he asked Humbert to release the signed over property. The friend believes Humbert refused," perhaps suggesting a motive for the killing.[76]

While such coverage hinted at the homosexual subtext of certain crimes, offering readers innuendo and suggestive details, some criticized the press for not being more explicit in its coverage of queer criminality. "The safety of children and woman is endangered because of the prudish failure of the newspapers to make any mention whatever of the astonishing number of cases of degeneracy and perversion which comes into our Magistrates courts and even into the higher courts," a lawyer told the *Brooklyn Eagle* in 1928.[77] "Degeneracy and perversion" were clearly codes for homosexuality. Queer men themselves were well aware of the dangers of being written up in the crime pages. Appearing in the news as the victim of an assault by the man you brought to your hotel room or apartment could destroy reputations, get one evicted or fired from work, not to mention the possibility of being charged with a felony and facing prison time. Such risks encouraged many victims of assault to be reticent in revealing the causes of the violence they suffered—leaving the entire attack a mystery.

Consider the assault on C. Payson Gibbs in a Boston hotel, which made the front page of *The Boston Globe* in April 1926 under the headline "Wealthy Mill Man Beaten Up." Gibbs was one of the "wealthiest men" in Biddeford, Maine, the article noted, but while police pointed to robbery as the motive, "there was considerable mystery attached to the case." Visiting Boston on business, Gibbs met a mysterious companion while crossing Boston Common. The next morning, he was found by hotel staff in a semiconscious state in his room. "After telling his story as best he could," the newspaper reported, "but without giving the names of any one who had been with him last night, or who he might suspect of having beat him, Gibbs was taken to the hospital for treatment."[78] The next day, Gibbs furthered the mystery when, the *Globe* reported, he "was unable to give police any idea of how he received his injuries." After he returned to the hotel from the hospital, Gibbs "checked out of his room" and, the article added, "[a]s far as could be learned at the hotel last night, he left for his home."[79]

Such mysterious newspaper accounts were familiar enough by the early 1930s that they formed a key part of the plot of Niles Blair's 1931 novel *Strange Brother*. Described by its publisher as "a brave and daring story about the dilemma of an intermediate man in modern society," it was one of many gay-themed novels published in the late 1920s and early 1930s during what George Chauncey has termed the "pansy craze"—an era when homosexual cultural expression, including drag balls, campy cabaret performances, and serious novels and plays about gay experiences, were in vogue.[80] In Blair's novel, the queer protagonist, Mark Thorton, navigates his desires amid a hostile and unsympathetic society. In a letter to his friend Peggy, Mark recounts his aimless cruising around the city at night seeking to find "someone suffering like myself," adding, "I get so worn out with thinking of sex." For Mark, homosexual desires are "not a phase of life, as it ought to be, but life itself."[81]

Mark finds some solace for his condition, albeit one framed by personal tragedies. He notes that the city's heat wave makes front-page news, but "turn the page and you see" other stories, ones with headlines like "'Kills Two, then Self, in Madman Fury. Teacher Vanishes. Leaves Suicide Note. Doctor and Father Die in Suicide Pact." The stories define both Mark's fears and realities, for he reads in them his own queer struggles and a similar tragic ending. One article in particular, about two naval lieutenants who commit suicide three days apart, one in London and the other in Annapolis, affects Mark most deeply. "Doesn't that seem strange to you? Do you see the story behind it?" Mark writes in his confessional letter. "Or do I imagine it because I am what I am?"[82] As Blair makes clear, Mark is not simply imagining the homosexual undertones in such news accounts. Rather, the novel presents the mysteries and silences in such news stories as evidence of queer experience. While *Strange Brother* ends with Mark's suicide—much like many queer-themed novels of the time—Blair also shows that underneath the tragedies, behind the headlines of sailors and civilians coming to violent ends in public parks and posh hotel rooms, the crime stories reveal fragments of queer life hidden between the lines.

War on the Sex Criminal

Defining Psychopaths and Sex Deviants in the 1930s

"THE MOST COLD BLOODED KILLER"

When Lawrence Shead did not show up for work one September morning in 1933, his boss, Charles Dooley, became concerned. Thirty-five-year-old Shead was the manager of the Warner Brothers Garden Theater, an ornate movie house built in 1916 in the center of Paterson, New Jersey. Shead grew up in Norman, Oklahoma, but had left in the early 1920s, working first in Los Angeles before moving east. He had only been living in Paterson for six months and his black-and-yellow roadster, which he parked behind the Garden Theater, still bore California license plates.

According to *The New York Times*, when Dooley and other theater employees sought Shead out at his apartment, they found him "lying unclothed on a bed in the two room apartment." He "had been hit heavily with a blunt instrument. His clothing was missing, and detectives said there were indications that money and valuables had been taken." Readers found a more gruesome image of the crime scene in the New York *Daily News*. "On the bed in his blood-splattered apartment," the tabloid reported, "the stripped and battered body of Lawrence Shead was found late last night by friends who broke into his suite." The newspaper reported that the murder occurred at the "height of a riotous party which kept neighbors awake." The next day, "an electric iron was identified as the weapon used to bludgeon the life from Lawrence A. Shead." Police were searching for a man named Kenneth Neu, described as a "tall Southerner, who had been Shead's guest."[1]

The front page of the *Daily Oklahoman* in Shead's home state declared, "Norman Man Slain in East." "Shead's face and head had been battered by a sharp instrument," the paper reported, adding, "police believe the first blow stunned Shead as he rested on the bed." *The Indianapolis Star*, the Indiana city where Shead's brother lived, reported that the theater manager returned home early Sunday morning with two men. "His apartment bore evidences of a party," the newspaper noted, "and was said to have been ransacked." The article included a small photograph of Shead, dressed in shirt and tie, square jawed, handsome, and smiling.[2]

The theory that Shead was surprised by his attacker was a constant one in the press. The *Central New Jersey Home News* published a detailed account of the crime and investigation. Police believed Shead had been "stunned by the first blow and offered no resistance" to the violent and fatal beating. The article also noted that "six suits, shirts, underwear, and various other personal belongings had been taken," furthering the belief that robbery was the motive for the attack. Police had sent out an all-points bulletin for Kenneth Neu. According to a friend, Shead had spent the evening in New York City with Neu, whom he introduced as a "friend from the south." Investigators were "reading through a packet of letters found in Shead's apartment which may throw additional light on the mystery."[3]

Ten days later and 1,300 miles away, the beating murder of Sheffield Clark at the Jung Hotel in New Orleans made local headlines similarly for its mystery and brutality. The Jung Hotel billed itself as the South's largest and finest hotel. Its advertisements in the 1930s promised guests an oasis from the hardships of the era, with the saying "Old Man Depression Overlooked the Jung Hotel."[4] The hotel manager had discovered Clark's corpse propped up in bed, dressed only in his underwear. He had been dead nearly two days. Maids had alerted the management after they had entered his room several times, and each time believed he was simply asleep. A clean sheet had been pulled up tightly around his neck, and his head placed on neatly arranged pillows.

The Times-Picayune of New Orleans offered readers a long and detailed account of the discovery and police investigation. It included a grainy photograph of room 657, where Clark was murdered, taken from the hallway through the open door, which gave readers a vaguely voyeuristic view into the room. According to the newspaper, "the murderer had struck down Clark as he sat, unsuspecting, either at the foot of the bed or at the small writing table near it. Heavy blows that fractured the skull had rained upon the stunned man." The article added that there was "a deep cut above one ear" and "bruises of powerful fingers upon the throat showed that strangulation had been a contributory cause of death."

Sixty-seven-year-old Clark had been in New Orleans on business. Founder and owner of Sheffield Clark and Company, a large manufacturing agency, Clark lived in Nashville, Tennessee, where, *The Times-Picayune* noted, he was an "old and honored citizen." A veteran of the Spanish-American War, Clark was described in the article as "prominent in the social life" of the city, including memberships in the Belle Meade Country Club and Hermitage Club, "an exclusive men's club of Nashville," as well as the local Presbyterian church. The article added the fact that Clark was a "Mason in high standing."

The Times-Picayune spared few intimate details about the crime scene, including a letter Clark received from his wife that was "rescued from the waste basket and pieced together." Editors reprinted the letter in full, making public a sorrowful account in which Clark's wife remembers the funeral of their child twenty-five years earlier. "How I wish I could be in New Orleans with you," she wrote, "It will ever be a city of dreams come true to me." She closed the letter, "I love you—love you—with all my heart, and pray God to watch over you and keep you safe from harm."[5]

Crucial to the police investigation was the testimony of Albert Sims, an

African American parking attendant at the Jung Hotel. The killer had taken the victim's car keys and parking ticket, and Sims would tell the police the young man who showed up to retrieve his car was "dark complexioned, looked about 25 years old about five feet six or seven inches tall, weighed about 130 pounds and was dressed in a dark suit." The man claimed to be Clark's son, and asked Sims "directions for reaching a night club on the highway leading north out of New Orleans."

Police had devised three theories of the crime. First, that Clark had picked up a hitchhiker on his way from Nashville to New Orleans, someone who won Clark's confidence and "gained admittance to the hotel room of the victim." Second, that the killer was a "hotel prowler" who found his way into Clark's room without his knowing it. And third, that a mysterious and "fair woman in black," whom a hotel porter noticed in the lobby before the crime, had plotted with a male companion to murder and rob the business-man. According to a bellboy, Clark had asked him to invite the woman up to his room. The bellboy told Clark "it was against the rules of the hotel to bring a woman to the room of a guest." He told police he "had never seen the woman before, did not know her identity and that she vanished from the lobby shortly after" he noticed her.[6]

Police departments across the South were notified of the crime via tele-gram and asked to watch for Clark's black Chevrolet sedan, readers of Clark's hometown newspaper *The Tennessean* learned. "Had the suspect not taken the parking ticket," the paper noted, "and removed the car, police would have no clue at all in one of the city's most baffling mysteries." It added that Clark's son Sheffield Clark Jr. arrived in New Orleans by airplane. "He was notified by telephone of his father's death, but he was stunned upon arrival here to learn that Clark was the victim of murder."[7]

The same day Clark's assailant gave the parking ticket to Albert Sims, a bellboy at the DeSoto Hotel in New Orleans found in a guest room a blue shirt, polka-dotted necktie, and shirt-collar band that was monogrammed "Sheffield Clark Sr." A ten-story Romanesque building, the DeSoto stood in the heart of the city on Poydras Street and had hosted the wealthiest visitors for over two decades. The press reported that the room was registered to

Bill Williams from Jacksonville, Florida. Williams had been at the hotel for several days, and told acquaintances he was in town on a three-month leave from the Chinese army, where he was an aviator. According to one press report, Williams was often seen "flashing a roll of money."[8]

A week after Clark's body was found in the Jung Hotel, New Jersey police stopped a black Chevrolet sedan with Tennessee license plates just outside the entrance to the Holland Tunnel. Driving the car was twenty-six-year-old Louis Kenneth Neu, whom newspapers would later describe as an "aspiring radio crooner." Along with Neu, police arrested twenty-five-year-old Eunice Hotte, a "New Orleans waitress, who had driven north with Neu," and nineteen-year-old Harold Parks, whom the pair picked up just outside of Philadelphia. "Parks, who was wearing a naval uniform," *The New York Times* noted, "said he had been discharged from the Navy last spring but that he wore the uniform when he went hitch-hiking because it got him more rides."[9]

Once the suspects were in custody, detectives noticed red stains on Neu's trousers. According to the *Times*, when one of the detectives asked about the stains, "Neu, smiling, promised him a sensation if he were permitted to wash. True to his promise," the article added, "he told of the Shead murder." But it was not only Shead's murder to which he confessed. It was also Sheffield Clark's murder, shocking detectives in his matter-of-fact recounting of the two crimes as well as his calm demeanor as he detailed the gruesome and fatal beatings.

Accounts of Neu's strange confession, combined with his movie-star good looks, quickly made this double murder a national story. A photograph that circulated through the Associated Press showed a relaxed and handsome Neu, dark-haired and wide-eyed in an open-collar shirt. The New York *Daily News* did much with this image, publishing a similar photograph of a smiling, slightly unshaven Neu, and describing him as "the most cold blooded killer" Jersey City police ever saw." "If I'd gone on any longer," the newspaper quoted Neu, "I'd have killed somebody else," adding, "I promised this girl I'd show her a good time on Broadway, and my funds were getting low."[10]

The *Los Angeles Times* picked up on the story, describing how "a young singer from the South who wanted to be a Broadway crooner completed a 3500-mile round trip today—with a murder charge against him at the end." Readers learned that Neu came to New York looking for singing work. In Times Square, he met Shead. According to Neu's confession, the night of Shead's murder, the two "drank, then quarreled, then fought." Shead, the article added in an oddly passive voice, "was hit on the head with an electric iron and killed." In New Orleans, with his money nearly gone, Neu "went to Clark's hotel room and asked for money. Rebuffed, he said he hit Clark with a blackjack and choked him."[11] What drew the men together in apartment bedrooms and hotel rooms was not immediately reported in the press.

While Neu was indicted in New Jersey for first-degree murder, he was eventually extradited to New Orleans to stand trial for the murder of Clark. As one report noted, police in New Jersey "admitted a strong case of self-defense could be offered in the Paterson killing," because Neu confessed he killed Shead "in a drunken fight." But it wasn't only intoxication that cast suspicions over Neu's motivation for killing Shead. It was also Shead's sexuality.

The *Times-Picayune* detailed Neu's encounter with Shead in a number of articles. Neu described how Shead tried to get his guest drunk with strong whiskey cocktails. Neu objected, claiming he was going to see his grandmother, who lived in Brooklyn, and he did not want to visit her "with whiskey on my breath." Getting Neu intoxicated had, according to his confession, ulterior motives. Neu detailed that Shead insisted he spend the night with him, and then reached out and "threw his arms around his waist." Neu then "struck the theater manager and cursed him and they started fighting out toward the kitchen. Neu picked up an electric iron, hit Shead on the head, and grabbed him by the throat. He said the theater manager struggled into the bedroom where he fell on the bed." Neu added, "What happened afterward is not very clear in my mind. I became terribly frightened and took all his clothing, money, suitcases, and watches and then got the car and left Paterson."[12]

A week after *The Times-Picayune* reported the drunken fight in Shead's apartment, the paper published another version of the encounter, based on more details of Neu's sworn confession, that continued to portray Shead as an unstoppable and violent force. Neu "spent two days" at Shead's Paterson apartment, "and on the last night after each had a few drinks, Shead 'propositioned' him," provoking a "maddening exchange of blows."[13]

Arriving at the New Orleans train station after his extradition, *The Times-Picayune* reported, Neu was greeted by "a large crowd [that] was awaiting to catch a glimpse" of the killer. The newspaper published two large photographs of Neu and Clark on its front page, both looking younger than their age, both in shirt and tie, each smiling for the camera. The article noted that the confessed murderer was delighted as he got off the train and "called out 'Hello, gang,'" to the onlookers, adding the fact that "to newspaper reporters and photographers he told jokes." A more disturbing detail was that the killer crooner was dressed in "one of the suits of Shead, his Paterson victim," a detail that the press noted without comment.[14] "I'm ready to pay the price," Neu told police and reporters. "Whatever is coming I'll try to take it like a man."[15]

Born in Savannah, Georgia, Neu was married with two children, although he was separated from his wife. According to press reports, he had worked "as an oiler and marine refrigerating engineer until last year, when he became ill." One article reported that acquaintances considered him a "young man of intelligence and a 'good mixer.'" In New Orleans, he performed as a "singer several months ago in a nightclub."[16] In fact, the night before Neu murdered Clark, he went to the Club Plantation and "sang several numbers over the radio." Afterward, he returned to the DeSoto Hotel, where he had registered as Bill Williams, the aviator in the Chinese army.

To the New Orleans detectives, Neu told of how he first met Clark at the Jung Hotel, and *The Times-Picayune* reported Neu's description. "I found a seat in the lobby. An elderly gentleman, whom I later learned to be Mr. Sheffield Clark, took a seat near me," Neu related. "After sitting together for about five or ten minutes, Clark engaged me in conversation about the model of a truck which was parked near the hotel." The two talked for about a half hour, discussing politics and international affairs.

After their conversation the two separated, but Neu would return to the Jung Hotel and go directly to room 657—he had remembered Clark's room number from the key he spotted in their initial meeting. His description of their room encounter was both odd and vague. "I sat down with my face to the window," the article reported. "His clothes were hung on another chair. He sat on the bed and faced me." The press did not offer an explanation as to why Clark, an "old and honored citizen of Nashville" and "a Mason in high standing," would be sitting on the bed in his underwear with a man he had met only a few hours earlier. Despite all the details the article offered about Neu's confession, this remained a mystery.

After having a drink, Neu told Clark that he was in "desperate circumstances and had to leave New Orleans immediately." Clark refused his request for money, prompting Neu to threaten him. The businessman ordered him out of the room and as he stood up to use the telephone, Neu attacked him. "I struck him with the billy which I had concealed in my pocket. I then grasped him by the throat, and struck him again and fell over him on the bed." He continued to hit Clark, explaining, "I don't remember how many times I struck him, but I realized that I had killed him." He arranged Clark's body on the bed so it looked like he was asleep, and then took forty-nine dollars in cash and the keys to Clark's car.[17] Neu drove to Eunice Hotte's apartment, from which the two traveled north to New York City. Hotte worked at the club Neu performed at and would later testify that, on their drive north, Neu "was singing most of the time and seemed to be enjoying himself," noting that he appeared "perfectly normal."[18]

In commenting on the arrest of Neu, the editors of *The Times-Picayune* made an intriguing contrast between real crimes and fictional ones. "Through years of following imaginary crimes as an amusement, a large section of the public naturally is ready to take an avid interest when a tragedy of unusual horror breaks close at hand, and to wonder why the clues so generously provided in fiction are not also to be found in the vicinity of the actual slaying." In making such a distinction, the editors promoted a story of law and order amid the turmoil of the Depression and reminded readers of the diligence of the New Orleans police. "Most real crimes," the editorial concluded, "are solved by the police and not by brilliant amateurs, and there seems to have been no laxity by our local force once the tragedy was made known."[19]

Men and women began lining up outside the Orleans Parish courthouse on December 13, 1933, at 8:00 a.m. The large and imposing sand-colored building was only four years old. In the 1930s the courthouse included the Orleans Parish prison, a small chapel, and the execution chambers. Its flat art deco façade was offset with twelve fluted Corinthian columns at its entrance. Carved in the frieze and framed by two stylized and foreboding pelicans were the words "This is a Government of Law Not Men."

"There was a craning of necks as the prisoner entered the courtroom," *The Times-Picayune* reported about the crowds who filled the corridors of the courthouse. As he did on his arrival, Neu wore "the suit he took from his victim in New Jersey and the tan shoes, now dyed black, that once belonged to Clark."[20] With Neu's signed confession, the question for the court was not whether Neu had killed Clark, but whether he knew what he was doing was wrong. While the presiding judge, A. D. Henriques, had determined that Neu was sane to stand trial, his sanity at the time of the murder was not a settled matter. That question was precisely the issue for the jury to decide.

While its legal definition varied across states, insanity defenses in general required defendants to prove that they had diminished capacity to tell right from wrong at the point of committing the crime. From its origins, the legal claim of insanity relied on vague and often contradictory understandings of mental disease. Through the nineteenth and early twentieth centuries, insanity was understood as a somatic condition, something that was inherited and often could be read through bodily gestures, facial contortions, or general behavior of the criminal himself. The criminally insane lacked any rational, normal thinking, so the theory went. But insanity could also be read through the horror of the crime itself—particularly in cases of temporary insanity, when the killer had lost all rational thinking in a moment of passion.[21] In either situation, in the courtroom a defendant could only be found rational or insane. There was no space in between.

While Neu's confession was admitted into evidence, his lawyers argued that he was suffering from a deteriorating mental disease, the evidence of which was found in physical examinations. According to the *Atlanta Constitution*, Neu's lawyer, Clarence Dowling, argued that his client "had been mentally abnormal all his life." In support of this argument, Dowling put on the stand a series of witnesses, starting with Neu's aunt. She testified to a moment when Neu "chased his grandmother around with a horse whip" when he was fourteen years old. Dowling also presented Neu's army record, showing he had been discharged in 1926 as "unfit for service as a soldier" because of a diagnosis of psychosis, which the military considered permanent. Readers also learned that despite the discharge, Neu "enlisted several times at various places under assumed names, after having deserted other commands, and that he had suffered a head injury while in the service by diving into shallow water."

One of the more outlandish efforts by the defense included the testimony of two newspaper reporters who stated that in interviews with Neu, "the defendant had told them of numerous 'love affairs,'" a claim that another witness, a shipmate of the defendant, disputed, stating he "didn't know of any love affairs that Neu had any time" on their voyage together. It was unclear from reports how either the excess or absence of such affairs would have confirmed or denied sanity. However, such efforts did point to the ways sexuality played a role in court in determining one's mental competence.

Perhaps the most direct evidence of insanity came from two local expert witnesses, Dr. Randolph Unsworth of the De Paul Sanitarium for Mental Diseases and Dr. Forest Johns, director of the laboratory of clinical pathology at Tulane University. Unsworth, the *Atlanta Journal* article continued, "produced a chart listing numerous alleged abnormalities of the defendant's life" and concluded that his mental capacity had "slowly been deteriorating" since his childhood. The chart was, unfortunately, not reprinted in the article. Neu "had never been a normal person," Unsworth concluded. Dr. Johns testified he had examined "spinal fluid" and concluded that Neu suffered from "a diseased condition of the brain" that was "rarely cured and gradually destroyed the brain tissue."[22]

Dowling also pointed to Neu's actions after the murder, appealing to the jury's conception of what an insane man might do after brutally beating and strangling another man in a hotel room. For Dowling, it was Neu's calm, seemingly rational behavior after committing such a horrible crime that offered the best evidence of his insanity. In his closing argument, detailed in *The Times-Picayune*, Dowling stated that "the elevator girl in the hotel testified that when he rode down the elevator he appeared perfectly calm and unruffled. The negro boy in the hotel parking lot testified that Neu smiled frequently during his conversation about his victim's car." Such details led Dowling to ask: "Are those the actions of a sane man?"[23]

For the prosecution, Neu's guilt was not a question of insanity but one of criminal intention. "I don't care what this expert tells you," Assistant District Attorney Bernard Cocke told the jury, "all of Neu's actions at the time he murdered Clark and during the days preceding and following the murder were the actions of a sane but criminally inclined individual." Buttressed by Neu's detailed confession, the prosecution dismantled the defense's evidence, noting that "the army record specifically states that further hospitalization and institutional care is unnecessary." He criticized the aunt's testimony, noting that "not once did his aunt say that she considers Neu insane."

Cocke also dismissed the defense's expert witness testimony. Dr. Johns's pathology examination was called into question, because such tests often proved inconclusive. In turn, the prosecutor also poked fun at Unsworth's evaluation. "Dr. Unsworth testified that he decided Neu was insane because he flushed red about the chest and neck," he reminded the jury in his closing arguments. "I get red when I argue a case. But I hope, gentlemen of the jury, that you do not consider me insane." In siding with the prosecution, *The*

Times-Picayune was equally dubious of the defense's expert testimony, describing it as "a desperate last minute attempt to save Neu from the gallows."

The clear theme of the trial coverage was a general suspicion of psychological theory. "Every desperate criminal pleads insanity after he has gotten in the hands of the law," Cocke argued, "but insanity as a defense has become such a fakery that citizens of this state have come to regard it with suspicion." Cocke's most compelling argument for Neu's sanity was also one of the most shocking. According to *The Times-Picayune*, Cocke told the jury, "Neu resented the physical advances made on him by Lawrence Shead, the first man he murdered, and," Cocke continued, "resenting these advances started to fight. Seeing that Shead was getting the best of him, he killed him." In this line of reasoning, Cocke appealed to the all-male jury by putting them in Neu's place at that moment with Shead. Killing Shead, he argued, "was what I might have done or you might have done under the circumstances. If Neu's story concerning his encounter with Shead is correct, then he did not commit a crime. But he believed he had committed a crime, so he fled to New Orleans." Cocke added, "Arriving in New Orleans he found himself in need of money, so he purchased a blackjack for the purpose of getting money out of someone. Nothing abnormal about that—merely a criminal tendency." The assistant district attorney's claims about Neu's sanity depended on convincing the jury that killing another man who comes on to you proved, in Cocke's words, "beyond doubt that Neu was a normal person."[24]

The jury spent five hours in deliberations. At one point, they requested clarification from Judge Henriques of the legal definition of insanity. At 9:13 p.m., they returned a verdict of murder, which carried the penalty of execution by hanging. It is unclear what persuaded the men to this verdict. Was it the argument that Neu's calm demeanor was indicative of his rationality? Was it the weak expert testimony offered by the defense? Was it, perhaps, the prosecution's key argument that a violent and murderous attack on another man's sexual solicitation indicated a certain rational normality? What was clear from the press reports of the trial was that Clark's status as a wealthy, married man protected him from any suspicions about the possibility of a sexual encounter between the two men in room 657 at the Jung Hotel.

As the verdict was read out, Neu turned to the jury and shouted, "Gentlemen of the jury, you have my best wishes." Afterward he asked the news photographers to wait to take a photograph of him smiling, which they did. A beaming Neu filled the front page of *The Times-Picayune* the following day. On his way out of the courtroom, accompanied by police guards, he sang "at the top of his voice" "Sweet Rosie O'Grady," a popular waltz ballad from the late nineteenth century.

Fourteen months after his conviction, on February 4, 1935, Neu was hanged at the Orleans Parish jail at 12:05 p.m. Newspapers around the country reported the execution, referring to him as the "debonair night club entertainer" and the "singing slayer," and describing how he was "nattily attired, his black hair almost glowing" as he stepped upon the steel trap of the gallows. One report noted that he woke early on the day of his execution. "I like to have everything just right," he was reported as saying, "even a hanging."[25]

"INSPIRED BY A DISEASE"

Neu's case presented readers with a powerful paradox of the criminal—a charming and handsome singer who was also a cold-blooded killer. Debates about his sanity in court and in the press reflected this paradox, as legal definitions of insanity were weak in defining his personality and the brutality of his crimes. Reports of his crime and the courtroom debates portrayed a growing tension between law and psychology in the understanding of criminality in the Depression era, where mental illness was an increasingly complex theory in the courtroom and on the crime pages.

These tensions were hastened by the rise of "new psychology" in the United States through self-help books, films, popular literature, and confession and romance magazines bringing theories of psychoanalysis to the

broader public in the 1920s and 1930s. Central to these new ideas was a focus on the psychosexual aspects of personality development, and how childhood development was a key influence on adult behaviors. The reviewer of
two new texts about abnormal psychology declared in *The New Republic*
in 1922, "Everybody who is anybody, or wants to be, has a 'psychology'
today, and makes knowing remarks about other people's." He continued
with such a skeptical tone: "Speculation and dogmatizing about the patterns and processes of the conduct of men has a contemporaneous vogue the
terms of which are symptomatic. Men have ceased to be clear in their hearts
about their own motives and actions, and have become suspicious of those
of their fellows."[26] Such ideas would only grow through the decade, even as
their scientific merit was often questioned. "Perhaps the popularization of
the theories and findings of the New Psychology has reached a saturation
point," wrote one commentator in 1927, "and we are feeling the need for
more substantial and plain, if less tempting, food. It is certainly somewhat
trying to be reminded in every new book on psychology of the abnormal
characteristics of pyromaniacs and homosexuals." The connection between
criminality and homosexuality was not uncommon, reflecting an increasing
public rhetoric that placed homosexuality within a continuum of mental
illness and criminal threats. But these books also highlighted another reality
about deviancy in the era as both a form of public spectacle and private outrage: such literature, the commentator concluded, "reminds one too vividly
of the Coney Island show booths with their monster men and women."[27]

These criticisms not only pointed to how titillating books about new
psychology, with their theories and descriptions of all kinds of deviancy,
proved for readers, but also how such books, as well as similar magazine articles, came to define the boundaries between normal and abnormal personalities. By the Depression, the crime pages offered readers gruesome stories
of murder and violence, as well as ideas about the psychology of criminality
and sexuality.

Months after Kenneth Neu was executed, reports of a bizarre double
murder-suicide in Los Angeles made front-page news. The *Los Angeles Times*
called it "Hollywood's most fantastic shooting affray," and detailed how

William Howard, a twenty-eight-year-old secretary-chauffeur and an ensign in the naval reserve, shot and killed Paul Ivar, a twenty-five-year-old "dress designer-by-appointment to Hollywood film actresses," at a dinner party Ivar was hosting at his apartment. After shooting Ivar, Howard leaped from an apartment window, escaping in his car to the home of Henry Bolte, a law professor and political candidate, where he shot Bolte in the back, afterward turning the gun on himself. Bolte would linger in the hospital for a few days before dying from his wounds. The murders led to a host of articles across the country filled with all manner of theories about the motives for such a crime.[28]

Ivar's murder came nearly a year after Hollywood instituted its infamous Production Code, a policy promoted by Catholic interests that set new standards for both the content of films and the image of Hollywood actors. The code censored all kinds of behaviors on screen, including profanity, ridicule of the clergy, plots that involved interracial couples, scenes of childbirth, most forms of nudity, and of course "sex perversion." Such rigid norms were a response to the destabilizing economic pressures of the Depression and to what many saw as the social excesses of the 1920s.[29] Not only did the Production Code prohibit the display of homosexuality on screen, but more profoundly it banned the mere inference of such behaviors. Once the code was put into effect in July 1934, any suggestion of homosexuality on screen ended.

The associations between Hollywood and sexual perversity simmered in press reports of the Ivar murder. "Sensation Near in Hollywood's Crime Mystery," the *Chicago Tribune* declared. *The Boston Globe* described Ivar's "shadowy past," which included unspecified thefts. A mug shot of him from a previous arrest accompanied the article, his round face casting a raised eyebrow of disgust at the police photographer. Many press reports noted Ivar's working-class background, often quoting the victim, who had described himself as "born of nobody but with a terrific ambition to be a somebody."[30]

The New York *Daily News* headline declared, "Bare Bizarre Trail in Movie Slaying." The tabloid reported that while police believed that money was the motive for the murders, "officers were still mystified over the relationship between the four men involved," adding that Ivar was "a neurotic young man with a flair for feminine accoutrements and effeminate companions, police said." The term "neurotic" was code for a host of sexual and gender transgressions. According to the *Daily News*, the investigation uncovered a "colony of neurotics" in a "Laurel Canyon hideaway who admitted they knew Ivar intimately." Two of the women, the article added, "were said by police to attire themselves habitually in male costume." According to one of the women, "All the boys knew Paul."

Equally strange was the case of William Howard. The press quoted a cousin of Howard who described the killer as "a peculiar man, who never associated with women and never intended to marry." Howard had met Ivar several years earlier, when Ivar was "a habitué of questionable resorts frequented by feminine men and masculine women." According to police, Ivar and Howard had been "cruising around the city" when they met a tall blond sailor, later identified as N. C. McDermitt. The *Chicago Tribune* gave even more precise details of the pickup: "The sailor said he did not know Ivar or Howard until last Sunday when they 'picked me up when I was on my way from San Pedro to Los Angeles.'" The dinner party, the press reported, was in McDermitt's honor, though the sailor fled the apartment as soon as he heard gunfire.[31] Despite these earlier suggestions of sexual and gender deviancies, the *Los Angeles Times* would report months after the killings that authorities believed "Howard killed Ivar and Bolte because he was desperate in need of money," as both the victims owed the young chauffeur money for work he had done. The killing was a moment of rage brought on by undue pressure "to satisfy creditors who were crowding him. Then," the newspaper added, "he killed himself."[32]

More often than not in the 1930s, the crime pages offered readers contradictory theories about mental illness that borrowed from both disease theories and the newer psychosexual development ideas in relating sexual deviance to the causes of criminality. In June 1936, Albert Walter led police to an apartment in the Nob Hill district of San Francisco, where he confessed to the beating and strangulation of Blanche Cousins. Newspapers termed the crime the "stocking murder," referencing how Walter strangled

Cousins with a silk stocking. In his confession, he claimed that he killed Cousins because she resisted his sexual advances. Cousins had left her small town in Idaho and met Walter on a transcontinental bus to San Francisco. The son of a wealthy Boston family, Walter was described in news reports as polite and good-looking. He had been married in New York City a few years before the murder, but, as *The Boston Globe* reported on its front page, he had a habit of disappearing. According to Walter's father, the assailant had only one fault and that was "wanderlust." In an interview with the *Globe*, his father claimed Walter "had been across the country a score of times. He was known to make mysterious disappearances from home and then turn up later seeking forgiveness." But, the father added, "there was nothing criminal in that."[33]

The peculiar behaviors of Walter were precisely what the press found most compelling. Some newspapers referred to his mental instability as his disease—a disease brought on by a trauma in his early teen years. "Walter said an incident in his relationship with a woman when he was fourteen years old caused him to turn against the opposite sex," *The Boston Globe* noted. The *Los Angeles Times* took a more critical tone, calling the twenty-eight-year-old Walter a "Lothario" who "hated women." The article described how Walter has spent most of his life bent on a "series of revenges" against women, each "inspired by a disease he had contracted at 14."[34] One of the more compelling and perplexing aspects was Walter's continued insistence on being executed, a claim many articles related as evidence of his mental disease. The *Los Angeles Times* reported a familiar refrain from the killer: "I regard the death sentence as the penalty for all of my crimes. I am a lost man."

Throughout the press coverage of his trial, accounts of Walter's childhood made implicit and explicit references to his homosexuality. An Associated Press report noted how Walter's father asked the court to have his son declared insane. "He frequently received letters from men," his father testified. In these letters "Albert confessed all his misdeeds, desires, and diseases—and all his uncontrollable homosexual desires," adding that the letters "told of the terrible mess he had made of his life and showed no escape from himself except suicide."[35] The court ultimately rejected the father's plea and sentenced Walter to death. In December 1936, he became the two hundredth man to be hanged in San Quentin since the prison began executing prisoners in 1893.

"SEXUAL PERVERT"

While Albert Walter symbolized the perceived figure of a violent, woman-hating, and mentally diseased homosexual, reports of his crime also pointed to a more monstrous figure: the sex criminal. Embodying a number of anxieties about aberrant masculinity, the sex criminal translated the social and economic turmoil of the 1930s into problems of gender and sexual nonconformity. In statehouses, newspapers, and psychiatric journals, the sex criminal was most acutely defined in a neologism of the era: the sexual psychopath. Such a figure embodied a wide range of mental and physical characteristics and exhibited such harmless behaviors as voyeurism, masturbation, and sodomy to the more violent offenses of rape, child sexual assault, and murder. By the late 1930s, newspapers and magazines, such as *Collier's*, *The Nation*, *Christian Century*, *Newsweek*, and *Literary Digest*, were offering readers all manner of commentaries and discussion about the problem of sex crimes and sexual psychopaths.[36] While criminologists, psychiatrists, and lawyers would debate the origins of and responses to the sexual psychopath for decades, at its core was an understanding that sexual and gender deviancy caused violent criminal behavior.[37]

Though the figure of the sexual psychopath embodied the broader public debates about deviancy and normalcy, it also fueled a sex crime panic that took hold in the press in the late 1930s. Sex panics had ebbed and flowed in the press since the late nineteenth century, often directed to the bodies of women and the problems of female prostitution. Sensationalized news accounts of the murders of young women were coupled with commentaries about female purity, the dangers of women in public spaces, or moral outrage about the scourge of prostitution. In reporting on such murders, newspapers not only shaped the meanings and interpretations of the crimes but also, in more subtle ways, conveyed ideas of female virtue and the dangers of women going out alone. These panics, with their definitions and proscriptions about femininity, had the effect of controlling the behaviors and boundaries of women's bodies in public.

In the 1930s and 1940s, however, sex crime panics were more often focused on controlling abnormal forms of male sexuality. The images of transient men, out-of-work men, and men who lived beyond traditional family structures were of particular concern, a subject of interest for social scientists and criminologists. Increasingly, the contrasting attributes of either feminized men or overly masculine ones were viewed as symptoms of violent criminality.[38] Often these panics were prompted by sensationalized accounts of sexually motivated child murders or, like Walter's killing of the young Blanche Cousins, the violent murder of women—crimes that fanned the fears of a broader threat of sexual perversion in the community.[39] The arrest of Albert Fish in New York in 1934 for the murder of twelve-year-old Grace Budd, for example, captured headlines for nearly two years, until his execution in January 1936. Accused of murdering and cannibalizing Budd, the sixty-four-year-old Fish confessed to other child killings, details of which filled the press. With the public preoccupied by his case, fueled by sustained news coverage, Fish came to embody the monstrosity of the sex criminal, linking in the popular imagination the horrors of sex offenders with child killers.

Such sensationalized media accounts also threw out a big net, one that included all forms of aberrant sex, from the violent to the consensual, as a form of mental illness and criminality. Within such sex crime panics, queer men were often the most vulnerable targets of police roundups, mob vigilantism, vice purges, and forced incarceration in psychiatric institutions to undergo extreme treatments. Annual arrests for disorderly conduct and sodomy in New York City between 1936 and 1938, when sex crime panic was at its height, were nearly double that of arrest rates in 1932. In such a climate, queer men were trapped within these panics and the image of the sexual psychopath, reinforcing public opinion that male sexual and gender deviancy in general, and homosexuality in particular, was a powerful menace in need of increased policing and legislative action.[40]

The abduction and murder of ten-year-old Charles Mattson in Tacoma, Washington, in December 1936 continued to stoke these fears. While initially the investigation involved only the local police, it quickly enlisted the help of J. Edgar Hoover's FBI and soon garnered national headlines. Within weeks, Mattson's body was found in a wooded area fifty miles outside of Tacoma. Press accounts of the crime offered gruesome details, including how Mattson was found naked with his hands bound, his skull crushed, his teeth knocked out, and his face and body badly bruised. The coroner also noted that there was a nonfatal stab wound in his back. President Franklin Roosevelt called the murder "ghastly" and pledged a relentless search by the FBI for the killers. Employing the help of a psychiatrist, FBI agents developed a profile of the killer as a "sexual pervert" with "sexual abnormalities." Despite a dragnet that involved detaining and eliminating nearly 24,000 suspects, the killer was never found. Nonetheless, the FBI used the search to expand the growing archive of political radicals and subversives that Hoover had begun in the 1920s to include sexual degenerates, homosexuals, and others detained or arrested for sex crimes.[41]

For some, the national panic around Mattson's murder pointed to a hypocrisy in the claims for law and order. Voicing views not uncommon in the African American press at the time, the editors of the *Pittsburgh Courier* criticized a justice system that made sex crimes a national concern but continued to ignore the brutality and constancy of African American lynchings. The editorial referenced the public lynching of Claude Neal in Marianna, Florida, in 1934. Arrested on rumors he raped and murdered a local white woman, Neal was forcibly removed from his jail cell by a vigilante mob, then tortured, castrated, and hanged in front of the county courthouse before a large and enthusiastic crowd. The story of his lynching was widely reported in the press. Recalling Neal's lynching, the *Pittsburgh Courier* editors questioned Roosevelt's public response to the Mattson murder and asked, "Did President Roosevelt consider this atrocious mob murder 'unbelievable and ghastly'?" They continued, "To say that such a crime as the murder of the

Mattson lad is 'unbelievable,' in a land where hanging, torture and burning are the customary methods of dealing with Negroes suspected of crimes, is to set one's self down as either an ignoramus or a hypocrite."[42]

"LET'S CLEAN UP THIS TOWN!"

In the wake of the Mattson murder, commentaries about how to deal with sex criminals ranged from increased policing and harsher penalties to forced medical treatment. An editorial in the widely influential *Saturday Evening Post* advocated the view that sex criminals should be executed. "Most of the sex killers are psychopathic personalities," it proclaimed, adding, "No one knows, or can even closely estimate, how many tens of thousands of them are loose in the country today." Pointing to two highly publicized murders of children in New York City, the editorial declared that "the medical profession agreed that there were no reliable mental, medicinal, or even surgical cures for such men" who commit sex crimes. "Is there any reason," it concluded, "why the law should not make the death penalty mandatory in such cases?" adding that there was a dire need for legislation giving "society a guaranty of protection against such mad dogs through extermination."[43]

In contrast to such dire criminal justice approaches, others argued for stricter medical treatment. In 1937, the well-known and respected science journalist Marjorie Van de Water published a series of syndicated columns entitled "Sex Crimes" suggesting several reforms. Drawing on the increase of sex crime stories in the newspapers, Van de Water claimed that "murder is adding its horrors to the attacks upon little boys and girls and are [sic] daily becoming more numerous." She argued that police were calling upon the expertise of psychologists and sociologists "to advise and join forces against this evil that is endangering women and little children." Van de Water offered ten ways social scientists could aid in the fight against the sex crime problem, including empowering a board of "qualified individuals" to handle the nonviolent cases so as to avoid court trials and civil action. The recommendations of oversight of nonviolent behaviors—including masturbation, public sex, exhibitionism, and sodomy, for example—betrayed the ways such editorials aligned violent crimes with a range of harmless sex acts. Van de Water suggested local and state agencies needed to develop a reporting system to local health departments of all cases of "sex perversion" in the same way "that cases of smallpox or scarlet fever are now reported." She suggested that a night hospital could be set up, and that "sex deviants could be required to report at a certain hour each evening, and there they would be compelled to remain until morning. Since," she concluded, "most assaults upon women occur during the evening and night hours."[44]

As Van de Water's columns were finding eager readers in the fall of 1937, J. Edgar Hoover called for his own "War on the Sex Criminal!" in the pages of the *Los Angeles Times*. Hoover stoked the fears of readers by claiming that the "sex fiend, most loathsome of all the vast army of crime, has become a sinister threat to the safety of American childhood and womanhood." In the belief that sex criminals become more dangerous over time, the FBI director called for more concentrated surveillance and policing as the smallest crime is a "blazing signpost pointing to a future of torture, rape, mutilation, and murder." But this policing was not simply the task of law enforcement. Hoover argued for a large network of psychiatrists, criminologists, and local communities, all vigilantly attentive to the sex criminals lurking around them. "Since the sex fiend may strike anywhere," he wrote, "every community should devote itself to the segregation of all suspected persons." The article was accompanied by an image of a well-dressed woman clutching a young girl, both faces frozen with fear as the shadow of a large hand reaches toward them, an aesthetic that could easily have come from the publicity departments of a Hollywood studio. In a tone of exasperation, Hoover concluded, "the present apathy of the public toward known perverts, generally regarded as 'harmless,' should be changed to one of suspicious scrutiny."[45]

Such articles were a key part of Hoover's efforts to consolidate an image of the FBI as America's trusted law enforcement agency. Ever since its launch in the 1920s, the agency had been viewed with suspicion by Congress and some in the press. The presence of a federal police force continued to raise concerns of government overreach and an undercutting of the authority of individual states over law enforcement and crime. Hoover employed the help of journalists and public relations specialists to create a narrative that emphasized responsibility and scientific police work while offering up Hoover himself as the epitome of law and order. Hollywood films in the 1930s gave us the G-men—clean-cut, heroic, and thoroughly masculine. It was an image Hoover exploited well throughout the decade as a national brand, including a G-men radio show, pulp novels, magazines, toys, and even bubblegum cards.[46] The war on sex criminals was undoubtedly a vital part of this public effort by the agency to establish its authority over a wider net of criminality—beyond gangsters, political radicals, and outlaws—to include urban vice and the policing of the gender and sexual norms of the nation.[47]

But vigilance had its price. The increased sensationalized press coverage of sex crimes prompted concerns about the possible effect the gruesome stories might have on readers. The editor of the *Green Bay Press-Gazette* voiced the opinion of many newspaper editors when he argued the value that sex crime stories had in combating the epidemic. "It must be printed," he argued in relation to sensational accounts of murder, "if public opinion is to be aroused to deal with this social menace." The editorial concluded, "[I]f printing the news means fanning the fire in some cases, it also furnishes the only method by which the fires can be controlled and restrained."[48]

Those fires burned strong in August 1937, when a "crowd of one thousand men and women attacked John Ploshay" after he was accused of molesting a woman and three girls in a New York City subway station. The story appeared in newspapers across the country. Reports described Ploshay as a "51-year-old Queen's [sic] laborer," who was knocked nearly unconscious in the attack. *The Washington Post* declared the crowd tried to "lynch the man" after someone shouted he was a "sex maniac." This was echoed in *The Oakland Tribune*, which noted the "men and women attempted to lynch a man accused of molesting a woman."[49] According to the Associated Press, Ploshay's face was "bloody and swollen and his coat and shirt ripped," add-

WAR ON THE SEX CRIMINAL | 69

ing that "public resentment against repeated sex crimes" was the source of the crowd's anger, and that some in the crowd shouted "let's hang him." The *New York Herald Tribune* related how one man who initiated the attack had suspected Ploshay of "being one of the sex offenders he had been reading about in the newspapers."[50]

Inevitably, such fevered fears and violent attacks were also directed at queer men, including a highly publicized mob assault on actor William Haines and his partner, Jimmie Shields, in El Porto, California, a seaside town just south of Los Angeles. Throughout the 1920s, Haines's handsome face and playful, comic acting had endeared him to audiences, making him one of the most popular actors of the silent film era. When the talkies arrived, Haines's adjustment to the form was difficult, not only for the new acting demands, but also because of the changing gender norms for male actors. As the Production Code went into force, Haines became a victim of the new morality standards, particularly in his refusal to adapt to the expectations of leading men: tough, masculine, and thoroughly heterosexual on screen and, more imporant, off. He had rejected efforts by MGM studio chiefs to marry and end the constant rumors about his bachelor status. In a 1932 *Vanity Fair* profile, the writer described Haines as "muscular without being athletic," adding, "when he walks there is a certain grace that suggests delicacy. There is masculinity in his actions, yet a definite tendency towards femininity in his thoughts."[51] Haines's last film was released in 1935, after which he built a successful interior decorating business, working with many of the same studio executives he did as an actor, only without the confinement of the Production Code.

In the mid-1930s, Haines rented a summer house in El Porto and would often host a number of gay male friends visiting from Los Angeles. News reports of the attack in June 1936 described how a group of local men and women approached Haines and his friends as they walked back home after a dinner. "We don't want you to live here," the crowd shouted. "We'll give you just an hour to get out of town."[52] Confused, Haines tried to make a joke about the comment. One man struck Shields in the head. As Haines leaped to protect him, he was also hit in the face. "I realized the men were drunk,"

Haines told a reporter later, "and to fight them might result in fatalities. So when I was struck, I decided to remain in a prone position."[53] As the crowd followed Haines, Shields, and their friends back to the house, they threw eggs and tomatoes at them. Haines was bleeding badly from a cut on his face, but he and the others gathered their belongings and packed their car amid a growing crowd that shouted, "Let's clean up this town!"

A front-page article in the *Los Angeles Times* about the attack included a large photograph of Haines. "Memories of a harrowing experience with an angry mob of men and women last night haunted the eyes of Charles William Haines," the article related.[54] *The New York Times* described how "a shouting, jeering mob, about 100 men and women, severely beat William Haines, former motion picture star, and Jimmy Shields, a companion, near Manhattan Beach and drove them and nineteen friends out of town."[55] News of the attack circulated through the Associated Press to small-town and big-city papers, including Haines's hometown of Staunton, Virginia. The front page of that town's newspaper, *The News Leader*, reported that several men in the crowd "openly boasted of taking part in the mobbing, saying they were members of a so called 'White Legion.'" The article added that one man in the mob shouted at Haines and his friends, "We've been waiting for a chance to get you."[56] References to the White Legion and white supremacist groups in the area were repeated in many of the initial reports. "Some wild, untrue rumor must have stirred them up," Haines was reported as saying in many of these reports, "It might have been some sort of clan or secret organization." Haines added, "It was a lynch mob all right."[57]

According to the *Los Angeles Times,* a local resident claimed that Shields subjected her son to "moral mistreatment" at his home, sparking the mob attack. But this was not the first such accusation in the area. There were several local accounts of "sex perversion" in the local press that summer. As Haines biographer William Mann notes, "[T]he very next week, Dr. Frederick Klaus, the highly respected principal of Pier Avenue School in neighboring Hermosa Beach, was arrested on a morals charge. G. R. Smith, a Hollywood banker and the father of a fourteen-year-old boy, claimed Klaus had improperly touched his son. Then, in July, A. W. Shade, a music teacher at Union High School, was accused by parents of conducting classes in an 'improper manner' and was put 'under advisement.'" As Mann concludes, "suddenly Manhattan Beach seemed in the midst of an epidemic of child molesters." The deputy district attorney questioned a number of witnesses to the attack, including Haines and Shields.[58] In the end, there was little evidence to proceed with criminal charges, and the incident quickly faded from the news.

"SORDIDNESS BEHIND THE GRIM WALLS"

The same week that readers were learning of the mob attack on William Haines, the trial of James Day for the Illinois prison murder of Richard Loeb made front-page headlines across the country. The murder had captivated and shocked the country that winter of 1936. The *Chicago Tribune* reported that the thirty-year-old Loeb was "slashed to death yesterday with a razor wielded by one of his fellow convicts in the Statesville penitentiary near Joliet." The newspaper offered grotesque and riveting details of the prison attack in the shower, describing the "ferocious cutting" that involved "fifty-six slashes from one inch to two feet long" on Loeb's body. At the prison hospital where Loeb was rushed after the attack, the paper reported he whispered, "I'm all right, warden; I'll pull through."[59]

Few stories illustrated the horrors and threats of violent queer criminality so acutely as the murder of the notorious child killer. Born into a wealthy Chicago family, Loeb, along with friend Nathan Leopold, was serving a life sentence plus ninety-nine years for the 1924 kidnapping and murder of fourteen-year-old Bobby Franks—a "thrill kill" that generated national and international press coverage in what newspapers deemed the "crime of the century." Leopold and Loeb—who, when they killed Franks, were nineteen and eighteen, respectively—possessed exceptional intelligence and social privilege. Leopold graduated from college at the age of eighteen, could speak eleven languages, and had published articles on ornithology, his passion for birds. Another passion was his charming and handsome friend

Richard Loeb. The youngest person to have graduated from the University of Michigan, Loeb was similarly intelligent, but coupled such talents with an interest in sports and a fascination with true crime and murder mysteries. It was Loeb's idea to create the "perfect crime" as a scientific experiment—a seemingly motiveless crime that would never be solved. With their capture, trial, and imprisonment, Leopold and Loeb had become national crime figures in the 1920s not because they typified gangsters or outlaws—figures popular in the press—but because the two young men of social privilege, wealth, and keen intellect didn't fit the image of the cold-blooded killer. The two were eventually sentenced to serve at the Statesville Penitentiary.

Twenty-three-year-old James Day "was a far different sort from the slayers of the Franks boy," the *Chicago Tribune* wrote. Orphaned at a young age and raised by his uncle and aunt in the rural poverty of West Virginia, Day was sent to reform school twice in his early teens, where, the newspaper noted, he was a "frequent offender of school rules and was regarded as 'insubordinate.'" After an armed holdup of a gas station attendant in 1932, Day was sentenced to ten years in prison. "He was always hard to handle," his uncle was quoted in the press, "I did my best to keep him out of mischief. But he became a thief." The uncle added, "His letters from prison indicated that he was getting along all right there and trying to get out and go straight."

With the tone of a good mystery, the *Chicago Tribune* editors raised the central question of the murder: "What had happened in the shower room?" To pursue this grim plot, the *Tribune* drew on Day's own confession, helping readers to imagine the scene of the attack with all of its salacious details. "Loeb brought it on himself," declared Day. "This morning I saw Leopold and Loeb chatting together and eating in a cell. I've had trouble with Loeb before; we had a fight once. He said he'd like to settle our difficulties and I said that would be all right. 'Meet me in my private bathroom after dinner,' he said. I told him that would be all right. After dinner I went to the door of the room and waited several minutes for Loeb. He came, took the key from his pocket, and unlocked the door. I went in with him and he locked the door on the inside. We undressed and got under the shower. Then he showed me the razor and told me if I did not do what he told me to he would kill me with it. I waited for an opportunity and kicked him hard. He fell to the floor and the razor dropped from his hand. I seized it."[60]

One report by the Associated Press noted that investigators had interviewed Loeb's cellmate, who would later testify that "Loeb never had a razor" and that Day had "initiated the date in the shower."[61] But these reports quickly disappeared as editors relied on Day's testimony, and his claims of self-defense, in constructing the details of the attack. Day's explanation of events would become the dominant story of the crime as it made front-page news in nearly every paper across the country, even traveling as far as the Manchester *Guardian* in England and the English-language *North China Herald*.[62] Many of the articles included a darkly lit photograph of the shower, with arrows pointing to the scene of the crime, helping readers imagine the bloody battle that Day described. In large block letters, the New York *Daily News* headlined its story "Loeb, First Thrill Killer, Slain," eclipsing coverage of the other news of the day, the funeral of King George V of Great Britain, which appeared on page two. *The Washington Post* offered a salacious scene of two "nude combatants" engaged in a "razor battle." The article related Day's vivid description of the scene: "Blood flew in my face, steam was in my eyes, but I kept slashing." His statement, the newspaper added, "shocked authorities in its allegations of sordidness behind the grim walls."[63] Even in small-town papers, the story commanded attention. "Richard Loeb Is Slashed to Pieces in Row with Convict," declared the front page of the *Pottstown Mercury*, an industrial town in eastern Pennsylvania, where readers learned how the fatal attack was a result of "Loeb's persistence in pursuing Day over a long period with improper advances."[64] Similarly, the *Manitowoc Herald Times* in Wisconsin noted the young Day "was driven to razor killing by indecent advances."[65]

Few newspapers explored the possibility that Day's attack was intentional. Instead, for some editors, the murder offered an insight into the psychology of sexual deviancy. The *Corsicana Semi-Weekly Light*, published in a small oil town south of Dallas, Texas, described how Loeb asked Day to "submit to an indecent act. Day refused. Day said Loeb then came up with a razor. Day kicked Loeb in the groin. They fought for several minutes." Day had been examined by the prison doctors, the newspaper added, who testified that he appeared to be suffering from a "panic reaction" and that he exhibited "an egocentric personality" but concluded that Day was "sexually normal."[66] Similarly, the *Alton Evening Telegraph*, in a small town on the Illinois side of the Mississippi River, offered readers a detailed accounting of the initial inquiry into the killing. The newspaper reported that, according to a psychiatrist, Day's attack "seemed in the nature of a panic reaction," adding that while Day was treated for hysteria in 1932, it was the doctor's impression that "Day was sexually normal."[67]

When Day's trial began in June 1936, claims of sexual normality would be central to his defense. According to the New York *Daily News*, on the witness stand Day would preface many of his answers by turning to the all-male jury and saying: "This won't be very nice, Gentlemen." The newspaper continued, "Then he would reply in the lurid jargon of men confined for years behind steel bars." The press coverage of the trial introduced readers to the vernacular of prison sexual codes. Articles related how Day testified on the ways Loeb threatened to spread the word that he was a "punk." "A punk," the *Daily News* informed its readers, "is despised by all prison inmates except the 'wolves,'" adding that Loeb was a "self characterized 'wolf,' a member of a prison pack preying on other men."[68] Mimicking this language in California, the *Petaluma Argus-Courier* recounted similar claims about "wolves" and "punks" for its readers, as well as Day's recounting of the fatal shower fight, testimony the paper characterized as "a vivid account of the killing." The article concluded with Day's central defense: "I was trying to save my dignity and my life."[69] Similar to many newspapers across the country, the New York *Daily News* reported Loeb's unseemly and horrific proposition: "Then Day paused, turned theatrically towards the jury, and said, 'In plain words, gentlemen, he told me ————.'" While the editors left the comment out of the article, it did note that "the courtroom buzzed with an undertone as the bailiff rapped for order and several of the ever-increasing audience of women departed as they have on previous days." Readers were left to imagine the shock of Loeb's "plain words" in what the empty line implied.[70]

In these accounts, the press helped construct the narrative of Day as a naïve prisoner who responded to Loeb's offer of friendship only to become a victim to Loeb's desires. Day had initially wanted to participate in a correspondence school, a program that Loeb had started in prison. Over time, Loeb's friendship and mentorship turned into threats. "Something more has grown between us," Day recounted on the stand about Loeb's sexual proposition, adding that Loeb wanted to "talk about the sex problem in jail."

In his closing arguments, Day's attorney, Emmet Byrne, told the jury, "Loeb's only wish was to educate poor boys in degeneracy." He directed the jurors to consider Loeb's earlier crime: "You have a right to take in the background of Loeb. When he stood there in the bathroom facing the defendant with a razor in his hand, he was a proven murderer, and proven pervert." He concluded by casting doubt on one of the prosecution witnesses, Loeb's former cellmate, who had testified that Day's attack was part of a prison plan. "Why shouldn't he be bitter against Day?" he asked, "He is the widow of Dickie Loeb."

For his part, the state's prosecutor, Walter Herschback, a young and inexperienced lawyer, referred to Day as "Jimmy the Mutilator" and questioned his claims of self-defense. Although the defense attorney had tried to prohibit them, he pointed to photographs of Loeb's body that the prosecution provided the jury, black-and-white images taken in the prison hospital that showed the fifty-seven slashes on the front and back of his nude torso. The photographs, Herschback argued, were evidence that the attack was a calculated murder. "James Day is a cold-blooded killer," Herschback intoned. "He wants you to pin a medal on him while he yells 'hoo-ray I'm the man who killed Richard Loeb! Put me on the stage!'"

As the jury deliberated, a marching band was practicing outside the Joliet courthouse and the music filtered through the windows of the jury room. After fifty-eight minutes, the men of the jury returned a verdict of not guilty of murder. When the decision was announced, the *Chicago Tribune* reported, "there was a burst of handclapping from spectators in the crowded courtroom."

Day's attorney heralded the verdict. "Under all the laws of God and man," he told the press, "Day should have killed him." In an unfortunate turn of phrase, Day himself told reporters he was "tickled to death." He added, "I've known all along that I did what any other normal man might have done under the same conditions."[71]

"MOST DEPLORABLE DEPTHS"

Questions of normality and abnormality had been central to the 1924 trial of Leopold and Loeb. In trying to explain how such privileged and intelligent young men could have committed such a heinous act, the press pointed to a host of social influences from too much education or too many detective novels to not enough parental control. In the 1920s, Leopold and Loeb became symbolic of the excesses of modern youth who had abandoned the sexual and social moralities of their parents' generation.[72] The editor of the *Daily Capital Journal* in Salem, Oregon, summed up the full measure of their corruption. "These youths are typical of the decadency that always accompanies a high state of civilization," the editor complained, adding, "In all ancient civilization, there were cults devoted to the monstrous and horrible gratification of the instincts of perversion. History is replete with the obscene orgies and bloody rites of mysterious cults, some of which made a religion of sexuality."[73]

The young men's lawyer, the famous and outspoken Clarence Darrow, successfully argued that while the boys were guilty, they were not insane. An insanity plea, with its demands that the defendants be proven without rational thought, would be a difficult one to make, Darrow surmised. Given their class privilege and exceptional intelligence, Darrow knew that neither a jury nor a judge would be persuaded that Leopold and Loeb lacked rational thought and didn't understand that the kidnapping and murder of Bobby Franks was wrong. In claiming the two were "abnormal," he had hoped to save the men from the gallows, by offering a less specific defense that relied not only on questions of right and wrong, but also on the emerging theories of new psychology that viewed criminal behavior as a problem of childhood development and environmental factors.

William Randolph Hearst, the mogul of yellow journalism, offered Sigmund Freud a large sum of money to comment on the trial for his newspaper. The famous psychoanalyst refused, writing Hearst: "I cannot be supposed to provide an expert opinion about persons and a deed that I have only newspaper accounts to go on and have no opportunity to make a personal examination."[74]

Despite Freud's refusal, the trial was filled with dozens of medical and psychological experts who examined, evaluated, and testified about the nature of the mental health of Leopold and Loeb. Darrow enlisted testimony from William Alanson White, the president of the American Psychiatric Association and superintendent at St. Elizabeths Hospital, who found in Loeb a disordered personality in which his intelligence and emotions had not been integrated in his childhood development.[75] Two expert witnesses, Dr. Karl Bowman and Dr. Harold Hulbert, produced an exhaustive case study of the killers that found both young men were "mentally disturbed" at the time of the crime and had a history of such mental disturbances. The report painted an image of the two killers as lonely and troubled youths. Leopold was described as weak and sickly. Loeb was viewed as suffering from a lonely and isolated childhood. The doctors pointed to the unhealthy influences of nannies and governesses in the mental disturbances both men suffered.[76] Such interpretations were enough to convince the judge that both young men suffered from a number of developmental failures and were undeserving of the death penalty.

The trial testimony made for compelling reading, as the press offered a host of psychological theories about criminality, many of which pointed to the stresses of modern life. The *Chicago Tribune* noted that Loeb was "almost without emotions," his "imagination has always made him the superior," and he "has always been fond of crime stories." While the press was restrained in reporting on the more explicit testimony in the trial about

Leopold and Loeb's homosexuality, readers did get hints of it through innuendo and suggestion. "Slayers 'King' and 'Slave'" declared one headline in the *Tribune*. The accompanying front-page article detailed expert psychiatric testimony indicating Leopold suffered an "inferiority complex," adding, "his abnormal sex life, his lack of physical prowess in athletics, the very differences which he seeks to make more marked, create this feeling of inferiority." The newspaper reported, "He is the slave, and his ideal man is king. And Loeb fits into this ideal."[77]

By 1936, however, after Loeb's murder at the hands of Day, such restrained comments on sexual deviancy were abandoned by the press, as newspapers characterized Loeb by the standards of the sexual psychopath and the Depression era's fears of sex criminals. In its article "Last of Loeb," *Time* magazine described Leopold and Loeb as "perverted Chicago youths" and noted inaccurately that they had "violated" Franks, arguing that "prison had only exaggerated Loeb's unnatural appetites."[78] The equating of the victimization of Day with Bobby Franks was common in the press.

The prison murder also prompted concerns about the policing of homosexuality within prison walls and the dangerous impact men like Loeb, or rather aggressive prison "wolves," had on "normal" inmates. In one interview, Chicago Mayor Edward Kelly told the *Chicago Tribune*, "Day, a young man, probably wanted to go straight. Now he is a physical wreck. There should be more watchfulness on the part of the guards and more guards if necessary. And the minds of the prisoners should be kept on a healthy plane."[79]

The threat of Loeb's sexual perversion was interlaced with his class privilege inside the prison walls. "Whatever else the murder of Richard Loeb in Joliet Penitentiary may reveal," wrote the editors of *The Hartford Courant*, "it has already shown that if money is allowed to count inside prison walls, it brings danger." Entitled "Luxury in Prison," the editorial warned of the problems that arise "when money talked with a loud commanding voice." The editors called on officials to "create a less degenerate and corrupting environment for those who in many cases will be turned loose again upon society."[80]

By February 1936, the governor of Illinois, responding to criticisms, appointed a commission to investigate policies of prison policing. Loeb's murder not only illuminated the failures of the prison system but also suggested the need for more intensified policing of homosexual activities.[81] A year later, the Illinois Prison Inquiry Commission published its 680-page report. Concerning homosexuals in the prison population, the report recommended that "if their abnormality is curable, they should be treated, and if not, they should be put under restraint for the protection of the other inmates, who have the *right* to protection." This segregation, the report noted, could be done by placing "mental and depraved homosexual perverts" in single cells in a special prison or in a separate section of existing prisons.[82]

The concerns about homosexuality in prison were not new. A February 1934 article in *Time* detailed a tour of New York City's Welfare Island Prison by the newly appointed commissioner of corrections, Austin MacCormick, who uncovered what the magazine called a "cesspool" of corruption and perversity. After describing the abuses of Italian and Irish gangs in the prison, the article detailed the "most deplorable depths" that the commissioner encountered. Into the mess hall "fluttered a huge chorus of perverts, their lips and cheeks blushing with rouge, their eyes darkened with mascara, their hair flowing long. In their cells were found heaps of feminine underclothes, nightgowns, perfume, lipsticks, suntan powder . . . *Unless close watch* was kept on these tainted characters, other prisoners would fight as desperately for their favor as they would for a woman's."[83]

But the problem of effete homosexuals in prison was not as troubling as that of the conventionally masculine ones—the so-called wolves that Loeb epitomized. The same year that Commissioner MacCormick was shocked by the prison conditions in New York, Joseph Fishman, one of a handful of federal prison inspectors, published *Sex in Prison: Revealing Sex Conditions in American Prisons*, a study funded in part by the Harry Frank Guggenheim Foundation. In pointing to the difficulty of policing homosexuals in incarceration, particularly those not outwardly feminine, Fishman cited county jails around the country where men who were awaiting trial were kept in the same quarters as those convicted of crimes. "The man awaiting trial," he noted, "may be not guilty of any offense, and legally may be absolved from having committed an offense but he is just as liable to leave the institution a confirmed homosexual, as one who has been confined a long time . . . No matter what happens to him in jail," Fishman bemoaned, "he has no redress whatsoever. He cannot even sue the city or the state."[84]

Fishman voiced a concern that was not uncommon in the era, and which was increasingly a topic of discussion among criminologists and social reformers throughout the 1930s. "Every year large numbers of boys, adolescent youths, and young men are made homosexuals, either temporarily or permanently, in the prisons of America," Fishman wrote. "This unfortunate condition is achieved not only through the negation of normal sex habits, but because of the constant talk concerning sex, enforced idleness, the loneliness in one's cell; and finally the relentless pressure of the 'wolves' or 'top men' housed among normal inmates in the prison, who 'spot' those among the younger prisoners whom they wish to make their 'girls' and who 'court' them with a persistence, a cunning, and a singleness of purpose which is almost incredible in its viciousness."[85]

Since the nineteenth century, social reformers had seen sex between male prisoners as a problem of morality and a threat to the discipline of the institution. By the 1930s, policing homosexual relations in prison raised more dire concerns about the nature of normal and abnormal sexual practices, as well as the causes of homosexuality. Increasingly during the Depression, sexuality was understood as a binary experience between heterosexuality and homosexuality—between normality and abnormality. But the prison experience unsettled such clearly marked divisions. The image of the prison "wolf" in particular questioned the divide between sexual categories. Male prisoners who, outside prison walls, were seemingly normal, masculine heterosexuals but inside prison engaged in same-sex encounters presented a troubling reality. Even more disturbing, the concern about homosexuality was as much about policing sexual deviants within prison walls as it was about theories of heterosexual normality. If men could be turned homosexual in prison, it lent credence to the theories of new psychology that sex desires were not in fact inherent, biological imperatives but rather affected by one's environment. Controlling the sexual deviant through forced segregation was an easier task than controlling the environment that made such sexual deviants. This problem would prove increasingly dire in the coming decades.[86]

The professional class struggled to respond to this conundrum. From the 1920s to the 1950s, Benjamin Karpman, the chief psychotherapist at St. Elizabeths Hospital in Washington, D.C., advocated for a view of homosexuality as a social problem rather than a mental disease. Karpman would become one of the leading advocates for the need for psychological treatment of sex criminals and a harsh critic of the criminalization of homosexuality in the years after World War II.[87]

Karpman saw a connection between the "so-called current wave of violent sex crimes" and the "sex life of prisoners," although he viewed this problem as a social rather than criminal one. We can see such tensions in an interview Karpman gave where he argued that as men in prison engage in "masturbation or homosexual practices for any length of time, they 'grow' or get fixed so much in the individual that even on discharge from confinement he often finds himself unable to return to normal sex activities." With a note of skepticism about the relationship between sex and crime, Karpman added, "[T]o that extent and perhaps to that extent only can we say that abnormal sexual life in prison contributes though probably rather indirectly to certain sex offenses."[88] Karpman's arguments epitomized the central tensions of the era between the law and psychology in the treatment of homosexuality. "When prisons are abolished," he maintained, "and hospitals take their place, when the warden, jailer, and the guard are replaced by the doctor and the nurse, abnormal sex practices in prison will disappear as the devil withdraws in the light of day."[89]

Karpman's theories reflected a growing shift among American criminologists and psychiatrists in the era, who drew on behavioral and developmental causes of sexuality and crime and advocated for psychiatric approaches to problems of sex criminals. While Karpman argued for the psychosexual and environmental influences on sexual deviancy, his views were one voice in a constellation of commentaries and editorials that offered readers an education in the causes of homosexuality. Such theories were often at odds with one another, reflecting the era's competing and uncertain understanding about the origins of sexual deviancy between biological imperatives and developmental models. They also reflected the tensions between psychiatry and criminology as they competed in the press and the courtroom to define the nature of homosexuality as either criminal behavior or mental condition in need of medical treatment, including everything from psychoanalysis and psychodynamic drugs to electroshock therapy. Queer men, arrested on any number of nonviolent offenses, would increasingly become specimens in such treatments meant to control and cure abnormal sexual desires. Debates about the legal and medical responses to sexual deviancy would continue through the 1940s and 1950s as queer criminality became a more visible public concern.

Behind the Headlines

*Homosexual Hoodlums, Working-Class Criminality,
and Queer Victims in the 1930s and 1940s*

"LUSH WORKERS"

On a humid evening in May 1936, Edgar Eckert, an assistant treasurer of the esteemed men's clothing store Rogers Peet and Company, was working late with his staff cleaning up the store's ruined stockroom. Recent storms had caused flooding at the Herald Square clothier, located on the corner of Thirty-Fifth Street and Broadway in New York City. Founded in the 1870s, Rogers Peet was known for its well-tailored business clothing. Like its rival Brooks Brothers, Rogers Peet offered traditional British-styled suits and shirts using imported fabrics. "Facing a new day, confident in your appearance, comes naturally when wearing Rogers Peet clothes," one advertisement from the era declared, adding, "They give a sense of well-being and comfort in the fullest measure to most men." In the 1950s, the song "Marry the Man Today" from the musical *Guys and Dolls* would immortalize the clothier as an example of the "better things" in life. Alongside golf, *Reader's Digest*, and Ovaltine, Rogers Peet was "[r]espectable, conservative, and clean."[1]

When the stockroom recovery was finished, Eckert and Gustave Fisher, the store's maintenance engineer, ate dinner at a restaurant on the east side. Afterward the two men walked to Forty-Second Street and Madison Avenue, where they separated. Fisher would later tell reporters he believed that Eckert was taking the shuttle train from Grand Central to Times Square, where he would connect with the Eighth Avenue subway to his home in the Bronx.[2]

Instead, Eckert walked west along Forty-Second Street, crossing through Times Square, which would have been teeming with late-night crowds of theatergoers and denizens of the many bars and cabarets in the area. It would have been impossible to avoid the prostitutes and male hustlers lingering along street corners, smoking cigarettes, and chatting up sailors and soldiers tipsy with liquor amid the bright lights of the square.

According to an account of the evening later published in *The New York Times*, a group of men began to follow the well-dressed Eckert. "About halfway between Seventh and Eighth Avenues, Eckert stopped, turned around, and, seeing the men, asked: 'Where is the Eighth Avenue subway entrance?'" The men showed him the entrance and continued to follow him to what newspapers would later describe as an "out of the way" place in the subway station—a small restroom "on the mezzanine floor, above the northbound platform, at a somewhat isolated point about halfway between Forty-second and Forty-third Streets."[3] Two of the men decided to leave. The other three followed Eckert into the bathroom. The details of what happened in that encounter remained a mystery.

The next morning a commuter found Eckert's body slumped in the corner of the restroom. His pocket watch, a gold medallion commemorating his service to Rogers Peet, and his wallet were missing. The medical examiner would later report the murder was "a typical case of manual strangulation."[4]

"Store Executive Slain and Robbed in 42nd St. Subway," the *Times* declared on its front page. The article quoted a colleague of Eckert who claimed the married man was always dressed well and "made a good appearance," leading "some cheap thug who was waiting in the washroom to imagine that a rich haul could be made from robbing him."[5] With its usual sensational tone, the New York *Daily News* proclaimed in large block letters across its front page, "Subway Robber Kills Merchant." The paper described the crime with tabloid drama: "A phantom strangler, lurking in the nocturnal shadows of the subway, murdered Edgar L. Eckert." While the article noted Eckert's body was found in the washroom, emphasizing the dangers of "tube thugs," the newspaper speculated that Eckert was "waiting for a northbound train in the subway when he was attacked and strangled." Readers were left to figure out for themselves how his body ultimately ended up in the out-of-the-way restroom. In dramatic prose, the article concluded that the crime had left the police as well as Eckert's widow, "prostrated at her home," without any clues.[6]

For newspapers beyond the city, the random act of violence in a New York subway station symbolized a host of urban dangers, but also the diligence of the city's police force. *The Plain Speaker* in the coal-mining town of Hazleton, Pennsylvania, informed its readers that "50 detectives began to search for the strangler" and had rounded up fourteen suspects, adding that "seven of the suspects were negroes."[7] The *Owensboro Messenger* in Kentucky reported that all the suspects had been "arrested in subway stations," emphasizing the quick response by the city police department. The Associated Press circulated a stylish photograph of Eckert dressed in Rogers Peet's finest. The caption informed readers that Eckert was the "victim of New York's most unusual crime of the year—a subway murder."[8]

Two weeks later, *The New York Times* reported that "a piece of cake" had led to the arrest of one of the murderers. Barney Omilaniwicz, a "gangly youth" of twenty-one, had gotten into a fight at a Times Square diner when the counterman accused Omilaniwicz of stealing the cake.[9] An argument ensued that prompted the counterman to take a knife to the younger man and pursue him down the street. Detectives took Omilaniwicz into custody, whereupon he confessed to his role in Eckert's murder. But this diner story may have been a bit of newspaper drama, as later reports discounted the tale, noting instead that Omilaniwicz was found by police in bed at his west side apartment.

Based on tips from men they detained in their search, the police arrested two other men involved in the murder, Edward Vespi, who often went by the name Tony West, and Philip Goldberger; they were both arrested in Boston, where they had fled after the murder. According to the *Times*, Vespi and Goldberger were picked up "outside a theater in the Scollay Square section, which borders the cheap rooming house quarter of Boston." A published photograph of Vespi and Goldberger shows the two men dressed in dark suit jackets and wrinkled felt fedoras, each staring off beyond the newspaper camera flash. A mustachioed Boston police captain stands stoically between them, one hand on each man's shoulder. The newspaper noted that Vespi and Omilaniwicz were both from Bayonne, New Jersey. Goldberger, it was reported, was homeless. All three men were eventually convicted of murder and sentenced to fifty years to life in prison.

In the press, police described the defendants as "lush workers," a term for men who robbed "late travelers" on the subways. One report noted that "sections where lush-workers congregated in Boston and Philadelphia have been watched for suspects" in the days after Eckert's murder, suggesting a much wider ring of police efforts beyond the Times Square area.[10] Such details underscored the law-and-order theme in reports of Eckert's murder, where the press emphasized the police investigation and the rapid arrests of suspects. But underneath this dominant narrative was another one with queer sexual overtones. While the "lush workers" preyed on subway travelers in the early morning hours, we can speculate that they were also targeting men cruising the subway stations, pretending to invite a casual sexual encounter as a cover for robbery and violence. The questions surrounding Eckert's murder emerged not only from the matter of motive, but also from the interactions that brought the victim and assailants together. Why Eckert wandered into an out-of-the-way bathroom when he most likely knew he was being followed by a group of men was a mystery the newspapers never resolved.

For astute readers of the details of Eckert's murder, the location of the crime would have given clues to its queer subtexts. Since the years after World War I, Times Square was known to be teeming with gay social life alongside its genteel theater-district character in the 1920s. With the end of Prohibition, the area took on a seedier and rougher character embodied in tawdry burlesque and cabaret venues that catered to a variety of denizens from out-of-towners and uptown slummers to sailors, soldiers, prostitutes, and queer men.

This change in the area during the Depression was hastened by a migration of young men to the city from rural areas and small towns looking for work, and many of these men supplemented their income by hustling.[11] One observer and client at the time noted that in the 1930s "the Square swarmed with boys," adding, "poverty put them there."[12] When the young Herbert Huncke, a writer in the Beat circle, arrived in New York in 1939, he landed in the center of the city. "I hadn't known anything about Times Square," he would later write in his autobiography *Guilty of Everything*. "In no time I became hip to the hustling routine, getting by fairly easily, meeting all kinds of people and having experiences."[13] Similarly, a participant in a study of "sexual deviance" conducted in the 1930s reported it was in Times Square where he "met a male prostitute," an "athletic and abnormal" guy who introduced him to other male prostitutes in the area.[14]

Along with the more commercial trade of male hustlers, queer casual pickups were particularly visible in the area. In his *Memoirs*, Tennessee Williams remembered how he and a friend cruised sailors and GIs in Times Square in the late 1930s. "I would make candid overtures, phrased so bluntly that it's a wonder they didn't slaughter me on the spot," he wrote years later, keenly remembering both the pleasures and dangers of such cruising. Oftentimes the men he met thought he was a pimp soliciting for female prostitutes. When they realized it was a gay invitation the men would laugh but then, "as often as not, would accept" and go along with Williams to his room at the YMCA.[15]

Queer men referred to the bathrooms in the Times Square subway station as the "sunken gardens" for the many sexual adventures that could be had in them. While the police were vigilant in their surveillance, routinely arresting men for solicitation, the intrigue and danger of the bathrooms held sexual possibilities for many men. This reputation extended beyond queer circles, as men who lived much of their lives as heterosexual could find quick and anonymous sex underground.[16] But the bathrooms were no utopia. Not only were men susceptible to police arrests, they were also victims of violence and robbery by "lush workers" targeting those who were cruising for sexual encounters.

"HOODLUM HOMOSEXUALS"

Amid the "war on crime" and the "war on the sex criminal," stories like Eckert's murder reflected a different kind of queer crime story. Public parks, entertainment areas, bars, and cafés were common settings for such accounts where queer men met their assailants, ending up together in apartments or hotel rooms. In contrast to sensationalized accounts of the individual sex criminal, these crime stories illustrated the problem of urban crime generally, and most acutely the dangers of working-class criminality. Often coded in their subtexts, these accounts hint at how queer men were targeted for robbery and violent assaults, offering a window into the vulnerabilities they experienced in the 1930s and 1940s when the sex crime panic was at its height. Crucial to so many of these stories were the mysterious and fatal encounters between working-class men and their wealthy companions.

A few months after Eckert's murder made headlines, in November 1936, a former actor and interior decorator named Walton Ford was found dead in his room at the Sutton Hotel, a stylish residence on Manhattan's east side, known in the 1930s for its young artists and writers seeking success in the city. Thirty-six-year-old Ford had come to New York fifteen years earlier from Roanoke, Virginia, and worked as a set designer and department-store window decorator. As *The New York Times* reported, "two unidentified men" had been guests of Ford's, leaving the apartment early the next morning. Hours later the hotel maid found Ford in his bed, his wrists and ankles trussed with a lamp cord, radio wire, and a belt, and "two neckties and a towel were tied tightly around his neck."[17] Ford's murder made news from Rochester, New York, and Oakland, California, to Palm Beach, Florida, and Manitowoc, Wisconsin. Such accounts offered readers morbid details of the hotel crime scene. The front page of the *Democrat and Chronicle* of Rochester, for example, reported that Ford was found with a cut on his forehead "in a blood splattered room of a midtown hotel."[18]

As with Eckert's murder investigation, the police rounded up and questioned more than a dozen men in the first few hours after Ford's body was found. Such roundups would have targeted queer men in the neighborhoods around Times Square, particularly the bars and cabarets where queer men socialized. Two individuals were eventually arrested and charged with the killing: Harry Marton and Walter Seymour, both nineteen years old. *The New York Times* reported that Seymour had been arrested before for "robbing intoxicated persons." Newspapers described how Ford met the two at a local bar and invited them back to his room at the Sutton Hotel. The police took the two men to reenact the crime at Ford's hotel room, where they explained that "after a few drinks, they strangled him, lashed him to his bed, and escaped with $40 from the bureau drawer and $1.65 from his pocket."[19] While readers could only speculate about the assailants and their victim, the facts of this encounter—of meeting in a bar and returning to the victim's apartment or hotel room, where an argument turned violent—were common details that pointed to the queer subtext of the crime stories.

Clues to this subtext were made even more evident in the sentencing of the defendants. Although indicted on first-degree murder, Marton and Seymour pleaded guilty to a lesser charge of second-degree murder. According to news accounts, Ford's relatives wanted to "avoid the possible notoriety of a murder trial."[20] The family's action underscores the kinds of shame and fear such crimes induced in the victim's relatives if the details of the crime were made public. It also meant that defendants were given lesser sentences for such brutal crimes.

This reticence was understandable in an era when queer men were so routinely portrayed as criminals. Claims of indecent or improper sexual solicitations made by the victims were increasingly present in such crime stories, making explicit the queer subtext, while also criminalizing the victim himself. In January 1940 the body of Harvey Shaw Hess, a thirty-two-year-old choir singer and assistant to a New Jersey state senator, was found on a snow-covered hill along the Schuylkill River in Philadelphia. Hess had gone out to a nightclub to celebrate New Year's Eve when he met Robert Hatry, whom newspapers described as a "big-muscled, 23-year-old West Philadelphia handyman."[21] After several drinks, Hatry invited Hess back to his apartment, where, *The Philadelphia Inquirer* related, some conflict ensued that prompted Hatry to strike Hess "on the jaw and he fell backwards, his head hitting the radiator as he toppled to the floor." Hatry removed Hess's watch (which he later hid in the bathroom of a local taproom), wrapped his body in a sheet, and drove out along the riverbank where, according to press reports, he "dumped him, clad only in trousers, over the retaining wall."[22]

Central to the murder investigation were uncertainties about what had happened in the apartment between the handyman and the senator's aide that led to the killing. In its front-page story, the *Inquirer* related how Hatry initially confessed that he had hit Hess after he had made "advances." After several witnesses testified to hearing loud noises in Hatry's apartment that indicated an extended battle between the two men, Hatry altered his confession, admitting that he had beaten Hess with a cast-iron laundry stand when the two got into an argument. The nature of the argument was never reported.

Hatry's defense soon fell apart, while suspicions over his own sexual deviancy rose. In contrast to initial reports, later articles noted that Hess's body was found "clad only in underwear," amplifying the sexual connotations of the crime. Now Hess's nearly naked body lying along the riverbank cast doubts about Hatry's defense, fostering the salacious conclusion that Hess had stripped naked either before the beating, or that he was undressed by Hatry afterward. Hatry's violent beating and murder of Hess seemed premised on what the state viewed as two equally vile motives: robbery or sodomy. Or both. "The Commonwealth argued," *The Philadelphia Inquirer* reported, "that Hatry took Hess to his apartment either to rob him or for an immoral purpose. In either case, the prosecution insisted, the 'slaying occurred during the commission of a felony and therefore was first degree murder.'"[23] In this line of reasoning, the state effectively argued—and the law supported—the claim that sodomy, which was illegal in all fifty states, was akin to violent robbery as a felonious offense. The assistant district attorney emphasized the sexual perversity of both the victim and the killer, arguing that the death penalty was "the only verdict compatible with this hideous and unnatural crime." His defense in tatters, Hatry eventually pleaded guilty to first-degree murder and was sentenced to life in prison.

Concerns about working-class criminality and homosexuality were significant ones for some researchers in the 1930s and 1940s. Amid the economic collapse of the Depression and the mass unemployment of men across the country, traditional gender roles were upended. Some psychologists and sociologists at the time theorized that unemployment caused neurosis among men, similar to the effects of shell shock for veterans of World War I. "I guess we'll all be wearing skirts pretty soon," one subject told a researcher in the early 1930s, adding that seeking government assistance was the "last resort in a losing battle to remain normal." As notions of masculinity lost their moorings in work life during the decade, concerns about joblessness and transiency among working-class men were often described as also problems of gender and sexual normality.[24]

A study based on the ongoing work of the Committee for the Study of Sex Variants in New York City, published in the academic journal *Mental Hygiene* in 1938, was one of the first of its kind to look at homosexuality among working-class men, albeit only those who had been arrested or sentenced for criminal offenses. Such studies illustrated how researchers of homosexuality often turned to places linked to criminality, like prison, courts, and mental hospitals, to find subjects and research respondents. Drawing on court records and individual interviews with men convicted of a range of felonies and misdemeanors, the study defined three types of homosexuals: the orderly homosexual, the exhibitionistic fairy, and the hoodlum.[25] While the authors claimed that the exhibitionistic fairy "cares little or nothing" for police arrests, the orderly homosexual, who concealed his homosexuality from all but a few close friends, was "haunted by a constant fear of the police and the blackmailer."[26] The authors also noted that despite such fears, "so great is the urge to homosexual expression that these men constantly take incredible risks in their search for new companionship." These risks included possible arrests, exploitation by blackmailers, and being beaten and robbed. And yet, the authors added, "they persist in exposing themselves to situations that seem dangerous beyond calculation."[27]

More troubling for the researchers was the hoodlum homosexual, whom they described in familiar, gendered terms from the era's crime fiction. Possessing a "rough, aggressive, 'hard-boiled' exterior," the researchers noted that the hoodlum was constantly "protesting his masculinity, and perhaps by boasting a little of the 'fags' he has beaten and robbed." The contrasts between their categories were stark ones. "The orderly and exhibitionist members of the homosexual underprivileged group are of interest to the police only as homosexuals and as nuisances," the researchers wrote; "the hoodlum elements are of interest as hoodlum and as a menace to society." They added, "The hoodlum homosexual must be regarded as a member of the criminal class. Contact with him by other homosexuals automatically brings the weaker men into criminal antisocial groups. Some notorious gangsters are said to be homosexuals."[28]

Whatever distinctions the study made between the different types of working-class homosexuals, the emphasis was on the problems each type presented for society. With regard to queer victims of assault, the study viewed many who fell prey to homosexual hoodlums as luckless and pathetic adventurers whose plight was of their own making. As the researchers concluded: "The earnings of the hoodlum homosexual are often supplemented by assault and robbery of clients or possible benefactors. The hoodlums know a client's fears to report his losses to the police, because he thinks that the police will look askance at a victim in the situation that made the robbery easy. There is a persistent rumor to the effect that the police permit these hoodlums a bit of latitude in the way of robbery and assault in return for their services as informers or 'stool pigeons.' No foundation for this rumor has been discovered, although it is widely believed among those who put themselves in a position to be victimized."[29]

"FAG HUNTING"

What was generally ignored in such studies of homosexuality were the more random acts of violence by those who targeted queer men for profit or sport. Recalling his childhood in New York in the 1930s, the writer Charles McCabe described gangs of high school boys who would go looking for queer men to rob and beat up, which he referred to as "fag hunting." Their victims were often effeminate men or men cruising along parks and side streets. Among his peers, McCabe related, queer men were so "universally despised, that aggression against [them] was viewed as a virtue," adding that the boys were empowered by their "religious training" or by "the whispered prejudices" of the time. "Depending on the situation," he added, "we could beat up the guy, or we could take his watch and his money. In some cases we could, and did, do all three."[30]

Such violence in the 1930s was not new. Queer men, particularly effeminate queer men, in earlier decades were often vulnerable to robbery and rape by Irish and Italian gangs in New York City, and by groups of young men looking to "roll a queer." While fairies, notes historian George Chauncey, may have been tolerated, they were often regarded as women, and as such "they were subject to the contempt and violence regularly directed against women."[31] Middle-class urban queers were particularly susceptible when they ventured into working-class neighborhoods, slumming for thrills and pleasures.

Such social dynamics played out with more explicitness during the Depression era, as fears of sexual deviants and sex crimes only fueled the sense of queer men as despised targets. In 1934, Robert Coates published the first fictional story of a queer bashing in American literature. In *The Autobiography of Alice B. Toklas*, Gertrude Stein wrote about Coates, a lesser-known figure among the American expatriate writers in Paris in the 1920s, "[W]e often met Coates hatless and redheaded in the most unexpected places."[32] Coates's early novels reflected his experiments in surrealism and modernism, but in the 1930s his writing used sparse and realist prose to explore the margins of society—what one critic described as his "dark psychological studies."³³ His story, "One Night at Coney," was initially rejected by *The New Yorker*, but eventually it was published in the more daring *American Mercury* magazine, and republished in *The American Mercury Reader* in 1944.

"One Night at Coney" begins with the image of two boys—one mulatto and one white—"dancing for pennies" in front of an evening crowd gathered at the boardwalk midway on Coney Island. Their movements, the narrator tells us, hint at the "sexual margins" of their play, but it is the "fairy" in the crowd that the story centers on.³⁴ This nameless "thin-bodied" man has an "abnormally round soft face and wide mouth" and wears a "deliberately shabby and disreputable-looking" raincoat. He watches the dancers with an uncontrolled enthusiasm, his body "rocking convulsively" while his delight "greased his face." Moved by the spectacle to seek a connection, he turns and speaks to a young "slick-haired and sharp-featured" Italian boy with the skin color of mahogany. "Let's do things together," the man says to the boy. "Let's wander down to Feldman's and sip a beer." The boy replies with an enthusiastic grin and a short hard punch to his face. The man is left to "twist and turn as he might" as the boys pursue him "towards whatever dark alley they might corner him in at last." The story's narrator expresses a feeling of empathy in his recognition of the man's "terrible aloneness . . . nowhere, not even in the thickest crowd, could he find a comrade, nowhere could he make a stand."

At the end of the story we are presented an image of a bruised and battered victim in the sad state of dissolve: "He had been down in the mud too, apparently, for one trouser leg was streaked with dirt, and his hands were grimy with it. His face was a mess, there was dried blood from his nose marking his upper lip, and one side of his mouth, and the fleshy part of his jaw had that pulped puffed look that you get not from one blow but from a hammering succession of them."³⁵ The story rests on a moral failing that is not just personal but social, as the narrator remarks, "[E]ven the cop on the beat will usually acquiesce in the right of every man to beat up the fairy who accosts him."³⁶

In contrast to Coates's story, accounts of horrific queer murders in the press rarely saw the queer men as anything other than willing victims of their own demise. In implicit and explicit ways, such queer crime stories, with their shocking descriptions of battered and beaten victims and mysterious sexual undertones, offered readers compelling examples of urban vice and crime. When drag performer Edward Dolan was murdered in his apartment in May 1937, the Associated Press reported that "the 57-year-old female impersonator was found strangled to death in his disordered lower East Side apartment yesterday, victim of Manhattan's latest bizarre homicide." The article described the victim's "lifeless eyes staring and his bare legs tied with a bed sheet," adding that the scene of the crime was "an unusual Ludlow Street apartment building known as 'the house of all nations' because of the cosmopolitan character of its clientele." Dolan, whom neighbors described as "amiable but eccentric," lived in the apartment with Kenneth Reese, a "37-year-old red-haired flashily dressed hospital orderly." *The New York Times* reported that neighbors complained about "a great amount of noise and commotion" in the apartment hours before his body was discovered. Neighbors also noted that Dolan "sometimes went out dressed in the attire of a woman" and that when questioned he said he worked as a female impersonator and "preferred to dress at home."[37]

A few months later, Claude Kendall, a publisher of risqué novels, murder mysteries, and confessional books, was found dead on Thanksgiving Day. Kendall lived alone at the posh Madison Hotel on Manhattan's east side, in what *The New York Times* described as a "$7-a-week-room." His body was found "battered and bruised with a bed sheet wrapped loosely around his neck." Kendall had attended a Thanksgiving Day party in the hotel and returned around midnight with two friends "with whom he had been drinking." But apparently Kendall went out not long after his friends left. "The night elevator operator gave a description of the man who came into the hotel with Mr. Kendall later," the *Times* reported.[38] Neighbors told police they heard noises and arguing in the early morning hours coming from Kendall's room.

"The homicide squad tonight swung into a search for a phantom-like slugger who slipped unobserved out of a small hotel early yesterday," *The Washington Post* reported in a language rich with fictional crime drama that was increasingly common in the press in the 1930s. The article added that Kendall was a "victim of as sinister a mystery as ever he produced in book form."[39] The "phantom" killer angle was repeated in several articles, which, like stories of Edgar Eckert's murder, dramatized the dangers of urban crime for readers inside and outside the city. The police rounded up nearly one hundred men in the neighborhoods near the hotel, *The New York Times* reported, but there were no reports of arrests.

In June 1942, Carl Broadland, a forty-year-old resident of Grand Rapids, Michigan, and a captain in the Salvation Army, was enjoying a two-week vacation in New York City. Broadland had checked in at the Times Square Hotel at 12:30 in the morning with two men "dressed in uniforms of British sailors," press reports would later recount. The sailors "stood aside while he registered, then went with him to his room." Later in the morning, when the front desk could not reach Broadland by phone, a bellboy entered the room to find him on the floor with two stab wounds in the chest. The New York *Daily News* reported that detectives found that the "two sailors left shortly after they went to the room," and the telephone had been "ripped from its wall bracket; otherwise there was no sign of a struggle." News of his murder circulated to Broadland's native Michigan and throughout the Midwest. The *Detroit Free Press* reported that Broadland had been active in the Salvation Army for thirteen years, where he had served as the "welfare and finance officer" for western Michigan. According to a report in the *Chicago Tribune*, police detained six British sailors, but "after lengthy questioning" they were let go.[40]

It was not only the ways such stories pointed readers to the seedier side of urban crime, but also how these stories, with their gruesome crime scene descriptions, aligned queer experiences with the tragedies of criminality. Few queer crimes stories illustrated this relationship as well as the brutal murder of Robert Byrne in his Hollywood home in the summer of 1939. Neighbors had called the police after they had not seen Byrne for a number of days. The body of the fifty-five-year-old man was discovered bludgeoned to death with a hammer, although police believed that given the conditions of his Sunset Boulevard residence, he "may have stumbled in a semi-conscious condition through the house for several days." The *Los Angeles Times* reported that that the victim, who was a "dog fancier" and "lived alone," "often entertained men younger than himself." Police were searching for the various "young men who assuredly frequented the Hollywood home," a point the article underscored numerous times. Readers also learned that on the apparent night of his murder, "evidence indicated that Byrne planned to dine with some person, a man or a woman, a table being set for two." In a phrasing rich with noir tones, the article related that detectives told a coroner's jury that Byrne died "ten feet from his telephone."[41]

A month later, the *Los Angeles Times* reported that the police had arrested Emacora Foschia for the murder, but gave no information on the suspect. Foschia was eventually released, and seven months later another article reported that police had now arrested forty-six-year-old taxicab driver Knud Troelsen in connection with Byrne's murder. The cabdriver denied any involvement in the killing and, according to the article, "said he was being persecuted for his labor activities." Detectives found "a quantity of women's clothing" in Troelsen's room and booked him for "suspicion of robbery, murder, and a morals charge." The article did not define what the morals charge was based on, although we can suspect that the pile of women's clothing had something to do with it. Troelsen was released soon after his arrest.

In February 1943, news reports of the arrest of Robert Harrington for the stabbing death of Barlow Bowen, a graduate student and former lieutenant in the army, noted that authorities were "questioning the youth regarding several unexplained local murders including the mysterious slaying of Robert Byrne." The *Los Angeles Times* described Harrington as a twenty-year-old "itinerate [sic] shoemaker and cowhand who once served a sentence in the Colorado reformatory for auto theft." According to the press, Bowen had picked up Harrington and invited him back to his room at the Claremont Inn in Pomona, California. Thirty-six hours later, police had arrested Harrington and took the suspect, still wearing his bloodstained clothing, to Bowen's room to reenact the crime, where he explained that after the two drank "three quarts of wine," Bowen "attempted to attack" him with a knife. In the ensuing fight, Harrington took the knife away and stabbed Bowen twenty times. At his trial, Harrington claimed "he struck in self-defense after Bowen made advances toward him." The jury found him guilty of the lesser charge of manslaughter.[42]

The image of the beaten and battered queer man could also be found in the era's popular crime fiction. Raymond Chandler's 1940 novel *Farewell, My Lovely* begins with his hard-boiled, thoroughly masculine detective Philip Marlowe's encounter with the effete Lindsay Marriott. As Marriott enters Marlowe's office, the private eye describes him as a "tall blond man in a white flannel suit with a violet satin scarf round his neck." Marriot also wore a "cornflower in his lapel" and his hair was arranged, "by art or nature, in three precise ledges." Later Marlowe describes him as having a "soft brown neck, like the neck of a woman."[43]

Marriott hires Marlowe as his bodyguard for an event. In a moment of confusion in the darkness of night Marlowe loses sight of his client, and Marriott is murdered. Coming upon his body, Marlowe describes the scene: "His hair was dark with blood, the beautiful blond ledges were tangled with blood and some thick grayish ooze, like primeval slime."[44] The murder motivates Marlowe to find the killer, only to uncover that Marriott was a blackmailer and "finger man for the jewel mob" who was known for robbing female socialites in Los Angeles.[45] In the figure of Marriott as both victim and criminal, Chandler harnessed a not uncommon image of gender and sexual deviancy in the era, one that often met with a tragic and gruesome ending.

"READ BETWEEN THE LINES"

The prevalence of stories of queer men beaten and brutalized by their working-class companions was the subject of a unique academic article published in 1941 in the *Journal of Criminal Psychopathology*. In "A Note on Homosexuality, Crime, and the Newspapers," sociologist F. A. McHenry argued for more explicit references to the queer subtexts of crimes stories—particularly when those crime stories involved working-class men. McHenry's article was the first scholarly work to consider violence against homosexual men, specifically, as a social problem. The "presence of homosexuality as a factor" in crime stories, McHenry noted, "has long been discreetly presented by our newspapers," adding that "in the past all reference to perversion as an element seems to have been avoided and only recently are the journals becoming more outspoken." But, he wrote, there was still "many an instance" where readers are unaware of the queer subtext that has been "part and parcel" of the crime. Unless readers were "sufficiently sophisticated to read between the lines," he cautioned, they were blind to the motives that underlie many crime stories.[46]

Echoing earlier, turn-of-the century social hygiene movements directed at female prostitution, McHenry argued that the "community would be better served if the newspapers would report these matters in full and would give the final disposition of the case." But it was not just concern for the safety of the community that motivated McHenry in his study—it was also the vulnerabilities of queer men. Queer men suffered intensely from "social ostracism," he wrote, which was compounded by a lack of frankness in the discussion of homosexuality in the press. While still framing homosexuality as a social problem, McHenry's ideas were radically unique in understanding the injuries that queer men endured, and how newspapers were complicit in these injuries. Homosexuals, he argued, "should be treated as a biological phenomenon [rather] than as an overt offense against the community."[47]

To demonstrate his premise, McHenry analyzed several newspaper crime stories, from front-page murders to smaller articles of assaults and robberies, pointing to the queer possibilities in each account. Along with stories he gathered from his own research, it is clear from the article that colleagues and friends also sent him clippings they encountered as well. For example, in one crime story about nine youths who robbed a man on a train platform, McHenry noted that the article "was sent me by a Western colleague with the penciled marginalia: 'Read between the lines!'"[48] The indication that McHenry and his network of colleagues were engaged in such reading practices, aware of the queer subtext simmering in the crime pages, illustrated how common such detection practices were.

Regarding an article concerning the assault and robbery of Truman Baker, a thirty-two-year-old unemployed clerk, by twenty-three-year-old Floyd Ingham, McHenry's interpretations were steeped with a heavy tone of irony and class awareness about the real dynamics that brought the victim and assailant together. "We next learn that Baker asked the boy to his home 'early today,'" he wrote. "The inference here is not difficult to make. They did not go there to discuss politics, and since Baker was unemployed, it is doubtful that he had an elaborate wine-cellar at home of quality surpassing the one of the tavern."[49] More intriguingly, McHenry demonstrated how to parse crime stories for their queer subtexts, specifically through the urban geography of the crime itself. In pointing out the place that Baker and Ingham met, McHenry wrote: "It is well known to the sophisticated round-towner in metropolitan areas that certain taverns are haunts of young male prostitutes and racketeers, waiting to accost or be noticed by passing homosexuals. One of these usually is particularly famous for its habitués: youth 'on the make,' sailors, marines, and a sprinkling of employed youths who add to their weekly income and to their pleasure of living, through their contracts made in this neighborhood."

But it was the age difference between Baker and Ingram that signaled the homosexual subtext for McHenry. "There is an apparent nine-year difference in the ages," he wrote, adding, "in this connection, one notes that the victim is usually a man between thirty and fifty years old, in cases of this kind." McHenry pointed to two reasons that this difference was key: "First, the homosexual has had behind him a sexual experience of perhaps fifteen or twenty years, in which he has gained sufficient courage to go searching among strangers for his *inamorati*. Second: he has passed the glow of youth in which he himself was the sought-out one; now he must perforce become the seeker. In such a situation, he appears usually to seek out robust youths in inferior financial circumstances."

Throughout the article, McHenry reminded readers of how queer men were vulnerable to assaults, blackmail, and arrest, leaving them prey to younger, working-class men's exploitations. In one account from a Midwestern newspaper about a man murdered in his apartment, McHenry noted, the killer fled the victim's apartment and, while escaping, accosted a man named Herbert Brown who was cruising along Duluth Parkway, "taking $1.50 from him." McHenry wrote, "Herbert Brown at about 4 a.m. sauntering along a parkway locally well-known to be favored by homosexuals and male 'pick-ups,' carried little money in his pocket, merely about the usual fee to be paid such an erotic partner." He added that the assailant took time from his flight from the apartment "to gather in a luckless homosexual who was engaged in an early morning search for romance and adventure."[50]

This characterizing of a queer cruising as a benign search for romance was quite an extraordinary claim in the era when homosexual encounters were viewed as a criminal offense and social threat. McHenry saw in the "illegality attached to homosexual relations" a tendency "toward other and infinitely more serious phases of crime."[51] While at the heart of his study was a concern for the ways working-class men fall into a life of crime by their easy associations with vulnerable queer companions who were targets of robbery or who might pay for sex, he also offered a unique idea for the era: in a world in which homosexuality was so despised, robberies of "luckless" queer men and violence can flourish.

One story that especially "stirred the public" (in McHenry's words) was the murder of Nazi diplomat Walter Engelberg in his Brooklyn home in the fall of 1939. According to *The New York Times*, police found Engelberg "lying on top of his bed covers in an old-fashioned nightshirt, his hands folded across his chest, with fingers extended. His face was covered with blood and his skull had been broken by a blow across the left temple which smashed his nose and left eye."[52] Across the country, newspapers reported the gruesome crime scene details. The *Weekly Town Talk* in Alexandria, Louisiana, was a particularly extreme example, as it related the medical examiner's report that Engelberg "had been struck at least three times while asleep, and that the blows with an 'ax or some other heavy weapon,' were so severe that the man was 'practically decapitated.'"[53]

Just days after Engelberg's murder made headlines, an anti-Nazi rally was held in Madison Square Garden, where, *The New York Times* reported, "20,000 persons filled every seat" to listen to prominent Christian and Jewish speakers "joined in protest against the persecution of Jews by Nazi Germany and in an appeal for the mobilization of the moral forces of the world against Hitlerism and Stalinism."[54] The December gathering was itself a response to a highly publicized and violent rally by the German-American Bund, or American Nazi party, earlier that year. On a February evening, more than 1,700 policemen encircled Madison Square Garden, standing between the entrance and scores of protesters outside and creating, according to the *Times*, "a fortress almost impregnable to anti-Nazis" as the "German-American Bund last night staged its much-advertised 'Americanism' rally and celebration of George Washington's Birthday." Inside, the hall was "decorated with American flags, a thirty-foot picture of George Washington" next to banners declaring "Wake Up America—Smash Jewish Communism" and "Stop Jewish Domination of Christian America." An editorial in the New York *Daily News* the next day termed the rally "Europe's Hatreds," characterizing the gathering and the rhetoric as a kind of foreign invasion rather than home-grown fascism. "It is to be expected that European hates will have repercussions from time to time in this country," the editors wrote, "with its heavy percentages here and there of people with recent European backgrounds." While the tabloid tepidly condemned such ideas, it concluded by praising the "superb police management of the whole affair."[55]

It was no surprise then that initial speculations in the press about the murder of Engelberg focused on fears of a vast network of Nazi spies, and the FBI's efforts to contain such a threat. *The Washington Post* proclaimed, "Police Brand Slain German a Nazi Spy," while *The New York Times* was a bit more tentative: "FBI Acts in Slaying of Nazi Aide Here; Spy Angle Traced."[56] New York tabloids fanned the fears of Nazi infiltration. The *New York Mirror* declared that Engelberg was associated with an "espionage ring having between 200 and 300 Nazi agents in the United States."[57] Many of the reports quoted the assistant medical examiner, who claimed that "Engelberg had been engaged in German secret service and espionage activities, and that a motive of vengeance for acts he had done in that capacity might have brought about his death."[58]

As the investigation progressed, however, another theory emerged that aligned the diplomat's spying with his sexual proclivities. Referring to an anonymous source, *The Washington Post* noted "a suggestion that Dr. Walter Richard Engelberg had used his post as first secretary of the German consulate as a façade behind which he carried on espionage was made official today as the authorities sought amid a mass of correspondence and pictures of nude men to identify the slayer."[59] References to Engelberg's photo collection would become a theme in the press. In reporting on the search of the diplomat's house, *Time* magazine noted, "Books and letters were everywhere—most in German, many on nudism. There were scores of photographs of naked men, many middle-aged. Neighbors had noted that no women went to see black-haired, squat Dr. Engelberg; that his servants were men, his numerous visitors were men."[60] Some press reports described an address book filled with names "on the physical details of scores of young men," concluding from such evidence that Engelberg was "obviously a homosexual."[61] Such clues to his sexuality were furthered by neighbors' accounts. The *San Francisco Chronicle* reported a common detail in the press accounts that Engelberg's house had "acquired a kind of sinister renown among the neighborhood children, who called it 'Hitler's House,'" adding, "it appeared that Doctor Engelberg entertained only men there."[62] Descriptions of the victim's belongings, his interest in nudism, and his all-male company explicitly framed the crime as one of sexual perversion. The deputy chief inspector told reporters that the police were "working on the theory that the killer is a degenerate."[63]

Claims of Engelberg's homosexuality were quickly connected to the political and moral corruption of Hitler's government. The influential radio journalist Walter Winchell broadcast his interpretation of Engelberg's fate to his national audience: "The murder . . . will be traced to the jealousy of his dearest Roehm mate." *Time* magazine published a photo of Engelberg's house in Brooklyn captioned with the same play on words, "Was it a Roehm-mate?"[64] The reference pointed to a widely publicized political struggle and purge in Adolf Hitler's Nazi party leadership in 1934, centering on Ernst Röhm (sometimes spelled Roehm in English), a World War I veteran and a close ally of Hitler in his role as commander of the Sturmabteilung, or S.A., which functioned as a paramilitary security force for the Nazi Party. Röhm's homosexuality was known among most of the party leaders. When rivals accused him of plotting to overthrow the Nazi government, Hitler ordered his execution along with nearly eighty-five other men, mostly homosexual party members deemed "radicals," in a three-day purge from June 30 to July 2, 1934, that would later be known as the Night of the Long Knives.

Rumors that Röhm and others were found in bed with young boys filled Nazi propaganda, underscoring the importance of the purge to clean the party of moral perversion.[65] *Time* reported Hitler's pronouncement after the executions: "I would like every mother to be able to give her son to the S.A. without fear that they would become more or less corrupted."[66] By 1936, Heinrich Himmler had established the Reich Office to Combat Homosexuality and Abortion, which gave Nazi leaders an official agency to arrest and imprison homosexual men with little evidence.[67] The reference to Röhm in reports of Engelberg's murder would have resuscitated the earlier analogies between Nazis and child-molesting homosexuals for American readers in 1939, connecting this foreign threat to the already circulating fears of violent, psychopathic degenerates within the local and national sex crime panic.

Police did not ultimately uncover a Nazi espionage ring behind Engelberg's murder; instead, they found a mysterious twenty-four-year-old unemployed Canadian boxer who went by the name Ernest Walter Kehler. Kehler confessed to the murder, claiming the attack was a moment of psychological distress brought on by Engelberg's sexual solicitation. Neighbors reported that Kehler was seen at the house several times. He and Engelberg had known each other for some time, and, as the tabloid *New York World-Telegram* reported, "Engelberg invited him to his home" the night of the murder, adding that the diplomat's "actions so enraged him, [Kehler] said that he 'went beserk' and his memory 'left him.'"[68] The boxer's uncontrolled rage toward Engelberg would be a constant theme in the press accounts. *Time* reported, "[T]he Nazi secretary whose curious hobbies included collecting books on nudism, photographs of nude men, made improper advances," and related Kehler's statement to the police: "'I hit the doctor with my fist,' the boxer confessed. The secretary's persistency enraged him. 'I reached for something that was on the table or the dresser . . . I don't know what it was . . . I lost my head.'"[69]

When the police found Engelberg, he was lying in bed on his back, hands folded over his stomach, and was believed to have been asleep at the time of the attack, putting into doubt Kehler's confession that he had to fight off the Nazi's sexual advances. The *New York Mirror* reported with subtle suspicion that Kehler had a "'social engagement' with the unconventional Nazi agent last Monday night, a few hours before he was beaten to death."[70] The *Brooklyn Eagle* recounted Kehler's signed confession, which noted that Engelberg, Kehler, and two other men attended a fight club in Jamaica, Queens, "after which they went to a Chinese restaurant on Jamaica Ave." At Engelberg's house the two men "ate again (chicken) and had several drinks. Dr. Engelberg and the prisoner then retired to the bedroom."[71]

Such inconsistencies prompted the press to question Kehler's claims about what happened. The New York *Daily News* published an extensive piece about the police investigation. Entitled "Will Justice Triumph?" the article detailed how the police took a "clueless case" and cracked it in six hours. In the style of true crime magazine writing, the newspaper offered readers a compelling story of detective work. Initially "the sleuths turned their attentions to Dr. Engelberg's den," readers learned, "the master bedroom which he had set up as an office." Two policemen fluent in German were enlisted to read through Engelberg's letters and journals. "Some of the letters helped further explain the absence of female touch in Engelberg's establishment," the article offered, adding, "two letters, signed by males, mentioned how lonesome they were for the doctor. Moreover, books and pamphlets found in the house substantiated the belief that the victim had been a homosexual." The article included a floor plan of Engelberg's master bedroom and a photograph of the house with the caption "Ladies not admitted."

In its conclusions, this article cast strong doubts about Kehler's motive for the attack, which the paper described as a moment when the diplomat "got fresh" with the boxer. It informed readers that Kehler's story of the events in the bedroom contradicted the police and coroner's assessment that Engelberg "never knew what hit him and that he was probably asleep at the time."[72]

Doubts about Kehler's confession were paired with uncertainties about his nationality and slippery identity. Different news reports claimed that Kehler was Swedish, German, and Canadian. He used several aliases, including Ernest Haas, and was described in many accounts as a "penniless boxer." A few articles reported that Kehler's wife and four-year-old son lived in a "cheap midtown hotel."[73] Such details raised questions about why a married man would spend his nights with an agent of the Nazi government and, more troubling, a homosexual?

Kehler's arrest recalled in the press an earlier, unsolved beating death: that of Max Morgenstern, a German émigré and foreign exchange expert who worked on Wall Street, the year before. Police had questioned Kehler in that case as well, but his association with Morgenstern was never made clear in reports. Morgenstern was found unconscious in his apartment on East Forty-Fourth Street, having suffered a concussion. *The New York Times* noted the injury was from a "single blow at the base of the skull," adding, "whether he had been attacked in his room or received his injury elsewhere was one of the many things that puzzled the police." Morgenstern never regained consciousness and died of his injuries two days after he was discovered. A neighbor noted that the fifty-year-old bachelor had been "in and out of his room several times in the evening" and returned in the early morning hours with a young man. Like the crime scene in the Nazi diplomat's house, police found no sign of a struggle in Morgenstern's room and concluded that "robbery apparently was not the motive." Although detained and questioned in Morgenstern's murder, Kehler was released when he had an "ironclad alibi"—again, news reports didn't offer details about the alibi.[74]

At the trial for Engelberg's murder, Kehler's attorney referenced the Night of the Long Knives, reminding jurors of the moral and political corruption of the diplomat. The defense's initial strategy was to raise questions about whether Kehler was even the killer, suggesting Engelberg's killing was politically motivated and ordered by Hitler himself. "It wouldn't be the first bloody purge by Hitler; he has purged many men before," the lawyer declared in court. But it was ultimately claims of self-defense against the diplomat's sexual advances that Kehler's counsel focused on, characterizing Engelberg as a "degenerate" and a "filthy beast." According to reports, his attorney argued, "when a beast attacks you are justified in killing him."[75]

This strategy worked. The jury was persuaded by Kehler's claims of self-defense and convicted him only on the lesser charge of manslaughter. Even though the jury may have sympathized with Kehler, the judge remained dubious. In published reports, he stated, "[T]he defense plea was plausible, but he slipped that in," adding, "I don't believe a word of it. This was a clever, shrewd murder."[76]

The social scientist F. A. McHenry also saw the case with a dubious eye toward Kehler's confession. "It is scarcely conceivable," he argued in his article about homosexuality in the crime pages, "that the boxer, who had been a hanger-on at coarse and outspoken midtown resorts and gymnasiums, and who had ridden the rods to New York from his native Canada some time before, was unaware after one visit to the consular official's home that he was homosexual." He pointed to the very brutality of the crime to surmise Kehler's intentions. "The fury of the assault," McHenry wrote, "betrayed a towering emotional force of rage or disappointment or indignation behind it."[77]

In the conclusion of his article, McHenry acknowledged the continued limitations of press standards in making explicit the queer undertones of crime stories. But he also expressed the hope that such standards might change. "The restrictions placed upon a publication by what constitutes good taste, the type of reader whom the paper reaches, the problem of suit or libel," are all obstacles, McHenry argued, "to the frank publication of articles which are known to have strong homosexual backgrounds." He added, "[P]rogress toward frankness will be in direct proportion to the general attitude of the public toward such themes."[78] While this "frankness" would take decades to achieve, what would become more prevalent in the queer crime stories were claims of violent homosexual panic against alleged indecent advances from the queer victim. In the years after World War II, this defense strategy in both the courtroom and the crime pages would increasingly define the boundaries between queer men and normal men as one marked by deadly violence.

Terror in the Streets

*Indecent Advances, Homosexual Panic, and the Threat
of Queer Men in Post–World War II America*

"A FANTASTIC STORY OF HOMICIDE"

The headlines in *The New York Times* on the morning of August 17, 1944, were consumed with news of the successful landing of the Allies on the southern coast of France. Troops battered through a concrete wall the Nazis had constructed along the beachfront near the port city of Nice, promising a turn in the protracted war. Only one article on the front page was devoted to another subject. Headlined "Columbia Student Kills Friend and Sinks Body in Hudson River," the article described how a nineteen-year-old undergraduate had stabbed his older companion several times in the early morning hours in Riverside Park on Manhattan's Upper West Side.[1]

The article identified the student as Lucien Carr. A handsome and erudite teenager from an old and prosperous St. Louis family, Carr possessed a mixture of delinquency, good looks, and intellectual charm. The companion was thirty-one-year-old David Kammerer, a tall, lanky man with dark red hair and a high-pitched voice who was a friend of the writer William Burroughs. The two lived near each other in Greenwich

Village, where Kammerer worked as a building janitor in exchange for a small apartment. Burroughs biographer Ted Morgan describes Kammerer as "friendly, open, and exuberant," and, like Burroughs, a "fellow outcast from St. Louis society."[2] Kammerer was from a middle-class family, earned a PhD in English, and had taught literature and physical education at Washington University in St. Louis. He had been infatuated with Carr ever since the two met in a summer camp for boys, when Kammerer was an instructor and Carr a student. He adored Carr's lean, athletic grace. The young Carr, always mature for his age, enjoyed the attentions and literary conceits of the older man.

While the two began a friendship that was both encouraged and monitored by Carr's mother, Kammerer's interest turned into a compulsive attraction. He followed the young Carr across the country, from prep school in Andover, Massachusetts, to the University of Chicago and Bowdoin College in Maine, before moving to New York when Carr entered Columbia University. Morgan related that while many believed these moves reflected Lucien's attempt to "get away from Kammerer," others were dubious, for "when you saw them together, they seemed to be the best of friends, drinking and horsing around."[3] At the West End Café, a bar near the Columbia campus where writers and artists socialized in the summer of 1944, they would talk of their literary idols and mentors, fostering the myth of the romantic rebel in the tradition of Rimbaud and Baudelaire. When Carr drank, he was known for his unpredictable behaviors, chewing glass shards or throwing plates of food on to the floor.[4] It was at the West End Café that Carr and Kammerer drank and talked late into that August night, before they ambled a few blocks over to Riverside Park.

Relating the tragic events that followed, *The New York Times* called the murder "a fantastic story of homicide" and described how Carr had confessed to the killing even before Kammerer's body surfaced in the Hudson near Seventy-Second Street. Recalling a script from one of the era's film noir thrillers, the account continued: "Working with frantic haste in the darkness, unaware of whether anyone had seen him, the college student gathered together as many small rocks and stones as he could quickly find and shoved them into Kammerer's pockets and inside his clothing. Then he pushed the body into the swift-flowing water."⁵

Drawing on Carr's confession to Assistant District Attorney Jacob Grumet, the article described Kammerer as "a homosexual who had recently earned his living by helping the janitor at 48 Morton Street." It added that the former teacher's "personality steadily deteriorated during his year in this city, until he was little more than a derelict, barely keeping himself alive by his janitorial work."⁶ Carr claimed that over the years of their acquaintance, Kammerer had several times "made improper advances to him, but that he had always rebuffed the older man." "In desperation," the article related in describing the brawl in the park, "Carr pulled out of his pocket his boy scout knife, a relic of his boyhood, and plunged the blade twice in rapid succession into Kammerer's chest." The detail of the Boy Scout knife would be repeated in subsequent accounts, serving as a powerful symbol of Carr's youth.

Over the next few weeks, this local crime made front-page headlines beyond New York City, including in Carr's native St. Louis, where the press described him as a "member of the pioneer St. Louis family."⁷ As the story circulated nationally through the Associated Press, the focus was often on Carr's youth and his claims against Kammerer. *The Daily Times* of New Philadelphia, Ohio, for example, proclaimed, "Student Held in New York Murder," while the *Baltimore Sun* declared, "Murder Laid to Sophomore," and the *Wilkes-Barre Times Leader* headline referred to the "Confessed Slayer of School Teacher."⁸ *The Plain Speaker* of Hazleton, Pennsylvania, made little doubt about the nature of the crime in its headline "Admits Killing of Alleged Pervert," informing readers that "the slain man was a homosexual who 'hounded' the student."⁹ These regional stories often portrayed Carr as a troubled teenager whose violence was an inevitable result of the "pervert's" obsessions.

The use of the term "improper advance" in Carr's confession was not new to crime stories in the 1940s. Terms such as "improper advance" or "indecent advance" had already appeared in both sensational queer crime stories and smaller accounts in the 1930s and early 1940s and were increasingly used by defendants in court as a justification for their violent actions. Since the late nineteenth century, such terms were common in the press to describe verbal and physical assaults on women. They connoted criminal actions that simmered with sexual abuses too shocking to make explicit. In the mid-twentieth century, they also served as shorthand for a host of heterosexual behaviors that made the dangerous seem harmless. In 1958 in Texas, a Dear Dorothy columnist in the *Denton Record-Chronicle,* for example, offered advice to a young female reader on her concerns about her boyfriend's improper advances on their most recent date. Entitled "Should Girl Forgive Boy After Improper Advances?" the column suggested that her boyfriend's behavior was probably just an effort to see if she "were like some of the girls who helped him gain his 'fast' reputation."[10]

Questions of purity often underlay claims of improper advances, particularly to describe heterosexual behaviors that crossed racial boundaries. In 1945, a few months after Kammerer's murder made national headlines, editors at the *New York Amsterdam News,* the African American newspaper, were dubious about the assault charges against Charles Johnson, an African American teenager who was arrested in Fulton County, Georgia. The article detailed the court's indictment, which described how Johnson made "improper advances to a white female using vulgar and obscene language and urging her in four different telephone conversations to meet him for the purpose of having illicit relations with her." The article concluded that no evidence was produced about the vulgar language, and, in fact, the woman he called claimed he used "endearing names in beseeching her for a date."[11]

Borrowing from such earlier uses, editors increasingly applied terms like "improper advance," "indecent advance," or the more direct "homosexual advance" to define the sexual provocation in queer crime stories in the 1940s and 1950s. Such terms used in the press and by defendants in the courtroom during the postwar years embodied a host of perceived threats of sexual deviants on the home front. Some of these claims were anchored to the dubious psychological theories of homosexual panic developed in the 1920s, while others simply drew on the growing prejudices of the time about the violent nature of homosexuals.

Initially, Assistant District Attorney Grumet had doubts about Carr's defense, telling *The New York Times* he "was uncertain whether he was dealing with a slayer or a lunatic."[12] This uncertainty about whether the crime was the work of a vulnerable teenager or a crazed, psychopathic killer would become the compelling question for detectives and journalists alike. It wasn't Carr's guilt that was in doubt. Rather, the real mystery of the crime rested on Carr's motive, and whether his claim of improper advances was a justified reason for self-defense. Solving this mystery depended on solving the riddle of Carr's sexuality.

Initial press accounts of Kammerer's murder hinted at Carr's queerness, portraying him as "a pale slender youth" who embodied the paradox of effete intellectualism and brutal violence.[13] The press also described Carr as "refined," "a frail blond youth," and a "slender, studious youth," "whose frail build and earnest expression might easily arouse sympathy."[14] Such descriptions framed Carr as anything but the normal American teenager. This image was amplified by references to his intellectual and erudite nature. *The New York Times* described Carr as "a quiet, well-behaved intellectual type" who had been classified 4F by the Selective Service on medical grounds—preventing him from military service.[15] The *New York Herald Tribune* offered readers details on his philosophical and literary tastes. "Most of the time the slender, studious youth stared steadily at a book he clutched in his right hand," the newspaper proclaimed in recounting Carr's demeanor at his arraignment hearing, adding that the book "was a copy of 'A Vision,' a philosophical treatise by William Butler Yeats and his constant source of solace since he came to the District Attorney on Tuesday to tell the story of the killing."[16] The article later noted that Carr unsettled his questioners in the district attorney's office with his "liberal use of polysyllabic words and deep philosophical observations."[17] In these accounts, Carr's acute intelligence was as much a symptom of his abnormality as his unmanly body.

A long article in the *St. Louis Star and Times* expressed these concerns more explicitly. In noting how university officials described Carr as "happy go lucky" and "a nice guy" as well as a "cultured gentleman," the newspaper also raised doubts about such claims. There were concerns among some officials, the article noted, "that he had a great deal of money for which he did not have to work, that he lived apart from his mother even though she was in New York, that he was free—perhaps too free—to lead his own kind of life, free entirely from direction or brake." One "middle-aged woman" at the university who praised Carr's taste in poetry, art, and music noted that "New York is a bad place for the young with money. They can lead such Bohemian lives. Carr impressed me favorably and yet—well he had temperament and temper, and too much money."[18] The intermingling of unmonitored, youthful freedom, a comfortable, bohemian life, and an uncertain personality cast Carr as a careless young man with unconventional tastes.

Police and editors may have been dubious of Carr's claims of self-defense precisely because of where the murder took place. Since the 1920s, Riverside Park was known as "a major cruising area and social center especially for seamen and their admirers," writes historian George Chauncey. The "[t]wo landmarks in the park, Grant's Tomb at 122nd Street and the Soldiers and Sailors Monument at 89th Street, were especially renowned as meeting places in the gay world."[19] In the 1933 surrealist novel *The Young and the Evil*, written by Charles Ford and his lover Parker Tyler, two queer characters wander into Riverside Park in the late-night hours, only to be assaulted by a group of sailors. Frightened and injured by the attack, the men are ultimately rescued when two detectives arrive and arrest both the sailors and their victims for disorderly conduct.[20]

But if officials were skeptical of Carr's account, the New York tabloids were more willing to embrace his defense, presenting the teen as a helpless victim of a psychotic homosexual attack. Initial stories in the New York *Daily News* and the *New York Mirror* emphasized Kammerer's deviancy and Carr's desperate defense to protect himself. While the *Mirror* called the crime a "twisted sex murder," with its titillating intersections between deviancy and violence, the *Daily News* described Carr's stabbing as an "honor slaying."[21] Alongside a photograph of Carr standing on the river's edge pointing out to police where the murder took place, the *Daily News* contrasted the "mild" expression on Carr's "young face" against the "33 year old former English teacher" who, Carr claimed, was "a homosexual."[22] In drawing this contrast between youthful innocence and sexual deviance, it was often difficult to discern who was the real victim of the crime.

By September, when Carr entered a guilty plea of first-degree manslaughter, Kammerer's compulsive perversities had become the central rationale for Carr's deadly attack. Crucial to this version of the crime was Carr's emotional state. *The New York Times* revised its tone from earlier reports and described how the assistant district attorney believed that Carr "had not intended to kill Kammerer, a homosexual, but that Kammerer for more than five years had persisted in making advances to Carr, which always were repulsed. Kammerer's persistence," the prosecutor added, "had made young Carr 'emotionally unstable.'" Reports of his plea hearing offered readers details about the many ways that Kammerer "'hounded' the youth with his attentions," detailing how Carr's mother had tried to separate the two a few years earlier when, she claimed, Kammerer's attentions had driven the young Carr to attempt suicide. In her testimony, Mrs. Carr described Kammerer as a "veritable Iago" who had corrupted her son "purely for the love of evil."[23]

Gone from these accounts were Carr's erudite interests, descriptions of his frail, effeminate body, his 4F status, and other "queer" attributes that cast earlier suspicions about his sexual and gender normality. No longer were the tabloids calling the killing a "twisted sex murder." Instead, Carr was increasingly portrayed as a troubled teen, whose naïve relationship with a homosexual had driven him to commit such violence. The "honor killing" interpretation, coupled with his emotional trauma, turned the case from murder to manslaughter—and Carr from a crazed homosexual killer to a misguided youth who had endured the threat of mental and physical harm.

In the months prior to the murder, through his friendship with William Burroughs, Carr had met fellow Columbia student Allen Ginsberg as well as Jack Kerouac, who had entered Columbia several years earlier on a football scholarship but dropped out after an injury and was now in the merchant marine. In the years to come, they would emerge as the leading voices of the Beat generation of writers, but in the summer of 1944 Kerouac, especially, would prove a useful asset in shaping the story of Carr's defense. Carr told police he had visited both Kerouac and Burroughs in the early morning hours after he left Riverside Park, and both were soon arrested as material witnesses. When Carr showed up at Kerouac's door, the two walked to Morningside Park to bury Kammerer's glasses and get rid of the Boy Scout knife by dropping it down a storm drain. Then they spent the day drinking, visiting the Museum of Modern Art, and going to the movies before Kerouac persuaded Carr to go to the police and confess.

Because of his role in these events, this would be the first time Kerouac's name appeared in the newspapers. Unlike Carr's, Kerouac's sexuality was never in question: nearly every article noted that the handsome Kerouac was soon to be married. "When Judge Sullivan fixed bail, Kerouac whistled," the *New York Herald Tribune* reported, adding, "He said he returned from sea last Saturday and that he and his fiancée, whose name he did not disclose, planned to be married today."[24] While he was still being held as a material witness, "[t]he police escorted Kerouac to the Municipal Building on Tuesday to witness his marriage to Miss Edith Parker of Detroit and then took him back to Bronx prison."[25] Such public displays of heterosexuality countered suspicions the prosecution and the detectives might have had about Carr's defense.

In fact, the twenty-two-year-old Kerouac was struggling with his own sexual desires that summer, torn between his feelings for Lucien Carr and pressure to marry the wealthy Edie Parker. Kammerer had become intensely jealous when both Kerouac and Allen Ginsberg competed for Carr's affection. Ultimately, Kerouac and Carr formed a close relationship. Kerouac affectionately called Lucien "Lou," and Carr returned such affections with his usual impertinence, calling Jack his "has-been queen."[26]

Such playfulness underscored Kerouac's conflicted feelings about his own queer desires—what one biographer terms Kerouac's "homophobic homoeroticism." As a Columbia football player, Kerouac had participated in a drunken gay-bashing binge in Greenwich Village with some of his teammates.[27] In later years such violence gave way to a series of guilt-ridden homosexual encounters. A few years after Kammerer's murder, Burroughs

Fig. 53.—Tensions of facial muscles showing desperate striving as a defense against fear of becoming effeminate and homosexual. His final solution was suicide.

Illustration from *Psychopathology* by Edward Kempf *(C.V. Mosby Company: St. Louis, 1920)*

Fig. 71.—Terrific striving to become omnipotent as a defense against fear of homosexuality and impotence.

Illustration from *Psychopathology* by Edward Kempf *(C.V. Mosby Company: St. Louis, 1920)*

"Third Sex Plague Spreads Anew!"
Brevities (November 2, 1931)

Louis Kenneth Neu in New Orleans courtroom for the slaying of Sheffield Clark Sr.
(AP Photo)

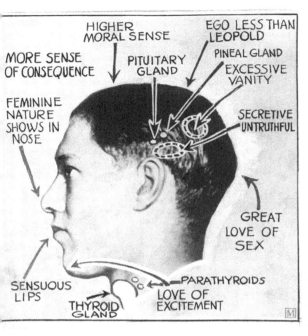

A phrenology diagram of Richard Loeb
(Photo by New York Daily News *archive via Getty Images)*

"Subway Robber Kills Merchant" (Edgar Eckert murder), New York *Daily News* (May 15, 1936)

Ernest Kehler brought to New York police headquarters to face charges of slaying Dr. Walter Engelberg *(AP Photo/Murray Becker)*

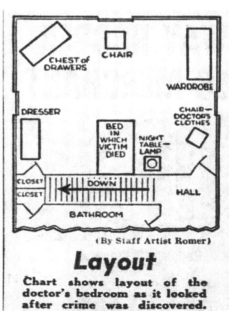

(By Staff Artist Romer)

Layout

Chart shows layout of the doctor's bedroom as it looked after crime was discovered. No article had been disturbed, and there were no signs of a struggle.

"Layout" (floor plan of Engelberg's bedroom), New York *Daily News* (January 21, 1940)

Jack Kerouac and Lucien Carr on the Columbia University Campus, New York City
(Photo by Allen Ginsberg/Corbis via Getty Images)

"Ace Detective Trails Clue to New Motive in Slaying of Dancer" (Burt Harger murder) New York *Daily News* (October 8, 1945)

"Haeberle Believed Murdered by Man He Greeted as Friend" (front-page artist rendering of Harvey Haeberle murder), *The Washington Post* (February 27, 1948)

Ralph Edward Barrows in a train at Hoboken, New Jersey, as he leaves for the state prison at Elmira, New York *(AP Photo/Anthony Camerano)*

"Pervert Colony Uncovered in Simpson Slaying Probe" (William Simpson murder), *Miami Daily News* (August 8, 1954)

"Twilight Men" (Van Vechten Scrapbooks), Yale Collection of American Literature, Beinecke Rare Book and Manuscript Library, Yale University

"The Village Meets Harlem" (Van Vechten Scrapbooks), Yale Collection of American Literature, Beinecke Rare Book and Manuscript Library, Yale University

brought Kerouac to a gay orgy and, with Ginsberg, to the Everard baths on West Twenty-Eighth Street, one of a number of bathhouses in New York in the 1940s and 1950s that discreetly catered to gay men. The baths, with their admission tickets and locker rooms, offered an openness where men could explore homosexual encounters and avoid the potential of violence or arrest that hovered over cruising in public parks or subway bathrooms. After one outing to the baths, Kerouac announced to Ginsberg he was ready to embrace the full range of his sexual desires and let his fears of homosexuality "dissolve."[28]

Yet, tinged with such private explorations were anxious public expressions. In his 1958 novella *The Subterraneans*, the Kerouac character encounters a sexual solicitation by a man in Riverside Park, the same park where Kammerer had been murdered. "How you hung," the man asks, to which Kerouac replies, "By the neck, I hope."[29] The novel also included an account of a well-known tryst between Kerouac and the young writer Gore Vidal in the Chelsea Hotel. In the novel, Kerouac portrayed the encounter with decidedly vague descriptions, casting his protagonist in the position of rough trade—a role that accommodated queer sexual forays while not threatening his essential heterosexuality.

Years later, Vidal would recount his version of the incident in his memoir *Palimpsest*. In August 1953 Vidal was drinking with Kerouac and Burroughs at the San Remo bar in Greenwich Village. After Burroughs left, Kerouac suggested the two get a room at the Chelsea Hotel. Vidal described the hotel encounter as "classic trade meets classic trade," prompting an awkwardness about "who will do what?" While the term "trade" referenced the image of working-class men who have sex with other men for pay (often assuming the active role in sex), it also embodied a queer hypermasculinity against the more effeminate gay men. In Vidal's retelling, Kerouac submits to Vidal's more aggressive play. "Jack raised his head from the pillow to look at me over his left shoulder," he wrote. "He stared at me for a moment—I see this part very clearly now, forehead half covered with sweaty dark curls—then he sighed as his head dropped back onto the pillow."[30] Although just a few months after this encounter Kerouac would refer to Vidal as a "little fag" in a letter to the literary critic Malcolm Cowley, the night at the Chelsea Hotel would exemplify the unease that Kerouac felt toward his homosexuality throughout his life.[31]

In 1944, this unease was not only a private matter but also one for the detectives. When police arrested Kerouac as a material witness, they held him in the Bronx jail. "During liberty period," according to Kerouac biographer Ellis Amburn, young, good-looking "Mafia hit men went to Jack's cell and attempted to seduce him. A friendly plainclothesman had already warned Jack that the 'stoolies' had been promised fifty years off 199-year sentences if they could prove that Jack was gay."[32] This experience would remain vivid for Kerouac when he wrote his fictional autobiography *Vanity of Duluoz: An Adventurous Education, 1935–46* in the late 1960s. In one scene, as he and Carr (named "Claude" in the book) are waiting for the arraignment hearing, Carr whispers "out of the corner of his mouth: 'Heterosexuality all the way down the line.'"[33] This pledge becomes a refrain for the two as they sat in front of the detectives investigating the crime. In a conversation with the lead detective, Kerouac portrayed the interrogation as chiefly an exploration of his sexual preferences:

> Me and O'Toole go in the other room, he says: "Sitdown, smoke?," cigarette, I light, look out the window at the pigeons and the head and suddenly O'Toole (a big Irishman with a gat on his chest under the coat): "What would you do if a queer made a grab at your cock?"
>
> "Why I'd k-nork him," I answered staightaway looking right at him because suddenly that's what I thought he was going to do. (Note: "k-norck" is Times Square expression for "knock," sometimes known, as "Kneeazorck.") But anyway O'Toole immediately takes me back to the D.A.'s office and the D.A. says "Well?" and O'Toole yawns and says "O he's okay, he's a swordsman."[34]

At the end of *Vanity of Duluoz* Kerouac upholds the commitment he made with Carr in 1944: heterosexuality all the way. "Claude was a nineteen-year-old boy," Kerouac writes, "who had been subject to an attempt at degrading by an older man who was a pederast, and that he had dispatched him off to an older lover called the river, as a matter of record, to put it bluntly and truthfully, and that was that."[35] The term "pederast" illustrated the anxious distinction between a tough masculinity Kerouac valorized and the effete and unmanly homosexual, who inflicted both physical and psychological harm on normal men, that he saw in Kammerer. This was the cornerstone of Carr's defense as his psychological trauma became a strong mitigating factor in the court's decision. The mental damage caused by Kammerer's actions pointed to the growing understanding that homosexuals were predatory figures whose behavior could turn even the seemingly normal and reasonable man into a killer. "He has gone through a terrible experience," Carr's attorney stated, "but medical experts say he can be rehabilitated."[36] The judge agreed and sentenced Carr to eighteen months in the Elmira Reformatory in upstate New York.[37]

In a journal entry composed a few days after the murder, Allen Ginsberg wrote, "The libertine circle is destroyed with the death of Kammerer."[38] On one page he pasted the newspaper article from *The New York Times* reporting on Carr's indictment for murder, placing it among a series of entries detailing dreams he was having about his lonely outings in the city, each haunted by Kammerer's death. He also recorded notes for a novella he wrote for his creative writing class—a work that shocked many faculty in the English department for its queer content. In a section entitled "Death Scene," Ginsburg transmuted the violence into an erotically charged moment caught between murder and sex: "Choose to present me with your pecker or your knife," Kammerer whispers to Carr in the darkness of the park. In response, Carr's eyes "maddened in conflicting ecstasies of fear and desire."[39] While Ginsberg's retelling may have been part of his own infatuation with Carr, it illustrated the nervous tensions between embracing and repulsing homosexual desires.

Just months after Carr's sentencing, Kerouac and Burroughs began their own fictionalized account of the event in a novel that alternated narrators, each writer composing different parts of the story. Entitled *And the Hippos Were Boiled in Their Tanks*, the book was finished in the spring of 1945 and was sent off to the publisher Simon and Schuster. Rendered in a matter-of-fact style of detective fiction, the novel focuses on two characters modeled on Carr and Kerouac who are trying to get a post on a merchant marine ship and sail off to France. The murder scene is moved from the riverbank of a park frequented by queer men to a warehouse in Greenwich Village. After breaking into the warehouse, Phillip and Al (the character names for Carr and Kammerer) find a hatchet and start breaking windows. On the rooftop Al confesses that he wants to ship out with Phillip, and "do things you do." He then tries to put his arm around Phillip. "I still had the hatchet in my hand," Phillip confesses later, "so I hit him on the forehead. He fell down. He was dead." The Burroughs character provides Phillip an alibi for the murder. "Do you know what happened to you, Phil?" he says after hearing the confession, "You were attacked. Al attacked you. He tried to rape you. You lost your head. Everything went black. You hit him. He stumbled back and fell off the roof. You were in a panic." Later, the Kerouac character gives Phillip a more precise defense: "Al was queer. He chased you over continents. He screwed up your life. The police will understand that."[40] And indeed, the police do believe his story of panic. The court sentences him to a few months in a mental hospital—a judgment that gives everyone around Phillip a bit of relief as the characters move on with their lives amid the heat of the New York summer.

"What will happen, I don't know," Kerouac wrote to his sister after sending off the manuscript to the publisher, adding, "For the kind of book it is—a portrait of the 'lost' segment of our generation, hardboiled, honest, and sensationally real—it is good, but we don't know if those kinds of books are much in demand now."[41] Simon and Schuster passed on the manuscript, and Kerouac and Burroughs never did find a publisher for the book. The novel nonetheless betrays what the crime pages made certain—that claims of improper advances were useful fabrications by defendants, and that the story of a queer man's death was always partially his own fault. The contrasting motives between these two retellings is notable. Ginsburg's story reveals

Carr's homosexual panic, his repulsion at his own latent homosexual desires, as motivating the violent stabbing. For Kerouac and Burroughs, Carr's defense is a consciously constructed fabrication for a seemingly motiveless crime.

What actually prompted Carr's stabbing in Riverside Park that August remains a mystery. Once he completed his stay in Elmira, Carr kept his distance from the Beat circle, and he never talked publicly about the crime again. Perhaps Kammerer did accost Carr. Perhaps Carr, drunk and lacking self-control, had in fact finally exploded in a heat of anger and violence. Perhaps Carr's violence was a repulsion against his own homosexual desires. "Like the rest of the University world, we are completely mystified at what happened," the editors of the Columbia University student newspaper had written soon after the murder, adding, "there is a complexity to the background of the case that will defy ordinary police and legal investigations. The search for a motive will dig deep into the more hidden areas of the intellectual world."[42]

"EACH CLAIMING TO HAVE STRUCK THE FIRST BLOW"

The story of Kammerer's murder and Carr's defense marked a gradual shift in the nature of queer true crime stories in the 1940s and 1950s. While claims of improper or indecent advances illustrated individual encounters, they also pointed to an increasingly common rhetoric in queer true crime stories where fears over the public presence of queer men were part of larger social panics about the sex criminal and the psychopathic homosexual. Such news stories encapsulated a compelling and troubling idea in the popular imagination that took root in the 1940s and grew in the years after: assertions of heterosexual masculinity were defined by violent rejections of queerness.

In the fall of 1940, the badly beaten body of John Martin, a British citizen and steward on the *Queen Elizabeth* steamship, was found in the Hotel Belvedere in New York City. Martin was set to leave town the next day. Police would soon arrest two cowboys from Wyoming, who were in the city to perform a rodeo show at Madison Square Garden, for the crime. "Rodeo Performers Tell Police They Beat British Seaman for Improper Proposals," the *Brooklyn Eagle* declared in its headline. The newspaper described how Martin's body was found on the fourteenth-floor corridor of the hotel, where "a trail of blood led back to Room 1508." Four cowboys had had a party in the room the night before, one of many such parties in the hotel, which was hosting the cowboy performers. The cowboys told police that during the party Martin had made an "improper proposal," which sparked the attack, and police determined that Martin had been "dragged out to the corridor." The article noted, "The room gave evidence of a violent battle." Initially detectives confined all the rodeo performers to their rooms, placing police guards at the entrance of the hotel while they investigated the murder. This confinement was lifted to allow the cowboys to perform in that evening's show.[43]

The next day *The New York Times* described how two "cherubic cowboys" had confessed to the murder. The men had met Martin outside the hotel and invited him to their room where, after a "quarrel," "the cowhands decided to 'roll' the Englishman." The article described how one man held Martin while his "huskier companion punched the hapless steward until he slumped unconscious to the floor."[44]

Such stories often simmered with dubious details about assailants' claims of sexual provocation. Consider the murder of Patrick Murphy, who was found beaten and tied up in his basement apartment in Cambridge, Massachusetts, in the summer of 1945. Murphy had been beaten so badly, *The Boston Globe* reported, that part of his skull was crushed in from "heavy blows with a blunt weapon." When he was found, his hands were tied behind him with wire and his body "doubled over at the foot of his bed."[45] Three young men were soon arrested for the crime. A front-page article in the *Globe*, which included a photo of the three assailants smiling and laughing at the camera, portrayed the boys as psychopathic delinquents. They ranged in age from seventeen to twenty-one, and the oldest was a decorated navy veteran. Once arrested, the young men "showed no concern when arraigned on the murder charges," the article related, adding, "They were busy reading newspaper accounts of the crime, laughing and pointing out their photographs to each other."

Reports of their confession claimed that Murphy, who knew some of the men, had served them "coffee and sandwiches, but declined to give his guests beer or lend them money." The men alleged that Murphy made an "indecent proposal" to the navy veteran, which enraged him. But rather than leave Murphy's apartment, he instead hit his host and then "chased him around the apartment" until "knocking him unconscious on the bed," presumably while the other men watched. The article detailed how the sailor "pulled the cord out of the coffee percolator in the kitchen and tied it around Murphy's wrists and neck."[46] The men talked "freely after their arrest, describing exactly how they had committed the murder and each claiming to have struck the first blow." Newspapers reported that the men described Murphy as a "soft touch," an indication that the killers exploited Murphy's kindness and vulnerability.[47] The image of the killers as psychopathic delinquents was a powerful disclaimer to their defense. But it also pointed to a renewed element in such crime stories in the postwar years: the links between psychopathic violence, criminality, and sexual perversion.

Just months after reports of Murphy's murder, the shocking mutilation and murder of world-renowned ballroom dancer Burt Harger made headlines across the country. *The New York Times* noted that, with his dancing partner, Charlotte Maye, Harger performed at the Biltmore Hotel on Madison Avenue as "the dancing toast of the continent."[48] Other reports noted that he had "given command performances before the late King George V of England and the present King George VI" as well as the king of Sweden and the former King Alphonso of Spain, and was "well known in Paris night clubs, on the Riviera, in London's more ritzy theaters and night spots."[49] The son of a postmaster, Harger was raised in California and studied dance at Stanford University, eventually settling in New York, where he worked as a dancer on Broadway before his ballroom act with Maye.[50]

In late August 1945, Harger had gone missing. At about the same time, body parts started showing up on New York City shores. The *Times* reported, "The mysteries of the disappearance of Burt Harger . . . and the simultaneous discovery of a dismembered body in the Hudson River [and] in the Rockaway Inlet, Queens were cleared up yesterday when detectives arrested Harger's roommate on a charge of homicide."[51] Walter Dahl, a tall, well-built freight solicitor for the Pennsylvania Railroad, had lived with Harger for over a year in their fourth-floor apartment on West Forty-Sixth Street in Manhattan. He had purposely eluded police for weeks, but in October, he finally confessed to killing Harger with a hammer. According to the press, Dahl "dismembered the body with a razor and butcher knife, dropped the arms and legs off the Weehawken Ferry and the torso off the Staten Island ferry in packages."[52]

The New York *Daily News* reported that the "blond, wavy-haired" Dahl was "jittery almost to the point of hysteria" as he confessed to the killing of Harger. Quoting neighbors of the two men, the article described the killer as "good-looking but overly polite—he would bow from the waist and kiss your hand," but, the paper added, "his friendship for Harger they never questioned." Dahl confessed that Harger "made improper advances to him as both were ready for bed." When Dahl resisted Harger, according to reports, the dancer came at him with an ice pick. "Dahl said he hit him with a hammer several times. He saw the dancer was dead so he took the body in the bathroom and, with a kitchen knife, laboriously dismembered it."[53]

Named the "New York Torso Killing" by the press, the crime gained attention well beyond New York newspapers. "Broadway Beau Held in Murder," declared *The Star Tribune* in Dahl's native Minneapolis. The article described him as a "nattily dressed hanger-on in Broadway circles," adding that he killed Harger with a hammer after a heated "quarrel over their strange intimacy."[54] The *St. Louis Star and Times* included photographs of both Harger and Dahl, the dancer portrayed in profile in a publicity photograph wearing a tuxedo, while Dahl was captured in a casual moment in the police station, looking downward and wearing a dark fedora—his handsome face made lurid by the shadows. Dahl's self-defense alibi held little traction as "police discounted his story because the two had lived as roommates for fourteen months."[55]

The Philadelphia Inquirer offered the most titillating tale of murder and romance in their long article on the crime published in November. Rendered with the drama of crime fiction, the article begins with an episode of Dahl on a ferry in New York harbor, "between midnight and dawn of late summer." Setting the scene of a "ferry chugging over to Staten Island" engulfed in late-night darkness, the article noted that a man can feel very safe at such a moment, for "he can rest a carefully-packaged bundle upon the railing and permit the bundle to slip from his fingers over the side." The image of Dahl standing on the ferry deck, dropping "packages" into the harbor sets a compelling tone of luridness throughout the article. While it details Harger's career and his professional life with Charlotte Maye—Dahl had known Harger and his dancing partner for five years and together "they made a gay party"—the article focused on the seemingly inexplicable motivations that could drive a man to such a violent crime. We learn that Dahl had sought treatment for a nervous condition weeks after he killed Harger, that he sent fake telegrams to the apartment to alert police that Harger had been traveling on the West Coast, and that police had asked Dahl to tie a package in the interrogation room to see if they matched the knots found on packaged body parts that were washing up on the banks of the Hudson River and Rockaway beaches. "Tall, blond Walter Dahl," the article concluded, "made his confession finally after he had told several stories, each more fantastic than the other."[56]

In May 1946, a small article on page thirteen of *The New York Times* noted that Dahl was sentenced to ten to twenty years for manslaughter—a light sentence for such a gruesome crime. In urging clemency, Dahl's attorney, "although admitting the crime was a shocking one, declared the slain man 'dominated' his client."[57] The article did not give details for this claim, leaving more mystery about Dahl's motivations for the brutal crime. Dahl, who suffered from diabetes, would die in prison in 1949 from complications of the disease.[58]

In the murders of Murphy and Harger, claims of improper advances defined the salacious context of the crime and the motive for the violence as the story circulated in the press, even as such claims were dubious in explaining the murder. While much was left uncertain about what propelled the violent attacks in the apartment of each victim, the framing of the crime as an indecent or improper advance confirmed to readers the horrific and gruesome violence that marked such encounters. The more brutal the crime, the more frequently defendants claimed self-defense against the victims' sexual advances.

In March 1947, William Albrecht met Fiske Dellinger in a bar in Queens that one newspaper described as "a favorite hangout for musicians, stage folk, and other entertainers."[59] Dellinger invited Albrecht to his apartment after the bar closed. While walking across an open lot, Albrecht claimed Dellinger made "two improper advances to him and struck him," according to *The New York Times*.[60] In response, Albrecht hit his companion with a large rock and walked home, leaving Dellinger lying unconscious and bleeding on the ground where he eventually died. A passerby found his body early the next morning. The son of a prominent Boston family, Dellinger was a World War II veteran who worked for Scandinavian Airlines at LaGuardia Field. *The Boston Globe* featured a photograph of Dellinger in his military uniform and noted that the right side of his face was "crushed in," suggesting the attack was not a simple rebuke but a much more aggressive assault. The article added, "[T]here had never been any trouble between them before." The erratic and unexplainable violence that erupted between the two men, the news accounts suggested, was prompted by Dellinger's persistent sexual provocation.

One of the more remarkable cases of a violent defense against a "homosexual advance" appeared in accounts of the beheading of prison inmate Clarence William Redwine in Angleton, Texas, in December 1948. The story circulated through the Associated Press to a number of regional newspapers in the Midwest and the South. The *Chicago Tribune* announced on its front page, "Convict Decapitated Leaving Mess Hall of Texas Prison Farm." In Oklahoma, the *Miami Daily News Record* was even more explicit in its headline: "Texas Convict Decapitated; Sexual Attacks Are Blamed," as was the *Hope Star* of Arkansas, where the editors declared, "Murdered Convict Was Homosexual."[61]

From these articles, filled with ghoulish details, readers learned that amid a crowd of about two hundred inmates in the Retrieve Prison mess hall, "one prisoner slapped a hand over Redwine's mouth, while another cut off his head with a small knife." The head was then left on one of the dining tables, without, reports claimed, any of the guards noticing: "The decapitation last night of one of Texas' toughest prisoners today was blamed on homosexual attacks he had made on other prisoners." Reports related that Redwine had been "accused previously of two homosexual attacks."[62] Little else is explained about the attack, nor were there follow-up articles in the next few days. Beyond raising legitimate concerns about the management of the Texas state prison system, the story of Redwine's beheading, based on the claim that he had sexually accosted a fellow prisoner, would have little relevance aside from the sensational headlines of brutal violence and sexual deviancy.

"THE PROWLERS AND THE EXHIBITIONIST, THE BLATANT ACCOSTERS LOOKING FOR PICKUPS"

"Once a man assumes the role of homosexual," wrote the editors of *Coronet*, a widely circulated magazine, in 1950, "he often throws off all moral restraints," adding that such men "descend through perversion to other forms of depravity, such as drug addition, burglary, sadism, and even murder."[63] This progressive model of perversion, in which antisocial behavior spirals toward ever-increasing, dire forms of violence, was a prevalent idea in popular magazines and newspaper articles about sex crimes in the late 1940s.

As in the 1930s, the late 1940s witnessed renewed legislative actions on policing and treating the category of criminality known as the sexual psychopath. Across the country, states and cities enacted new sexual psychopath laws that conflated a host of behaviors, from rape and exhibitionism to public masturbation, sex with minors, public sex, and sodomy. In the years after the war, twenty-one states and the District of Columbia passed new laws aimed at such criminality.[64] Such laws often mandated broader surveillance and policing efforts of sexual deviants that disproportionally focused on queer men's visibility and activities in public. In Philadelphia in 1950, for example, police were arresting approximately two hundred men a month on charges of disorderly conduct or public indecency, numbers that the courts were struggling to handle.[65] While such arrests often targeted harmless interactions between queer men in public, the effect of such policing was to increase rates of arrests of "sex perverts," which in turn gave the impression that the city was being overrun with sexual deviants.

As he did before the war, FBI Director J. Edgar Hoover stoked such fears by writing dire articles warning about the safety of children. In "How Safe Is Your Daughter?" published in *The American Magazine* in 1947, Hoover fostered a fevered fear of sexual deviancy and the threat of a sexual psychopath around every corner. "The wartime spirit of abandon and 'anything goes,'" Hoover wrote, "led to a decline in morals among people of all ages."[66] In another article, this one from the early 1950s, Hoover would claim "the sex offender has replaced the kidnapper as a threat to the peace of mind of the parents of America."[67]

In Hoover's own Washington, D.C., concerns about sex crimes reached a fevered pitch in the late 1940s as Senator Joseph McCarthy was organizing his purges of Communists and homosexuals from the federal government. A 1947 editorial in *The Washington Post* echoed sentiments found across the country when it argued for a "comprehensive sex crime law" to protect "the people of the community." Noting that while "forty-seven states now have such laws," the city relied on "obscure common law provisions on sodomy." In its focus on sodomy, the editors betrayed the underlying motive for tougher sex crime legislation: more surveillance and arrests of queer men across the city. "Washington," the editorial claimed, "has become more or less a haven for sexual perverts and degenerates." While recognizing that some sexual perverts could be changed through psychiatric treatment, and supportive of suggestions that all sex offenders be "committed to St. Elizabeths Hospital" for long periods of treatment, the piece declared that stricter laws and enforcement were needed for "perverts who lacked the will or desire to change."[68]

The following year, President Harry S. Truman signed the Miller Sexual Psychopath Law. Named for its principal sponsor, Republican Arthur L. Miller of Nebraska, this law increased penalties for a host of behaviors deemed deviant sex crimes in the nation's capital. While its stated motive was the protection of children, the law was used to further criminalize consensual sex between adult homosexuals during what historian David Johnson has termed the lavender scare—that many-tentacled postwar force of executive orders, policy initiatives, and FBI surveillance across public and private sectors meant to identify and purge gays and lesbians within the federal government. While in the 1930s and 1940s, Washington was relatively tolerant and open to homosexuals—especially during the war years, when the federal government dramatically expanded its workforce, bringing thousands of young people to the city where many lived beyond the moral constraints of their hometowns and immediate families—the atmosphere changed after World War II ended. The purging of homosexuals from government employment had destructive effects on queer life throughout the city, as homosexuals were targets of suspicion, entrapment, stepped-up police arrests, and the victims of assaults and robbery.[69]

The same year that *The Washington Post* editorialized about the problem of sexual degenerates in the capital, the U.S. Park Police instituted a "Pervert Elimination Campaign" that led to the harassment and arrest of men in known gay cruising areas. Hundreds of men were arrested and charged with loitering, indecency, disorderly conduct, or other nonviolent violations simply by walking in parks, sitting on park benches, or talking with strangers. More troubling, many of the men arrested never went to court because the police didn't have enough evidence to convict; instead, the police held them in custody just long enough to fingerprint, photograph, and record the names and occupations of these men, adding information to an ever-growing "pervert file."[70] Across the country, such laws meant to target predatory sex criminals would, more often, simply criminalize the public visibility and presence of queer men.

Nowhere was fear of queer threats in public more acutely detailed than in a series of articles by journalist Howard Whitman entitled "Terror in the

Streets," published in *Collier's* magazine in the late 1940s. Known for fiction and investigative journalism that appealed to conservative middle-class tastes, *Collier's* had a circulation of close to three million readers at the time. "Terror in the Streets" presented a host of urban tensions, from gang violence, juvenile delinquents, and child molesters to sexual psychopaths and gruesome murders of women. With titles such as "Cleveland's Thugs Crawl in the Cracks of Sidewalks," "The Teen-Age Punks: S.F. Tries to Tame Them," "They Get Away with Murder, Pittsburgh," "Don't Go Out Alone at Night in L.A.," and the more direct "Terror in Washington," the series sensationalized an epidemic of urban crime across the country and fostered fears about social unrest in the postwar years. Taking a tough-guy journalistic approach, Whitman constructed an image of urban disorder and decay while drumming a constant beat for the need of an expanded police force in cities and small towns everywhere.

In 1951 Whitman's book version, also called *Terror in the Streets*, was published as a mass-market paperback, its pulp noir cover depicting a fairhaired ingénue stopped on a darkened city street as two men loiter nearby, one hiding just around the corner of an alley waiting to pounce on the woman as she looks back in fear. The book's cover copy promised the truth "about the epidemic of hoodlum crime . . . that is turning our cities into jungles."

The Washington Post described *Terror in the Streets* as a "frightening book" that points to a "dark place in our backyard and indicates how it might be cleaned up." *The Philadelphia Inquirer* framed it in more sociological terms, describing it as a "shocking nationwide study," and praised Whitman's call for more police in cities and towns. And the *Chicago Tribune* noted that the stories of violence that filled Whitman's book would be "familiar to any newspaper reader." The reviewer noted that "too often we are able to do little or nothing about potential sex criminals," adding, "even after they commit their crimes the laws are inadequate to deal with them."[71]

This helplessness in confronting the sex criminal threads throughout *Terror in the Streets* as Whitman conflated cases of child murderers, exhibitionists, sexual psychopaths, and homosexuals as interchangeable deviants who were all equally "repugnant to society."[72] For Whitman, the recently enacted Miller Sexual Psychopath Law represented a way forward for dealing with the sex crime problem, as he argued the more "liberal" view of the era: that sex criminals should be placed in "quarantine which can keep the sex offender out of circulation, not for months or years—but for as long it takes to get him well." Whitman applauded states that saw "the sex criminal as a mentally sick individual who imperils society . . . a sick person who is dangerous, like someone with smallpox, who must both be treated and quarantined."[73] Such quarantining would remove the lot of "sex criminals" to mental hospitals, where they would stay until the doctors and the state deemed them cured. If they never responded to the treatment, Whitman argued, they should remain in mental hospitals for the rest of their lives.

Central to Whitman's concerns about homosexuality was the anxiety of queer men "prowling" the streets for victims. In the chapter "Crime and the Homosexual," Whitman detailed his travels with vice squads in a number of cities, tracking cruising areas where queer men searched for sexual encounters. Describing such men as wolves, Whitman wrote that "instead of going on the prowl for females," the wolf goes on the prowl for boys and men. "He accosts and inveighs them in the cheap movie houses," he added. "He makes a flagrant display of himself in the public lavatories; he infests the most beautiful public parks, making them repugnant and fearsome to decent citizens."[74] But in his documentation, Whitman also detailed a geography of male cruising for his readers. "Here was a bus terminal in the heart of Pittsburgh," he complained, "where prowlers had made the lavatory a virtual mantrap." In Washington, D.C., he noted with exasperation that "one of the favorite prowling grounds is Lafayette Park—right across from the White House!" adding that the vice squad had recently picked up "sixty-five homosexuals" in a single night. In Detroit, Whitman detailed the "pathetic and horrible" encounters he witnessed in Grand Circus Park, Cadillac Square, and Capitol Park, noting that he saw "the prowlers and the exhibitionist, the blatant accosters looking for pickups."[75] The most concerning provocation of homosexual prowlers for Whitman was their influence on adolescent boys who encountered homosexuals in movie theaters or public restrooms or were picked up while hitchhiking. In numerous cases, their corruption hinged on their encounters with queer men, leading to increasingly violent behaviors.

Crime stories in the press of casual encounters between younger men and older queer men pointed readers to how pervasive the threat of sexual perversion was to the nation's youth. In December 1948, the *Chicago Tribune* related how forty-one-year-old John Dempsey was thrown from a fourteenth-floor hotel window by a companion named Robert Blaney. Described as a college student, Blaney confessed that he had met Dempsey in "a hotel restroom and took him to his room," where the older man "made improper advances." After beating Dempsey to death, he threw his body out the window, and, according to the article, "spent the evening in the same room with an unidentified girl friend." Headlines in the *Daily Chronicle* of Centralia, Washington, in 1952 described how Edwin Hanely, a twenty-two-year-old marine, bayoneted his companion, fifty-five-year-old Martin Zellmer, to death. Hanely, who was hitchhiking when Zellmer picked him up, claimed the older man had "driven off the highway, stopped his car, and made improper advances." The marine, who was AWOL from Camp Pendleton in California at the time, described how after Zellmer grabbed him, he told him he would "kill him if he did not lay off."[76]

In the summer of 1953, the murder of Reverend Robert Hodges, a Catholic priest, made headlines across the country. Hodges had picked up William Jackson Townsend, a twenty-three-year-old fugitive from the Indiana Reformatory, just outside of Kansas City. *The Arizona Republic* included a portrait of the square-jawed Townsend, looking serious and innocent in his mug shot, with his wide eyes and big ears. "The priest began making homosexual advances as they drove," the article noted, adding, "The slight young man, a convicted rapist, said he resisted."[77] In this telling, the convicted rapist appears more the victim of the crime than the murdered priest. Like numerous other stories of such deadly encounters, Townsend's violence in reaction to an alleged queer sexual solicitation was evidence of his sexual normality.

Sometimes, though not often, defendants retracted their claims that indecent advances had been made. In 1949, nineteen-year-old Arthur Hester admitted he killed his foster father, John Lord, a former dean at Texas Christian University. In testimony before his trial, Hester had claimed that he met his foster father at a theater, where Dr. Lord "made advances to him and suggested unnatural acts" in exchange for the use of Lord's car.[78] Later, the *Lubbock Morning Avalanche* reported, Hester admitted that he had concocted a story of sexual solicitation to avoid the death penalty. "Dr. Lord was not homosexual," Hester stated, recanting his earlier testimony, "and not at any time did he ever have unnatural sexual relations with me or conduct himself with any manner that would lead me to believe he was homosexual." While such stories were rare, as the legal consequences of changing prior claims were so great, Hester's retraction points to how easily youthful defendants could claim justifiable homicide against their victims by invoking the specter of queer sexual solicitation.

"CRUEL BLUEPRINT FOR DEATH BARED"

Queer crime stories of indecent advances reflected the social segregation of the news in the 1940s and 1950s. The visibility of African Americans in mainstream newspapers was limited and often relegated to defendants of violent crime. News accounts of African American victims beaten or murdered by their male companions only rarely made headlines beyond the African American press. When Romeo Mayfield, a thirty-four-year-old army veteran and liberal arts student at New York University, was found dead in his McDonough Street rooming house in Brooklyn in May 1949, the local, mainstream press ignored the crime, including the long-standing *Brooklyn Eagle*. The African American newspaper *New York Amsterdam News* reported on the murder, noting in its initial story, "Little could be learned about the student except that he reportedly had many male companions."[79]

A month later, the newspaper announced the arrest and confession of Thomas Taylor of Harlem. The headline, "Ex-GI Admits Sordid 'Act' Led to Death," made clear the relationship between provocation and brutal killing.

Mayfield "had been stabbed, strangled, and gagged with a sheet" by Taylor, who was a "former navy man and now a cook." Mayfield had met Taylor on a street corner in upper Manhattan a week earlier, at which time Mayfield invited him to Brooklyn. The article noted, "Taylor went to the McDonough St. address" the following week, where the two men had dinner, and Taylor "decided to stay with his new acquaintance all night." Echoing a continuing theme in such news reports, the two men got into a "quarrel" when "improper advances were made by the host during the night." The article described how "a struggle followed and Mayfield was stabbed in the neck and the back and then strangled. A twisted sheet was then thrust as far down the victim's throat as possible." After the strangling, Taylor stole clothing from Mayfield's room and left. Intriguingly, the newspaper noted that "a pair of army shorts worn by Taylor . . . had been left behind," and while police searched the partial serial number on the shorts, they "later learned that the shorts had also been stolen by Taylor." While the newspaper described the crime as "one of the most difficult homicide cases to solve in annals of Brooklyn police," the fact that it involved two African American men kept it out of the mainstream press.[80]

Crime stories involving black men and white men illustrated how racial and sexual discriminations played out in queer crime stories. In the summer of 1952, James Ernest Thompson, a twenty-three-year-old African American man, was on trial for the murder of Wilson Smith, a white resident of the tiny tidewater town of Heathsville, Virginia. *The Richmond News Leader* reported that Thompson, a native of Philadelphia, took the witness stand in his own defense, claiming, "he had never intended to kill Smith, nor to harm him seriously; his only purpose in fighting with the man was to defend himself against homosexual advances made by Smith." In a later report, the newspaper called it an "act of sexual perversion against him."[81]

The article detailed how Wilson picked up Thompson, who was hitchhiking from Richmond. In the car Thompson rebuked Wilson several times, eventually getting into the backseat of the car, where he "dozed off," only to be awakened by Smith, who had parked the car and was "partly undressed." According to Thompson, the two men fought, and Thompson hit Smith with "his fists, 'kneed' him, kicked him, and later struck him over the head with a large stick." After the attack, and as Smith lay motionless along the roadside, Thompson took his car back to Richmond and returned to Philadelphia on the train. When the prosecution questioned Thompson about why he didn't report what had happened at the time, he replied: "They would have hung me before I finished telling. Nobody would have believed that about Wilson."

Thompson's assumptions proved true. *The Richmond News Leader* recounted how the state presented more than twenty witnesses, many of whom testified to Wilson's character. Thompson's court-appointed lawyers called two local residents to attest to Smith's "alleged reputation in the community for perversion." One witness related that on two occasions, "fifteen or twenty years ago," Smith had made "unnatural advances" toward him. Another witness testified that Smith had a "reputation of being homosexually inclined when he had been drinking heavily," but added "he had never seen anything to indicate that the reputation was deserved." The jury sentenced Thompson to sixty years in jail.[82]

Often such crime stories varied in details and meaning across the mainstream and African American press. In 1956, *The Washington Post* reported on the murder of a fifty-two-year-old African American named Robert Freeman by three "teenage soldiers" in Washington, D.C. Freeman worked as a chef for the Southern Railway, and he met the soldiers at the Trailways bus station. The *Post* noted that the soldiers found out Freeman "kept several hundred dollars in his apartment," and that "police said the three planned on robbing Freeman." One defendant claimed that Freeman made "improper advances" leading to a "scuffle" that ended with Freeman being killed by a bullet to his temple.[83] *The Post* did not indicate that Freeman was African American, nor that the soldiers were white, but instead focused on the problem of the soldiers' criminality.

Taking a much different approach, the *Afro-American* declared in its front-page headline, "Cruel Blueprint for Death Bared." Quoting testimony from the investigative detective, the article related how the soldiers planned on robbing Freeman, because "they didn't believe he would say anything because he was 'a queer.'" The article described the killers as "blond 19-year-old soldiers." Freeman's neighbor told detectives she saw him get out of a "taxi and two men were with him in khaki," and later she heard "rumbling upstairs" and then "two shots."[84] The details of the two reports differ in many ways, most acutely where and in what manner Freeman was shot. While *The Washington Post* emphasized the lawless behavior of the young soldiers, the *Afro-American* found in the crime a story of victimization of a queer black man at the hands of his white companions.

When Joseph King, an African American native of South Carolina, confessed to the stabbing death of white business executive Harold Oerther in his Greenwich Village apartment in 1953, news of the crime made headlines far beyond New York City. Oerther and King met by chance as they took cover under a building awning during a sudden downpour. *The New York Times* noted King then "visited a bar with him and had accompanied him to the apartment." The article continued, "The slaying took place during a fight in the apartment."

While the *Times* only hinted at the underlying circumstances of the two men's fight, other newspapers were more explicit about the queer context. The Long Island newspaper *Newsday* reported the arrest on its front page. After the two men visited a few bars, they bought beer and returned to Oerther's apartment late Sunday evening. "Early Monday morning," the newspaper related, "Oerther made allegedly improper advances, picking up a knife," adding, "King snatched up a cast-iron skillet and struck Oerther so hard the utensil broke. King then wrested the knife from Oerther and stabbed Oerther repeatedly."[85] The newspaper published a large headshot of Oerther, smiling at the camera in his naval officer uniform. It also included a photograph of his distraught wife and stepdaughter arriving at the police station. Oerther and his wife, the article noted, were "estranged" and the family had moved to New Jersey, although the executive stayed in the Greenwich Village apartment during the week. The images of the smiling victim in his uniform and his distraught family were in strong contrast to the story of the African American killer, whose confessions about what happened in the apartment the newspaper cast in doubt.

With the headline "Advances Lead to Murder; Jobless Garment Worker Admits Village Slaying," the *Afro-American* emphasized both the class and race disparities between the two men in its lead: "A twenty-six-year-old unemployed garment worker," the newspaper reported, "confessed to stabbing and beating to death a forty-six-year-old, $10,000-a-year executive of an employment agency in his Greenwich Village Apartment after the white man made improper advances." The article also detailed that after King refused the advances, Oerther "threatened him with a knife."[86]

In King's native South Carolina, the front page of the *Index-Journal* announced, "Young S.C. Negro Arrested in Slaying of N.Y. Employment Agency Executive." The article included King's claim of sexual advances, but emphasized the brutality of the crime and the killer. "Oerther's body bore a number of knife wounds and showed evidence of a severe beating," the article noted. Readers also learned that when police found King, he was in a bar "reading a newspaper account of the murder," underscoring the cold-blooded nature of the "young negro" assailant.[87]

"STOP ME, FOR GOD'S SAKE BEFORE I KILL AGAIN"

In the summer of 1952, Chicago police were put on alert by the rantings of a man the press would soon label the "Hammer Killer." After an anonymous phone caller informed the police, "[i]f you want to see something bloody go to room 414 at the Loop Hotel," officers arrived to find the battered body of thirty-four-year-old Thomas Acton, his skull fractured by the blows of a hammer. In subsequent telephone calls to the police, the killer announced that he would kill again, directing them to the more fashionable Drake Hotel. Newspapers across the Midwest avidly reported the killing and the subsequent series of wild chases across the city. Most ominously, the press related how the killer in his desperate phone calls to police pleaded, "Stop me, for God's sake before I kill again."[88]

The Chicago police set up dragnets around the city and at several hotels. When they arrested a suspect, Owen Cox, he readily confessed to the crime.

Owen and Acton had met in Alabama and the two had traveled to Chicago together, taking a room in the Loop Hotel. He told police he had an "urge to kill" which, a newspaper noted, "culminated in the assault." Cox had "no remorse" for the murder; instead he told reporters he was glad Acton was dead, even while he begged to be executed.

Not long after the confession became public, the press offered up Cox as a case study of depraved and violent queer criminality. One report explained how the unmarried Cox "remained calm as he told them about his deviationist sex life and his crime."[89] In detailing Cox's childhood, his upbringing in a poor coal-mining family in West Virginia, his service in the war, and his many treatments in mental hospitals, the article pointed to his sexual deviancy as the cause for his brutal violence. The *Tucson Daily Citizen* explained Cox's desires more explicitly: "Police said he admitted he was a homosexual, and said they believed his 'urge to kill' came during periods of remorse after the sex act."[90] As the newspaper reports made clear, mental illness, a troubled childhood, lack of empathy, and sexual deviancy all interlaced to become factors in Cox's "urge to kill."

The news articles about Cox's violent crimes reflected an underlying but gradually compelling idea in the postwar years. Suggestions that his "urges" were both sexual and violent in nature pointed to a theory of his latent homosexuality. Within this theory, the compelling guilt of having sex with another man, or even being propositioned for sex with another man, provoked a violent, deadly reaction. Claims of the homosexual panic self-defense against indecent advances were as much about the actions of the queer victim as they were about the nature of provocation. But what was crucial to the idea of homosexual panic was how it made homosexual desires a lurking, unseen force of public danger.

Homosexual panic was vital to Whitman's concerns about sex crimes in *Terror in the Streets*. Whitman told his readers that when an older man seduces a younger man, the "result often is a fight or even killing." He wrote, "Men who naively fall for the prowler's come-on frequently fly into a rage when the reality of the situation finally dawns on them. They punch, beat, maul, and sometimes kill their would-be seducers."[91] For Whitman, this response was only natural, arguing that the violence was a reaction by the "so-called normal man's tremendous resistance to facing latent homosexual factors in his own make-up." Whitman then dove into a lesson in human psychology: "This is, of course, scientifically true. All human beings are mixtures of male and female, and the well-adjusted male is perfectly capable of recognizing homosexual components in himself while easily submerging them into a heterosexual cultural pattern, just as he may recognize, say, aggressive criminal components in himself and sublimate them in socially constructive activity."[92]

The problem with public homosexual prowlers, this logic suggested, was that they not only lacked the control of their own homosexual feelings but also prompted other men who possessed latent homosexual desires to lose such control as well. Such an idea astoundingly blamed the violence queer men suffered at the hands of their seemingly "normal" companions as in fact evidence of sexual deviance as well. "Often the men who fly into the blindest rages at the very thought of homosexuality," Whitman concluded, "the men who want to go around smashing homosexuals in the jaw, are, in actual fact, the men with the greatest unrecognized homosexual components in their own characters."[93]

In the 1940s, doctors began to reconsider and reformulate Edward Kempf's initial theories of acute homosexual panic, which he'd developed during World War I. Benjamin Karpman, the psychotherapist at St. Elizabeths who was a leading voice in the psychoanalytic treatment of homosexuality in the 1940s and 1950s, revisited Kempf's theories, noting that no one had "taken up the problem of acute homosexual panic" since Kempf's work. For Karpman, both theory and treatment needed to be rethought through a more precise psychoanalytic lens. Defining homosexual panic as a condition of latent homosexuality that is "pressing strongly to the surface for open expression but is held in check by the dictates of the super-ego with a sense of guilt," Karpman affirmed that within a state caught between two conflicting emotions, the patient is "thrown into acute conflict."[94]

World War II was a watershed moment in the use of psychoanalysis for the treatment of mental illness. At the beginning of the war, only thirty-five members of the Army Medical Corps had specializations in psychiatric practices. By the war's end, that number had grown to more than 2,400 army doctors assigned to psychiatry, prompting the creation of a new division dedicated to psychiatric treatment alongside medicine and surgery within the military.[95] This division was headed by William Menninger, the first psychiatrist promoted to the rank of brigadier general in the U.S. Army. Under Menninger's direction, these doctors treated a range of mental illnesses brought on by environmental and combat stress. The military doctors made use of short-term psychodynamic therapies, including psychoanalysis, and in this process gave birth to a new, younger generation of doctors who reshaped the understanding of treatment of mental illness. In his 1948 book *Psychiatry in a Troubled World: Yesterday's War and Today's Challenge*, Menninger detailed how psychiatric treatment had helped soldiers on the battlefront, and how it could be useful on the home front as well. For what he termed "neurotic reactions," Menninger advocated the practical uses of psychiatry beyond its application for severe cases of mental illness. Instead, psychiatry had a role in assisting people on an everyday basis to deal with "environmental stresses on the personality," adding that it could help with the "problems of the average man and to the large social issues which he is involved." "Psychiatry," he wrote, "must gain for itself an even wider acceptance and a more intelligent understanding by the public."[96]

The same year that Chicago was on edge with the violent threats of the Hammer Killer, the American Psychiatric Association published the first edition of the *Diagnostic and Statistical Manual*. The manual was based almost entirely on "Medical 203," an internal military guide composed under Menninger's direction that categorized a wide spectrum of mental illness that had, at the start of World War II, been a diverse collection of terms and treatments across the different divisions of the military. The *DSM-I*, as it became known, was the first effort to propose a consistent diagnosis and treatment of mental illness outside of the military and would become the standard guide for clinical practice for the next twenty years. In its appendix of supplemental terms, the *DSM-I* listed homosexual panic as a mental disorder alongside obesity, nymphomania, and kleptomania, to name a few.[97] While it did not define the conditions of homosexual panic, it did define the more common term of "sexual deviation." "This diagnosis," the handbook directs, "is reserved for deviant sexuality which is not symptomatic of more extensive syndromes, such as schizophrenic or obsessional reactions. The term includes most of the cases formerly classed as 'psychopathic personality with pathologic sexuality.' The diagnosis will specify the type of the pathologic behavior, such as homosexuality, transvestism, pedophilia, fetishism, and sexual sadism (including rape, sexual assault, mutilation)."[98] While this grouping of homosexuality with violence and assault formalized a postwar understanding of sexual deviancy as part of a spectrum of aggressive and dangerous behaviors, it also staked out a claim over the definition of sexual deviancy as a medical concern rather than a legal one.

Despite its listing in *DSM-I*, homosexual panic remained an uncertain condition in research and clinical practice. Writing in the *Journal of Mental and Nervous Disease* in 1959, Burton Glick, a clinical psychiatrist, noted that homosexual panic "is a phrase used often in teaching seminars, case discussions, and in the written descriptions of case histories," but, he added, there had been very little research on the condition since Kempf formulated his theories. "Homosexual panic," Glick wrote, "is apparently not recognized as existing by many of the standard psychiatric or psychological dictionaries," adding that in clinical practices the condition has "had many meanings attached to it, ranging from vague feelings of discomfort to truly horrifying fright accompanied by disordered thought and behavior."[99]

As with many psychological theories, Glick's theory of homosexual panic took on the nuances of its time and place. Glick distinguished two forms of homosexuality: the latent or unconscious homosexual, and the "manifest" or overt homosexual. He described latent homosexuality as a "passive-feminine attitude" that triggered a host of fears, including "castration, turning into a woman, complete subjugation with loss of will, [and] physical pain."[100] The impetus to such panic in latent homosexuals was linked to an exposure to "homosexual material"—a vague term that included everything from contact with homosexuals to the more nebulous presence of homosexual references that might trigger a man's anxiety with his latent desires. By contrast, the overt homosexual, Glick surmised, would not be triggered by such fears since he desired the passive role. Glick claimed that the mere presence of homosexuality—in any number of visible or suggested ways—was enough to provoke a violent, psychotic episode.

As the defense took hold in the courtroom, the legal appropriation of homosexual panic misconstrued the psychological theories themselves, constructing courtroom defenses and jury verdicts based on discriminatory understanding of homosexuality as an inherent, and often violent, threat.[101] The effect of this misrepresentation in both the courtroom and the press was to justify violence against queer men as an assertion of heterosexuality through claims of self-defense.

Throughout the 1950s and 1960s as the legal defense evolved, the integrity of heterosexuality in cases of homosexual panic depended on the "reasonable man standard," which argued that any "normal" man would be outraged by another man's sexual attraction, or mere suggestion of homosexual interest. Such a standard justified the violent attack as a reasonable response to such an emotional and psychological threat.[102] The reasonable man standard allowed all kinds of antiqueer violence to be defended, whether those charged were genuinely disturbed by the queer victim's flirtation or simply professed such emotional distress to cover their efforts at targeting queer men for robbery and assault. In providing a compelling alibi for acts of violence against queer men, claims of homosexual panic defense exploited ideas about queer criminality, turning the dead victims into the real culprits of the crime.

Stories of homosexual panic and indecent advances went beyond the crime pages. The premise of Richard Brooks's 1945 novel *The Brick Foxhole* could have come from any number of such queer true crime stories of the era. Brooks, who would later go on to be a well-respected Hollywood screenwriter and director, crafted a story of bored soldiers stationed stateside during

World War II. The novel's protagonist, Jeff Mitchell, travels to Washington, D.C., for a weekend, along with two of his fellow soldiers, Monty Crawford, a former Chicago police detective, and Floyd Bowers, a young and naïve son of the Deep South. The novel's plot is set in place when the three hitch a ride to the nation's capital with an effete and wealthy interior decorator named Mr. Edwards. In the car, Monty and Floyd goad Mr. Edwards with claims that they need money and that they are tired of women. In fact they gave "up girls altogether" but, they add, "A guy's got to have some fun."[103] Such conversation prompts Edwards to invite the soldiers back to his house in Washington, though Mitchell senses the danger in the invitation, for he had "heard about the pastime of some soldiers. Their treatment of sexual perverts. The way they regarded them. Jeff," the narrator adds, "was afraid for himself, too."[104] But as Floyd whispers in Mitchell's ear in the backseat of the car, the latter understands the crime that is unfolding: "We're set buddy," Floyd says. "I ain't beaten up a queer in I don't know how long."[105]

At his home, Edwards puts on a record of a "well known negro singer," enraging both Monty and Floyd, and prompting Monty to brag about African American and Jewish suspects he assaulted and murdered while in custody, describing such actions as a service to the citizens of Chicago. Mitchell leaves the apartment in a drunken haze, sensing what is to come next. A few chapters later, we learn of Edwards's fate as local news headlines declare, "Prominent Decorator Found Dead in Sordid Sex Orgy, Serviceman Believed Killer." Edwards was beaten with the "large, flat top of the toilet" that smashed his skull "like a cantaloupe."[106]

In his police interrogation, Monty points to Jeff Mitchell as the killer. "What if he did go into the bathroom with that bastid fairy," Monty sneered, claiming it was justifiable homicide: "What if Edwards made a pass at him? He was making goo-goo eyes at poor Jeff from the start. I don't blame Jeff. It serves Edwards right. They ought to kill every one of them fairies. There ain't a court martial in the world would do anything to Jeff for that."[107]

The novel makes clear that claims of indecent advances were not only dubious justifications of homicide, but also enmeshed with larger bigotries in the postwar years. It was not Edwards who was the threat in Brooks's novel, but the racist and anti-Semitic army soldiers. When the novel was turned into the 1947 noir detective film *Crossfire*, directed by Edward Dmytryk for RKO studios, the censorship of the Production Code meant that the murdered homosexual was replaced by a murdered Jew and the problem of anti-Semitism. Any reference to homosexuality was erased. Another significant change from the book to the screen portrayed racism and anti-Semitism as a problem of individual, psychopathic hate rather than a larger social disease. RKO's efforts to secure support from community leaders through advance screenings across the country, and an ad campaign that emphasized the "courage" of the film in addressing the problem of religious bigotry, helped make *Crossfire*'s controversial story one of the most successful films of the year. It was nominated for a number of Academy Awards, including best picture, best director, and best screenplay, and won the Best Social Film award at the Cannes Film Festival.

A few years later, the young writer James Baldwin composed a searing critique of contemporary fiction's depiction of violence against homosexuals in an essay published in the small but important postwar arts magazine *Zero*. In Raymond Chandler's detective novels, for example, Baldwin argued that the men and women are "surrounded by blood and treachery" and their connections have little to do with love or sexuality but rather with an "unbelievably barren and wrathful grinding." But it was in reflecting on the increasing presence of homosexual characters in postwar literature that Baldwin saw a more profound uncertainty with heterosexuality. "Let me suggest," he wrote, "that the present debasement and our obsession with the homosexual corresponds to the debasement of the relationship between the sexes." He provided as examples Gore Vidal's 1948 novel *The City and the Pillar*, in which, Baldwin noted, "the avowed homosexual . . . murders his first and only perfect love," and the dramatic conclusive assault in Charles Jackson's 1944 novel *The Fall of Valor*, where a married professor is nearly beaten to death after confessing his desire for a marine. "The violent resolutions," Baldwin wrote, "are compelled by a panic which is close to madness. These novels are not concerned with homosexuality but with the ever present danger of sexual activity between men."[108] As Baldwin saw in the literature, we might also see in the crime stories splashed across the front pages during this era when homosexual panic was imagined as both an individual and cultural trauma. While reflecting fears of sex deviants prowling around every street corner, accounts of explosive violence in the wake of indecent advances manifested larger ideas about the boundaries between normal men and queer men in postwar America. Crucial to these boundaries were the psychological imperatives that defined male heterosexuality through a violent disavowal of homosexual encounters.

The Homosexual Next Door

Kinsey and the Private Life of Sex in the Cold War

"GROTESQUELY BOUND TO HIS BED"

The Ambassador Hotel faced south along Franklin Square in Washington, D.C. Built in 1929 by the son of an Italian immigrant, the hotel had a distinctive and starkly modern orange brick and white stone façade. Its architecture avoided the ornate Victorian opulence of many of the well-established hotels in the nation's capital, like the Hay-Adams or the Willard. Instead, the Ambassador appealed to modern, middle-class travelers. It offered free radio service in every guest room, and by the late 1940s boasted it was "completely air conditioned." Guests enjoyed one of the first interior swimming pools in the city. Specially designed submerged lights illuminated the two-story art deco pool room in shimmering blue light. Guests also enjoyed the sleek cocktail lounge called the Hi-Hat Club, described in newspaper advertisements as "the most popular place in town."

The hotel made news in the summer of 1948 when Frances Gerson, a thirty-year-old woman from Cincinnati, jumped out a seventh-floor window to her death. *The Washington Post* described how "her body crashed against the window cornice of the Hi-Hat cocktail lounge and landed near the street curbing." She left a seven-page suicide note, claiming her ex-husband drove her to her death.[1]

A few months later the hotel would make headlines again when Doro-thy Kinsler, a hotel maid, entered room 604 and discovered the badly beaten body of Charles Hines. The forty-eight-year-old Hines was a house painter from Madison, Wisconsin. Days earlier, he was in North Carolina visit-ing his son, a marine stationed at Camp Lejeune. From there, according to his wife, Hines took the train to Washington to do some sightseeing. He checked into the hotel on a Monday afternoon, two days before he was found murdered.

Reports of the crime filled the front pages of the D.C. press for several days. In its extensive coverage, *The Washington Post* described how Hines was found dressed only in his underwear, "lying on his back on the bed. His head was covered with blood, which had dripped over the bed and onto the floor." More details illustrated the complex torture that Hines endured: "A rolled-up sheet covered his mouth and was tied tightly around his neck. His hands had been tied together with his own leather belt, which in turn was fastened by a hotel towel to the head of the wooden bed ... His feet were tied with a neck tie and then tied by a shirt to the foot of the bed." Besides such graphic descriptions, readers also learned about witnesses who saw Hines in the hours before his murder. John Bradley, a waiter at the hotel, told police he brought beers to Hines's room at four in the morning, where "perhaps two or three" men were with Hines. The police also interviewed neighbor-ing guests, though "none of them had heard any sounds of struggle."[2]

The press offered readers clues from the room itself. In one corner a gray suit was "laid neatly on a chair" with "brown shoes placed beneath it." There was a "half-pint bottle of Tuxedo whisky, about one third full" left on a table, and in the bathroom "four empty Schlitz beer bottles" along with a glass "which had contained whisky, another which had contained beer, and a third which apparently had been used only for water." While the room was in order and the furniture was not disturbed, police believed there was a fierce struggle, as "blood had splattered on the ceiling" and on the venetian window blinds, which were "about eight feet away from the bed." One of the more revealing details concerned the ashtrays. "About a dozen cigarette butts were found in the room," one article noted, adding, "none of them bore traces of lipstick, indicating Hines had had no women visitors."[3]

Two days after Hines's body was found, police arrested Crispin Barrera Perez for the murder. News reports described Perez as "a twenty-nine-year-old bartender" and "a swarthy and impassive student." The *Washington Evening Star*, which often avoided local crime stories on its front pages, opting instead to focus on politics and foreign affairs, reported that police had "a signed confession from swarthy Crispin Barrera Perez," and that he was "a well known figure in midtown bars." A photograph of Perez in police custody showed him wearing a dark sweater and tie and light-colored pants. *The Washington Post* noted that Perez had a common-law wife, who told police that he was of "Spanish or Mexican descent" and came to Washington from Texas. She also stated that Perez was known to get "crazy drunk."[4]

In his own statement to the police, Perez detailed how he met Hines in front of Playland, an amusement hall on New York Avenue, before heading to a local tavern where the two met "another man and two girls." After they all had dinner, Hines and Perez went to the Ambassador Hotel. There the two got into a fight because Perez stopped drinking. "Hines became angry," the newspaper reported, "and the fight began in which he struck Hines with a blackjack." Perez confessed that "'he couldn't remember' how many times he hit Hines."[5]

The story of Hines's murder remained on the front page for a few weeks. When a grand jury indicted Perez for first-degree murder in January 1949, it determined the motive "was robbery of a $300 finger ring" that Hines wore.[6] While the ring, described in earlier reports as worth $1,000, and Perez's drunken state pointed to the motive for the crime, many readers would have wondered how Hines came to be so sadistically tied up, with a bedsheet stuffed down his throat, if the crime was a simple robbery.

The robbery motive would define the story in reports beyond the nation's capital, offering readers gruesome crime scene details. In Hines's native Wisconsin, the *Green Bay Press-Gazette* reported Perez went with Hines to his hotel room "after noticing the expensive diamond ring." Readers learned how

Hines's body was "grotesquely bound to his bed," and how "a handkerchief, stuffed down Hines's throat before he was tied up with a tightly knotted bed sheet, asphyxiated him and was the immediate cause of death." Intriguingly, editors placed the story of Hines's murder next to the recent arrest of the dean of a Milwaukee vocational school for "taking improper liberties with a seventeen-year-old boy." The front page of *The Sheboygan Press* reported, "Hines's feet were bound together with a necktie," adding, "the dead man was clad only in his underwear." Even as many press reports pointed to robbery as a motive for the crime, the brutality of the killing remained a puzzling reality. The *Belvidere Daily Republican* in Illinois published a photograph on its front page of the police carrying a body bag out of the Ambassador Hotel, noting how a maid "discovered the blood smeared corpse." The newspaper reported, "Even after questioning Perez, detectives were unable to explain why he subjected his victim to such a sadistic beating."[7]

In May 1949, after doctors at St. Elizabeths Hospital examined Perez and declared him sane for trial, he pleaded guilty to a lesser charge of second-degree murder. In these later reports, there was no mention of Perez's common-law wife or the expensive ring. Instead, a different story emerged of the killer's motivation, of what led him to his encounter with Hines. *The Washington Post* related that Perez was a hapless victim of a "promiscuous" girlfriend. As he went out "hunting for her in the taverns and dives," he met Hines.[8] These later reports said little about robbery as a motive, pointing instead to the mental state of Perez. The *Green Bay Press-Gazette* reported the judge accepted Perez's plea of second-degree murder "because the prosecution admitted Perez's mentality was perhaps too low to permit him to form a premeditation necessary for first degree murder."[9] Did Perez's examination at St. Elizabeths, well-known at the time for its experimental treatments of homosexuals, account for the shift in the press reports to the killer's "low mentality," a term often associated with sexual perversion in criminology? The mysteries of the crime would linger even with this new interpretation of Perez.

Days later, *The Washington Post* reported, "[E]vidence that the murder was committed in the perpetration of a robbery was scant." The judge, the article noted, "believed the Hines family might be subjected to some 'embarrassment' if the first-degree trial were held."[10] Such coded language hinted at the sexual nature of the encounter between Hines and Perez, even as it left uncertain Perez's real motives in torturing and killing the older man. Instead of a trial, the judge accepted the plea deal and sentenced Perez to fifteen years to life. As had happened before in such crime stories, the family's fear of public testimony would continue the mystery of what transpired in room 604 of the Ambassador Hotel, as well as the motives for such a brutal and deadly crime.

The same year the Hines murder made headlines, the country had been embroiled in a discussion about the sex habits of men prompted by one disquieting book: Alfred Kinsey's *Sexual Behavior in the Human Male.* Published in January 1948, the 804-page book cost $6.50 (the equivalent of about $70 today). Despite its price and its dense, scientific rhetoric, Kinsey's study quickly became a bestseller. The book "precipitated the most intense and high-level dialogue on human sexuality in the nation's history," wrote Kinsey biographer James Jones, adding, "In boardrooms, in barbershops, in cafés, in grocery stores, and on street corners Americans could be heard reciting his findings on the incidence of masturbation, homosexuality, premarital and extramarital intercourse, and the like."[11] That August, *Life* magazine reported that Kinsey's study had garnered an "astounding number of reviews, critiques, summaries, interviews, and 'think pieces,' which has saturated every level of journalism from the tabloids to the most recondite scientific publication."[12]

It was Kinsey's findings about the widespread occurrence of homosexual practices that drew the most attention, prompting a rethinking of decades of ideas about the nature and origins of homosexuality, and making male sexuality a subject of public discussion in the postwar years.[13] The study produced the now famous Kinsey scale, a span from 0 to 6 marking a continuum between complete heterosexuality (marked as 0) and complete homosexuality (marked as 6). Men in the study were placed on the scale, generating statistical evidence of the prevalence and occurrence of homosexuality among American men. Kinsey and his associates used detailed survey questions about sexual practices as well as long face-to-face interviews with willing participants. One respondent explained that Kinsey, who was trained in the study of insects, brought to his research interviews a scientific reserve, void of moral or social prejudices. "If you told him you had licked someone's toes," the informant related years later, "he was fascinated to find out about it. And he was nonjudgmental. He wouldn't have been able to get things out of people unless he was the person that he was." Beyond interviews and personal case histories, Kinsey was also known to observe men having sex or masturbating. Kinsey approached "homosexuality just as calmly as he did his work with wasps," recalled the artist Paul Cadmus, adding, "he interviewed me about my sex life—how many orgasms, how big it was, measure it before and after."[14]

The Kinsey Report findings—that sexual experiences between men occurred across different ages of men's lives and were not as uncommon as many previous studies had suggested—cast dramatic doubts on not only contemporary theories about homosexuality as an aberrant behavior of a minority of men, but also the legal prohibitions that criminalized such behaviors. "The judge who is considering the case of the male who has been arrested for homosexual activity," Kinsey wrote, "should keep in mind that nearly 40 percent of all the other males in town could be arrested at some time in their lives for similar activity."

But it was not only what Kinsey's study revealed that was unsettling, it was also what it made uncertain. The possibilities that your coworker or neighbor could be a homosexual (or at least had engaged in homosexual experiences at some point in his life) upended earlier ideas that queer men manifested certain physical and psychological traits that were easily identifiable and, subsequently, containable. While Kinsey argued against punishing and arresting men for homosexuality, his study had paradoxical effects. For some it raised awareness and a new understanding about the prevalence of same-sex experiences in postwar America. But for others, it highlighted and confirmed the growing threat that homosexuals allegedly presented to the larger society. As historian Jennifer Terry notes, Kinsey's study gave evidence to the fear that homosexuality was a growing invisible menace, and that such sexual deviancy was right under the noses of authorities and innocent civilians alike.[15] Similar to Cold War fears about the Communist living next door, homosexuals were increasingly understood as a vast, undecipherable network of individuals who had insinuated themselves at all levels of society. "Persons with homosexual histories," Kinsey wrote in his study, "are to be found in every age group, in every social level, in every conceivable occupation, in cities and on farms, and in the most remote areas of the country."[16]

Underneath the radical and, for some, threatening findings of Kinsey's study was a more subversive argument about the private life of sex. Throughout his interviews, Kinsey and his colleagues gave a picture of homosexual practices occurring in homes and apartments between consenting adults or, through case studies of childhood experiences, between experimenting teenagers. Such an image countered the decades-long crusades that targeted homosexuality as a dire public problem of criminality, immorality, and disease. Within the mantle of scientific inquiry, the Kinsey Report revealed a stark contrast between actual sexual practices and the moralizing claims that framed discussions and public policy pertaining to homosexuality.[17] The argument that homosexuality presented no public harm, and was in fact a matter of private concern, would increasingly find expression in the Cold War and beyond as activists pushed for the decriminalization of sodomy and the end of forced psychiatric treatments of homosexuals.

"A HANDSOME YOUNG MAN WITH AN UGLY CRIMINAL RECORD"

In the same month that Kinsey's research on the sexual practices of American men prompted a national conversation, a twenty-two-year-old Gore Vidal published his third novel, *The City and the Pillar*. The publisher's advertisements for the novel declared, "Never before in American letters has there been such a revealing and frank discussion of the sexually maladjusted, of those of the submerged world which lives beneath the surface of normality."[18]

The novel tells the story of Jim Willard. Beginning with his high school sexual encounter with his best friend Bob Ford, we are taken along Willard's adventures from the late 1930s to the postwar years. In stark, realist prose, Vidal gives us a queer landscape of America—from bars in New York and private parties in Hollywood, to sailors on cruise ships and writers in New Orleans. This landscape—filled with effete queers, military men, and rough trade—put a homosexual social world at the center of a work of American fiction for the first time.

While Willard comes to his own sexual awakening through a series of queer encounters and relationships, it is his obsession with Ford that draws the novel to its tragic climax. After the war, Willard reunites with the now married Ford in New York, and the two have drinks in a bar filled with queer patrons. "Jim watched the people in the bar," Vidal wrote. "Some were very obvious. A pilot would squeeze in beside a sailor. They would have a drink together. They would talk. Jim could see their legs pressed together. Then they would leave together, their faces flushed and their eyes bright." Such encounters prompted Ford to ask, "That's sort of a queer-looking crowd," with Willard responding: "That's New York." Ford observes, "There're a lot of queers here. They seem to be everywhere now."

The two continue the night in a "dingy room in a large, not too respectable hotel," where Ford is staying. Their drunkenness builds Willard's confidence to try to replay their high school sexual encounter, an action that only enrages Ford. "You're a queer," Ford shouts, "you're nothing but a damned queer! Go on and get your ass out of here!"

His rage prompts Willard's own anger. Fury, Vidal wrote, "took the place of love." The scene boils toward the violent end: "Jim had Bob by the throat; methodically he began to choke him. Bob twisted desperately on the floor but Jim was too strong. Suddenly Bob's body became rigid; then, after a long time, he went limp and Jim knew that he was dead." Williard picks up Ford's body and puts him in bed. "He was very heavy. Jim arranged his arms and legs and put a pillow under his head. He kissed him."[19]

In a letter to Vidal, the writer Christopher Isherwood called it "one of the best novels of its kind yet published in English." But Isherwood also took the younger writer to task on the ending. "Dramatically and psychologically, I find it entirely plausible," he wrote. "What I do question is the moral the reader will draw. This is what homosexuality brings you to, he will say: tragedy, defeat, and death. Maybe we're too hard on these people—maybe we shouldn't lock them up in prisons; but oughtn't they to be put away in clinics? Such misery is a menace to society." Isherwood added that the success of a homosexual relationship "is revolutionary in the best sense of the word," for it "demonstrates the power of human affection over fear and prejudice and taboo."[20]

Vidal claimed that the ending had nothing to do with the publisher's expectation that a story of homosexuality end in tragedy—a common demand by editors at the time—but rather that killing off Ford was Vidal's own decision. "I had always meant the end of the book to be black," he wrote years after the novel was published, "but not as black as it turned out."[21] In 1965, his publisher brought out a revised edition, in which Vidal rewrote the ending from one of murder to that of rape.

While *The City and the Pillar* quickly became a bestseller, the critics were unanimous in their dislike, rehashing familiar criticisms about the morality of the book. *The New York Times* observed that Vidal had "produced a novel as sterile as its protagonist." The *Chicago Tribune* bemoaned the way it promoted the idea that "homosexuality is an admirable thing which ought to be not only tolerated but encouraged," adding that the novel is "wishy-washy, pretentious, ridiculous propaganda." The reviewer in *The Cincinnati Enquirer* found a new adjective for places that catered to homosexuals, describing the protagonist as one who "drifts away from home, drifts into various Sodom and Gomorrahish establishments in Hollywood and New York without motivation or even initiative. He is colorless to the point of invisibility." *The Hartford Courant* complained that the novel offered no explanation for the causes of Willard's homosexuality. "In spite of the author's explicit detail and conversation of his more intelligent characters," the reviewer wrote, "no psychic or physiological basis for homosexuality is indicated." In speculating about the cause of his homosexuality, this reviewer offered a strange aside: "The dominating character of American women is vaguely suggested as the reason why men are driven from heterosexuality. But this is absurd inasmuch as it is a well known fact that homosexuality is far more prevalent in European countries."

Perhaps the most cutting review was found in *The Washington Post*. "In attempting to keep his interest in homosexuality on an almost clinical level," the reviewer wrote, "Vidal accomplishes the nearly impossible task of raising a slimy subject to some degree of dignity. He makes the reader feel that his natural revulsion toward the half-world of sexual misfits is perhaps as boorish as race or religious bias." The reviewer deemed the novel more useful as clinical theory than literary art. "Gore Vidal should be able to get a degree from some university for this study in abnormal psychology," the reviewer concluded. "He has written some worthy footnotes to Krafft-Ebing. But the place for such a novel as this is in the stacks of the psychology library, not in the hands of effeminate boys, pampering their pathological inclinations."[22]

Life would imitate art throughout 1948 in a series of deadly and gruesome hotel murders with queer undertones. In February, the body of former navy lieutenant Harvey Haeberle was found in room 541 of the Henry Hudson Hotel in New York City. *The New York Times* noted that the thirty-five-year-old Haeberle, married and the father of two, "had visited Henry Hudson three times in recent months, coming alone and staying only a few days on each occasion."[23] According to the article, "Haeberle was found to be tied in a fashion borrowed from the Chinese, who used the same method to torture their victims to death. Clad only in his underwear, his hands and feet were tied behind him with strips of bed sheet and his belt and another piece of bed sheet were knotted around his neck. A chain strip running down his back linked the knots of the three separate pieces so that the slightest movement would tighten the strip around his neck."[24]

The description of Haeberle's body, tied and chained, dressed only in his underwear, and the reference to Chinese torture methods, conjured interlacing national and sexual deviancies for readers. The Chinese torture theme would dominate much of the initial news coverage. "'Torture Knot' Takes the Life of Former Iowan," declared the *Iowa City Press-Citizen* on its front page, describing how Haeberle was tied in a method "employed for centuries by the Chinese to torture victims to death."[25] A newspaper in Huron, South Dakota, related that "strips of bed linen were looped about Haeberle's arms and throat in a version of the Chinese torture knot," but added that the results of an autopsy revealed that "Haeberle did not die of strangulation but was smothered when his head was pressed into the mattress of his bed. The body was found face down."[26] Such details of the crime scene, published in small and large newspapers across the country, turned the New York City crime into a national story of foreign agents, brutal torture, and hints of sexual sadism.

In New York for work on a film for the navy, Haeberle was employed by the Naval Photographic Center in Washington, D.C. "He was not known to be carrying any classified or confidential matter," *The Washington Post* reported, hinting at the continuing links between national security and his killing. The newspaper enlisted an artist to render the crime scene of Haeberle's body garroted in bed. Next to a photograph of a smiling Haeberle, a front-page line drawing depicted a half-naked man, hands and feet bound behind him and twisted bedsheets wrapped around his neck. The image resembled an interrogation chamber rather than a midtown Manhattan hotel room. Readers learned that "a guest in the next room told authorities he heard a voice greet a man" who arrived at Haeberle's door around eleven at night. Another guest gave a description of a "swarthy-faced man, twenty-five to twenty-seven years old . . . [wearing] blue denim trousers." The visitor reportedly said, "Hello. Long time no see," just at the entrance to the victim's hotel room, leading police to believe that Haeberle knew his killer.[27]

The crime provoked an extensive investigation across thirteen states. Over fifty detectives and policemen searched the area around Times Square for clues to the killing. As the investigation continued, the image of the "swarthy-faced" man changed in the press to an "Unknown white man" of "United States nationality," and all suggestions of Chinese torture disappeared from the news coverage. Later articles pushed speculative headlines about urban crime, such as "Navy Man's Death Laid to 2 Thugs" even as detectives had not made any arrests.[28] After weeks of investigation, the New York City police, according to *The Washington Post*, "were without a tangible clue to the slaying."[29]

The press would connect Haeberle's murder to similar crimes that occurred in the early months of 1948, each involving a man tied up, half naked, and strangled or suffocated in a hotel room. In January Henry Cintron was lured into his assailant's room at the Hotel Alamac on Manhattan's Upper West Side where, according to reports, he was stripped, tied up, and tortured with broken glass and lit cigarettes. Later reports acknowledge that Cintron was working with police to catch two men who were extorting cash from wealthy male tourists.

Four men were arrested and charged in February for the murder of Kenneth Gray, a merchant seaman from Texas who was strangled in his Times Square hotel room in the same way as Haeberle. Readers learned that one of those charged, Bruce Bowers, was "a gaunt man, who is almost six feet tall" and, according to *The New York Times*, "addicted to pull-over sweaters." A police detective described Bowers as "'a floater,' a criminal type that floats from city to city and bar to bar seeking out robbery victims."[30] Bowers, along with the three others, targeted Gray because he saw him spending freely in the hotel bar. As the press reports made clear, the underlining motives in such crimes was to lure men into hotel rooms, torture them, and extort money. Despite such explicit motives, many readers would have wondered how the men all ended up in the hotel room together, and why the victims were often left tied up in bed wearing only their underwear.

The murder of Theodore Allen in an Albany, New York, hotel room in September 1948 echoed these earlier cases. Allen had worked in radio broadcasting for the National Broadcasting Corporation. Soon to take a position in radio communications with the State of New York, Allen was in Albany looking for an apartment for him and his wife. On the night of his murder, Allen's wife called the hotel front desk, concerned that her husband had missed their usual evening phone call. The desk clerk, according to reports, found Allen "trussed with a bed sheet rolled into a rope-like shape" and his hands "bound behind his back and the sheet looped about his neck and tied to his ankles." He was gagged with a bedsheet that was stuffed down his throat, and, the press reported, was strangled in a fashion that resembled a "Japanese noose." [31]

It was not a foreign agent who was arrested for the murder, but instead a twenty-year-old army recruit from Fort Dix, New Jersey, who pleaded guilty to a lesser charge of second-degree murder. He claimed self-defense, arguing that Allen invited him to his hotel room and "there made improper advances." [32] As was often the case, readers were left to wonder how a moment of rage prompted by homosexual solicitation could explain the tortured state of Allen's body.

These hotel crime stories were usually murders of married men, their queer undertones pointing to the unsettling reality that homosexuality could be found in the most seemingly normal of American men. Few stories embodied this concern more than the murder of fifty-six-year-old Colin MacKellar in his Waldorf-Astoria hotel room in November 1948. A wealthy Canadian businessman, MacKellar had traveled to New York City for work. Married with two kids in college, he was a member of a number of top social and business clubs in Montreal and lived in the upscale Westmount suburb of the city.[33] As *The New York Times* reported, MacKellar often stayed at the Waldorf-Astoria while "passing through the city on his way to meet his corporation's foreign accounts." The newspaper noted, "He was a distinguished looking man, about five feet eight inches in height, well-built, with thinning white hair, and to all appearances a thorough conservative." [34]

On his last visit to New York, the "thorough conservative" had two drinks at the Waldorf-Astoria hotel bar before heading to the posh, dark paneled Astor Hotel bar on West Forty-Fourth Street and Broadway. Along with the Top of the Mark at the Mark Hopkins Hotel in San Francisco and the Biltmore men's bar in Los Angeles, the Astor Hotel bar had gained a reputation as a gay meeting place during the war years.[35] It maintained this reputation after the war, although within more strict codes of behavior that segregated the queer patrons to one end of the bar and straight men to the other. Within this atmosphere, a stark and sad irony between male patrons emerged. While the straight men had the freedom to touch and hug their friends, the queer men were cautious of such public intimacies for fear of being asked to leave. "The management would cut us down a little bit when it felt we were getting a little too obvious," one patron recalled years later; "if you got a little too buddy, or too cruisy . . . too aggressive, they'd say cut it out men, why don't you go somewhere else?"[36]

It was in this casual but guarded atmosphere that MacKellar met Ralph Barrows, a handsome former high school football player. Tall and muscular, he looked much older than his age. Newspapers would later describe him as a "strapping nineteen-year-old Adonis." Press accounts detailed how, before meeting MacKellar, Barrows spent the day wandering Times Square, taking in a movie at the Loews Criterion, where he saw *Kiss the Blood Off My Hands*, starring Burt Lancaster and Joan Fontaine, about an ex-soldier who accidentally kills a man in a bar fight.[37]

Both Barrows and MacKellar would have known of the Astor Hotel bar's reputation as a place where queer men, sailors, soldiers, and civilians mingled, and would have understood the bar's etiquette between the queer and the straight sections. After a few drinks, the two left for other bars in the area, ending up at the Forty-Fifth Street Cafe. Unlike the Astor Hotel bar, with its more upscale patrons, the Forty-Fifth Street Cafe was known for its seedier clientele, including working-class gay men, prostitutes, and out-of-towners. *The New York Times* described it as "one of the characteristically dark spots common to either flank of Times Square. It features a pianist, a singing waiter, and female bartenders who work up to midnight. Its trade," the paper concluded, "except for Times Square 'characters' who are more or less habitues, is transient."

Barrows and MacKellar enjoyed a few more hours of drinking before the Canadian invited the former football player back to his hotel suite on the nineteenth floor of the Waldorf-Astoria. They got to the hotel "around 2 a.m. Friday," the *Times* reported, describing what transpired between the two men in the hotel suite: "They drank from Mr. MacKellar's bottle of Scotch, and eventually began to argue. What they argued about the police would not tell, if they knew. They said the boy admitted he got up and hit Mr. MacKellar hard on the jaw, with his fist, and that the executive fell." The article added, "The boy left the suite, clutching the bottle, and went to the residential hotel where his father lives. He slept most of the day, and in the afternoon went to see the motion picture *Sealed Verdict*."[38] The heavy silence around the reasons for returning to the hotel suite together in the early morning hours, and the nature of the argument, were central to much of the initial reporting. As the New York *Daily News* reported, "There was still a blank as to just what occurred in the hotel room."[39] While journalists refrained from explicit details in the early reports, they offered knowing readers enough of the queer social landscape to understand the subtext of the men's entertainment. In fact, it was a matchbook from the Forty-Fifth Street Cafe, found at the crime scene, that led police to the bar where the two men were last seen together, and eventually to Barrows's arrest.

The press pointed to a number of influences to explain Barrows's violent crime, including his interest in crime films, his divorced parents, and his father's lack of steady employment. His working-class background contrasted with the wealthy family man MacKellar. In this sense, Barrows embodied the era's concerns for working-class juvenile delinquency and sexual deviancy—two antisocial behaviors that were often connected in the crime pages. Readers learned that at sixteen, Barrows was discharged from the navy for being underage. At seventeen, he joined the army but was "marked as a mental case" and after a short hospitalization was discharged. The nature of his psychological treatment was not defined. The *Detroit Free Press* reported on Barrows's previous criminal convictions, including one in 1944 when he was arrested for impersonating a merchant marine, which led to his detention in a boys' reformatory, and another for criminal assault, a charge that was later dismissed "because the complainant refused to testify"—a fact that suggests the victim was trying to avoid publicity around the encounter. Months before his arrest in New York, Barrows was convicted for a series of robberies of men he met in bars in Grand Rapids, Michigan, encounters that had similar details to the one with MacKellar. It was this latter conviction that brought him east, as the Michigan judge sentenced him to three years' probation on the condition that he leave Grand Rapids to live with his father in New York.[40]

Alongside this image of the juvenile delinquent was also the paradoxical image of the all-American boy. The *Detroit Free Press* described him as a "handsome, neurotic" youth, and detailed how "his hands shook nervously as he lit a cigarette when he pleaded innocent" during his arraignment. In other press accounts he was described as "a strapping former high school football player" and "the hulking Ralph." Such descriptions accompanied by photographs of Barrows dressed in dark suit and tie, sitting at court or in his jail cell, smiling at the camera, portrayed him as both desirable and deadly. More important, his masculine, athletic image, coupled with his neurotic and criminal deviancy, epitomized a postwar fear: inside such all-American young men might lurk the possibility of sexual and social menace. Describing him as the "tall and handsome defendant," the *Daily News* reported that Barrows was ultimately "just a cheap mugger in dark alleys before his pleasing grin and ready fist sent him up the social scale of crime to murder at the Waldorf-Astoria."[41]

The press framed such a contrast as a symptom of his parents' divorce and a troubled childhood in which Barrows could never really fit in. Drawing on interviews with Barrows's mother, the *Daily News* recounted "the story of a youngster who literally outgrew himself, a little boy with a man's body who couldn't adjust himself to either a boy's or a man's way of living." The article added, "Ralph's trouble, said Mrs. Barrows, was that being so big for his age, he felt out of place with youngsters his own age and sought companionship among older boys." Articles highlighted Barrows's abnormal behaviors with phrases such as "wears pink shirt" or "no time for Dad," emphasizing how his upbringing was a key factor in his deviant psychology and lack of social conformity. Contrasting Barrows with his younger brother, who was "steady, dependable, a good student," Ralph was a social misfit. Barrows's mother once took him to a psychiatrist, she told reporters, "in an effort to learn the cause of his often peculiar behavior." But, she added, he was "never a normal boy."[42]

While initially Barrows pleaded guilty to manslaughter, claiming MacKellar had made "improper advances" in the hotel room, the police investigation dragged on for nearly a year, uncovering what the district attorney described in press reports as "new evidence" in the case. A second indictment charged Barrows with first-degree murder. "We can now prove that Barrows went to the room of MacKellar to rob him and, when the victim resisted, he was beaten to death," *The Gazette* reported in MacKellar's native Montreal. Part of this new evidence was, according to reports, the beating and robbing of Harold Heinmiller in New York in 1945, in which Barrows stole a watch and five dollars, though details about that earlier robbery and assault were scant in the press. With this new evidence, *The New York Times* questioned Barrows's initial confession, reporting "that the youth had told his lawyer that he had struck Mr. MacKellar in repulsing what he asserted were improper advances. Police, however, contend that the youth kicked the fifty-six-year-old Canadian in the stomach, after knocking him unconscious, in a blind rage when he had gone through his pockets and found no money."[43]

As Barrows's trial began in 1950, District Attorney Anthony Liebler, according to press reports, made a "determined effort to keep women off the jury. All women called were challenged." The jury would eventually be composed of only men, who were all asked by both defense and prosecution attorneys "if they would be influenced by any trial evidence of homosexuality," a detail that pointed to the key issue both sides would focus on.

In his statement to the jury, Liebler argued that Barrows targeted MacKellar for robbery. "He was going to take him over, this old man from the sticks who apparently was well-heeled, for he'd been paying for the drinks all night." The image of the business executive and world traveler as a man from the "sticks" was an odd one for the prosecution to make. Barrows's attorney argued that his client was fighting against the sexual advances of the older man, but also suggested the possibility that "some bellboy, some watchman, somebody else might have gotten into that room."

Press reports of the trial continued to show the paradox of Barrows, describing him as "a handsome young man with an ugly criminal record" and often referring to him as a "problem child." The *Detroit Free Press* described how "the young man looked pale in court" and was "dressed neatly in black." Like many press accounts of the trial, references to his divorced parents were a common theme. "With his divorced parents keeping vigil outside the courtroom," the article noted, "twenty-year-old Ralph Edward Barrows went to trial."[44]

The jury deliberated for nearly two hours, returning a verdict of first-degree manslaughter. The lesser sentence confirmed the jury's agreement that the killing was not premeditated and was committed in a heat of passion. At the sentencing hearing, the judge imposed a prison term of twenty to forty years. In referencing a psychiatric report, the judge declared that Barrows "showed practically no prospect of social rehabilitation." He also pointed to the defendant's history of arrests and convictions, stating, "All of this is coupled with a psychopathic, abnormal, sexually perverted and sadistic personality." The judge added, "In short, he is a sexual maniac, a menace to society—good looking, well-built, personable, ingratiating, and congenial, which makes him all the more dangerous." In imposing the maximum penalty for the crime, the judge concluded, "there is no special institution for sex maniacs like you."[45]

The journalist Jess Stearn recalled the MacKellar murder in his book *The Sixth Man*, an account of the homosexual social worlds of the 1950s. "I covered the story of a wealthy middle-aged visitor to New York," Stearn wrote, "who had met a husky young man in the mid-town bar and taken him back to his hotel suite. The older man had been killed for his pains, and the younger claimed improper advances. I couldn't help wondering," Stearn concluded, "why he just hadn't walked out, if that was all there was to it."[46]

The dangerous image of Barrows as good-looking, personable, and psychopathic would become a compelling one in the 1950s, in both the crime page and fiction. Alfred Hitchcock's film *Rope*, about two well-dressed and intelligent college men who enact the perfect murder by killing their friend, simmered with sexual perversions just beneath the dialogue. The film, which came out in the fall of 1948, not only had echoes of the Leopold and Loeb murder from the 1920s but also reflected postwar sensibilities about the psychological underpinnings of murder.

More acutely, the characters that suspense writer Patricia Highsmith created in the 1950s embodied this image of the psychopathic personality shrouded in the good-looking, congenial killer. The casual encounters between Guy Haines and Charles Bruno in her 1950 novel *Strangers on a Train* (which Hitchcock also filmed) depicted how easy it was for a normal man to fall into the trap of the seemingly charming but psychopathic, and queer, stranger. But few characters of the era illustrated the charming queer psychopath more than Highsmith's Tom Ripley in her 1955 novel *The Talented Mr. Ripley*. Ripley's working-class background and orphaned upbringing influenced his early criminal activities of mail fraud. But once Dickie Greenleaf's wealthy father hires Ripley to go to Italy and bring his bon vivant son back to the United States for the serious work of business, Ripley's deceits become violent. Highsmith captured the mood and fears of the era about the nature of sexuality and criminality as ever-shifting identities and uncertainties. Ripley's explicitly defined queerness is as much about his desires as his ability to perform any number of roles—including becoming Dickie himself. In thinking about his own sense of self, the narrator tells us Ripley "could look like a country gentleman, a thug, an Englishman, a Frenchman, or a plain American eccentric, depending on how he wore it." This seemingly easy masking of his psychopathic and queer tendencies in masculine respectability lay at the heart of Ripley's criminal intrigue. While Tom Ripley was a fictional creation, elements of the character could be found in many of the queer true crime stories of the era. *The Washington Post* called the novel "[a] fascinating tale of a repellent character," while *The New York Times* praised the book, describing Ripley as a "congenital psychopathic inferior" who builds an "intimacy with a wealthy youth that tempts him to murder."[47]

"HE WAS OFTEN SEEN ALONE,
AND RARELY WITH A COMPANION"

The same year that the press was reporting on the gruesome hotel murders, the army was lecturing its new recruits on the dangers of socializing with queer men. "You read in newspapers of fiendish and horrible sex crimes committed against men, women, and oftentimes, small children," an army lecturer said, adding that sometimes the victims were horribly mutilated. He concluded with a speculative claim that such violence "can be related to homosexuality."[48] These lectures, according to historian Allen Bérubé, "encouraged revulsion towards homosexuality and 'homos' as normal and manly . . . and gave explicit advice on how to spot them, reject their advances, and report them to authorities." Such warnings were part of the military's effort to weed out sexual deviants among new recruits, and they were coupled with an aggressive purge of homosexuals already occurring in the armed forces. Between 1947 and 1950, the army and navy annually discharged nearly one thousand men and women suspected of being homosexual.[49] Beyond the military, stories of violence and murder involving military men in the press pointed readers to the lurid realities that might be threatening the nation's sailors and soldiers.

The murder of John Boland made headlines in Boston in 1953. The twenty-six-year-old Boland was a graduate of Harvard and a national guardsman stationed at the Commonwealth Armory in the city. Neighbors told the police that Boland and another man came home around "2 a.m. and could be heard arguing a short while later." Reports also noted that police believed the "slayer might have been a chance acquaintance of Boland's, [who] accepted an invitation to go to his apartment and then robbed him after a fight."[50]

A few days later, police arrested John Effner, a sailor on the USS *Baltimore*. *The Boston Globe* described Effner as a "handsome," "tall blond sailor" and included an official photograph of him dressed in uniform. Effner confessed that after meeting Boland at a downtown pub they went to Boland's

Back Bay apartment on Marlborough Street, where the two "had a few drinks and then got into an argument." Effner claimed he grabbed Boland's homemade blackjack, which was constructed from wire, sheet metal, and lead, and attacked Boland, leaving him with a fractured skull and brain hemorrhage. Upon his arrest, Effner told police the beating was prompted when "Boland made improper advances." Newspapers from the suspect's home state of Michigan were more coy about the provocation. *The Lansing State Journal*, for example, described Boland as a "drinking companion," noting that the sailor "admitted beating Boland fatally and robbing him during an argument in Boland's room."[51]

Stories of strange and violent encounters in private spaces between military men and civilians were the more common queer true crime stories in the Cold War years. When twenty-five-year-old Eugene Hoover, an army veteran, murdered fifty-five-year-old James Mahoney in New Orleans in 1949, local newspapers described it as a "bizarre French quarter slaying."[52] Mahoney, "one of the wealthiest men in Bristol, Virginia," a small town on the Virginia–Tennessee border, was visiting New Orleans for Mardi Gras, staying at the stylish and upscale Monteleon Hotel. Newspapers detailed how Mahoney, a bachelor, was found naked on his bed, "his neck had been broken by twisting a hotel towel around it, and his head was battered badly enough to cause contusions of the brain." One article reported that there were "lacerations between two fingers," suggesting that Mahoney had "tried to ward off a blow."[53]

Described in the press as a "parking lot attendant," Hoover had just been released from a Veterans Administration hospital, "where he had gone for treatment as a mental patient." He told police he could remember nothing of the night's events. According to press reports, detectives administered sodium pentothal (truth serum) to uncover the facts of the hotel encounter. Under the drug's impact, Hoover related he went to Mahoney's hotel room and an "argument ensued as the two men lay nude on Mahoney's bed." The argument started when Mahoney "called Mr. Hoover a name," after which Hoover attacked the older man.[54]

The *Kingsport News*, a paper published down the road from Mahoney's hometown, in Tennessee, related comments from one of the detectives on the case. He described Hoover as "a really sick man" and that Hoover's wife "said he was 'definitely a mental case.'" The detective also said that the woman had left Hoover about a month earlier for "personal reasons" but planned on returning to him once he "had been cleared." She would eventually divorce him before the end of Hoover's trial.[55]

In court, Hoover offered an insanity defense, claiming he went into a rage prompted by Mahoney's indecent advances. The prosecution presented a psychiatrist from the Veterans Administration hospital who described the defendant as an "anti-social personality," "restless," and afflicted by "explosive behavior and irritability." However, the expert witness claimed Hoover didn't suffer from a "mental defect but rather a moral one."[56] Some newspapers excerpted parts of Hoover's medical report from the hospital, details of which were entered in the public record during the trial. Doctors described him as a "spoiled little boy" who would "cry, pout, and curse when frustrated." The report also noted that Hoover was brought up on disciplinary charges in the army for stealing a jeep. Most damning of all: Hoover admitted to "being a homosexual."[57] The hospital treatment he underwent was undoubtedly a response to this admission. According to one article, Hoover's wife testified about a dream he had where he committed "the perfect murder." In the courtroom, Hoover abruptly interrupted her testimony and "retorted that he was recovering from a shock treatment at the time of the nightmare."[58] Such treatments would most likely have been a response to Hoover's admitted homosexuality. Hoover was eventually convicted of murder and sentenced to life in prison.

The mysteries and details of violent sexual encounters were common in true crime stories, offering readers a window in the private, domestic space of the queer victims. In the fall of 1953, Elmer Schroeder was found beaten and strangled in his West Philadelphia apartment. *The New York Times* reported, "The body was found gagged and bound in the bedroom of the bachelor quarters."[59] Schroeder was a well-respected lawyer who had a career as a successful professional soccer coach in the 1930s and 1940s. A front-page article in *The Philadelphia Inquirer* described how "his skull was crushed" and a "sock had been jammed into his mouth and held there by a pajama coat knotted around his face." Readers learned that police were searching for Schroeder's ex-roommate. Schroeder, the article noted, was "unmarried" and had lived alone for years.

The article also detailed the well-ordered and "richly decorated apartment," the scene of the murder, with its floors "carpeted with rich oriental rugs. Hundreds of books lined one wall of the living room. A large collection of classical recordings were cataloged neatly. The furnishings were subdued but costly." Other details, such as Schroeder's gray trousers, a blue shirt open at the neck, blue socks, and brown oxfords, contrasted sharply with the description of his body having been "trussed in cords cut cleanly from venetian blinds in the living room." The merging of fashion, décor, and murder was a not-so-subtle indication for any reader looking beyond the facts of the crime. But if such details were not enough, the last paragraph would have confirmed the reader's suspicions. In describing a tavern where Schroeder was last seen in public, the newspaper noted the victim had "on previous occasions visited the bar several times with young men."[60]

Reports of the investigation filled the front pages of the *Inquirer* for days. Readers learned that detectives were unable to track Schroeder's activities on the night of his death. Schroeder's former roommate was "grilled" by police, but was later dropped as a suspect. At one point, the press promoted the idea that the killer was Basil Kingsley Beck, described as a "blue eyed fugitive," a "desperado," and a "youthful and bad-tempered roamer." Beck had escaped from prison in Kansas and was believed to be living in Philadelphia. The FBI had deemed him one of its most wanted criminals. Newspapers described Beck as "moving from rooming house to rooming house" in the city, adding that witnesses at the tavern where Schroeder was last seen identified Beck as "a drinking companion" of the lawyer.[61]

Such sensational leads lingered for nearly two years after Schroeder's murder. At one point, the press linked his killing to the 1954 murder and dismemberment of John Dopirak, a restaurant worker, merchant seaman, and air force veteran. Dopirak had met his killer, Francis X. Ballem, at a downtown bar. Ballem confessed to the murder after his arrest, and the newspapers, which referred to him as the "mad butcher" and "torso killer," made strong associations between the violent killing and the mysterious details of the two men's public and private interactions.[62]

Five years after Schroeder's body was found, police arrested Thomas Wetling, a sailor from the Newport, Rhode Island, naval base and a married father of two. Wetling's arrest came as the FBI, in a separate investigation, learned from one of Wetling's shipmates that the sailor had confessed to him of killing Schroeder. Newspapers reported that Wetling and Schroeder had had several outings together in taverns and bars in the city. *The Philadelphia Inquirer* related that on the night of the murder, the sailor had "visited Schroeder in his apartment and quarreled with him about money and other things. They got into a fight and Wetling left the lawyer tied up on a bed covered with blood."[63]

The state asked for the death penalty in the case. The assistant district attorney argued that the crime was "a willful, deliberate, and premeditated killing." On the witness stand, James Clifford Beardsmore testified he lent Wetling clothing after the sailor came to his apartment on the night of the murder. Wetling's clothes were "covered with blood," Beardsmore said. The press reported that the witness claimed the sailor told him he had an "argument with Schroeder, that he hit him several times and tied him up to prevent an outcry." But other witnesses were less determined in their testimony, and less certain in their ability to identify the sailor nearly five years after the fact. In his own defense, Wetling testified that he had never met Schroeder. According to reports, he also denied Beardsmore's claims that he told his friend about the killing. Wetling's testimony swayed the jury. *The Philadelphia Inquirer* reported that after twenty minutes of deliberations, forewoman "Emily Green, a laundry worker" delivered the verdict of not guilty.[64]

In a strange twist to Schroeder's murder, a year after Wetling's acquittal, he was shot and killed in Los Angeles by Donald Britton in a Hollywood Hills home the two had shared until six weeks before the shooting. The *Los*

Angeles Times described Wetling as a student at Los Angeles City College whose murder was prompted by an argument between the two men and "threats over financial matters." He "staggered out the front door and collapsed in the driveway." The two men had a business together in which they sold detective correspondence courses and detective equipment, the article reported. But oddly, the article did not reference Wetling's earlier arrest and acquittal for the murder of Schroeder.[65] *The Philadelphia Inquirer*, however, in its reporting of Wetling's murder, reminded readers of the grotesque details of Schroeder's crime scene. According to the article, Britton, an aviation engineer at Bendix, had served as a "character witness for Wetling" at his trial, suggesting the two men had a relationship long before he was arrested for murder. Wetling's wife, the article concluded, "had no knowledge of her husband's whereabouts until she received a telegram" informing her of his death.[66]

The same year Wetling was acquitted of murder, Jim Edmonds, a nineteen-year-old marine stationed in Washington, D.C., went on trial for the murder of George Lefebvre. Thirty-one-year-old Lefebvre served in the military during the war and was completing a degree in business at American University under the GI bill. News reports of Lefebvre's murder didn't appear until nearly two weeks after his death, when concerned neighbors in his Georgetown neighborhood contacted the police after they hadn't seen him for several days. *The Washington Post* reported that police found the man's "partly decomposing body, clad in underclothing . . . lying face up on the living room floor." Descriptions of the crime scene in a number of reports focused on one detail: a pink pillowcase. The *Post* noted that "[t]here were no marks of violence about the body or the apartment, but a pink pillowslip found looped about the man's neck indicated he might have been strangled."[67] Another article observed, "Lefebvre's body, a pink pillowslip looped about his neck and the ends twisted together, was found Tuesday in his three-room bachelor apartment. Police estimated he had been dead about ten days."[68]

A few days after the discovery of Lefebvre's body, police arrested Edmonds. Newspapers would describe Edmonds as "tall and handsome," and detail how "he wrapped a pink pillow case around the neck of George P.

Lefebvre, and twisted it until Lefebvre went limp."[69] With all of its gendered connotations, the pink pillowcase was a not-so-subtle detail that pointed readers to the queer subtext of why a bachelor might be murdered in his small apartment in Georgetown after picking up a marine in the early morning hours.

Recounting Edmonds's statement to the police, *The Washington Post* detailed how Lefebvre "lured" the marine to his apartment. While driving his white Chevrolet convertible along M Street back home to his apartment, Lefebvre noticed Edmonds standing at the corner. After parking his car, Lefebvre, tall, lean, and wearing horn-rimmed glasses, walked toward the husky Edmonds. Edmonds "had taken unauthorized leave from the Marine barracks" and had "visited two drinking places with a friend before he met Lefebvre," according to the article. Lefebvre asked him if he would like a cup of coffee. Edmonds replied: "What is your angle buddy?" "Nothing," replied Lefebvre, and the two went across the street to Lefebvre's apartment on the second floor of a brick town house. In the apartment, Lefebvre made them coffee, and seeing Edmonds was tired, offered him the sofa to sleep. "Then," the article reported, "Lefebvre attacked him on a daybed, and they struggled and rolled to the floor." According to his statement to police, Edmonds was "scared and mad" and, as the article noted, "the 200 pound Marine grabbed Lefebvre by the neck with both hands and squeezed for a long time, until his assailant went limp. Then Edmonds grabbed a pink pillow slip from the bed and wound it around Lefebvre's neck."[70]

"Marine Says He Strangled Nashuan in His Apartment," declared the *Nashua Telegraph*, Lefebvre's hometown newspaper in New Hampshire. The article offered a somber tone about the murder of a local resident, the son of a mail carrier and a veteran of both World War II and the Korean War. Echoing other press reports, the article related how Edmonds confessed to strangling Lefebvre after he made improper advances. But unlike *The Washington Post*, the *Nashua Telegraph* editors placed the word "improper" in quotation marks, raising a small doubt about Edmonds's testimony and the claims that their hometown veteran could have been guilty of such horrendous behavior.[71]

At his trial, Edmonds claimed both sexual panic and temporary insanity. He argued that he was mentally ill when he met Lefebvre, and that his companion's aggressive sexual solicitations pushed him into a panic state where he was not in control of his actions. He argued that he lost all memory of strangling Lefebvre, claiming, "I'm not sure how long I held him" on the floor.[72] His attorney portrayed Edmonds as a troubled young man who "saw his father kill his mother with a shotgun at the age of eight." Newspapers reproduced this sympathetic image of the killer, reporting how he cried in the courtroom as details of his difficult childhood were recounted.[73]

Assistant District Attorney Thomas Flannery interrogated Edmonds on the witness stand about his claims that he was suspicious of Lefebvre when he first saw him in his car. "A normal man, or normal stranger, in anyone's opinion," replied Edmonds, "is not going to ride up and down a street looking at a person without some reason." The prosecutor wondered why the marine followed Lefebvre to his apartment if he had such deep suspicions about Lefebvre's behavior. In questioning the interactions in the apartment, the prosecutor asked Edmonds if Lefebvre touched his "private parts" in a "friendly manner," adding, "he did not try to hurt you there, did he?" To which Edmonds replied, "no sir." Edmonds claimed Lefebvre allegedly came after him three times. The defendant stated he did "have fear that the man might be, as what I heard of, a maniac homosexual."[74]

District Attorney Flannery also raised doubts about Edmonds's recounting of the murder. "Did you kneel down beside the body and attempt to remove this thing from around the neck that you had put there?" Flannery asked regarding the pink pillowcase. When Edmonds replied no, Flannery rephrased the question: "Did you make any effort to revive this individual on the floor?" Again, Edmonds replied no. At that point, Flannery asked Edmonds to explain why, even at the moment with the lights turned on and Lefebvre lifeless on the floor, he didn't try to revive the victim. Edmonds replied: "After the way the man had 'did' me, sir; after the advances he had made; the way he had made them, I did not care." The prosecution countered: "Even after you had gotten up and he was defenseless on the floor you did not care?" Edmond replied: "Why should I care?"[75]

Although Edmonds was convicted of manslaughter in this trial, an appeals court set aside the verdict, citing certain psychiatric testimony that should have been excluded. At his second trial, Edmonds did not take the stand; instead he relied on expert testimony to explain his state of mind at the time of the killing. While a defense psychiatrist testified that "Edmonds had suffered from a mental disorder for forty hours before the crime," the prosecution's psychiatrist claimed he "was not mentally ill at the time of the crime." Amid such dueling interpretations, the jury convicted Edmonds of the lesser charge of second-degree manslaughter, and he was sentenced to twenty years in prison.[76]

While press accounts of queer murders in the 1950s were shaped by larger social narratives of sexual deviancy and masculinity, they were also influenced by political and social forces on the local level. The murder of twenty-nine-year-old John Murrett in July 1955 was a case in point. Murrett was found dead in room 709 of the Heidelberg Hotel in Jackson, Mississippi.[77] Initial reports of his murder in the local press pointed to robbery as the motive. The statewide *Clarion-Ledger* in Jackson described Murrett as a "lanky six-foot-seven-inch interior decorator" who was originally from Silver Creek, New York. The article also interviewed friends of Murrett who described him as "quiet and pleasant" but added that "he was often seen alone, and rarely with a companion." Before moving to Jackson, the article noted, Murrett had "taught painting and sculpture in South Carolina."[78]

The *Daily Messenger* of Murrett's native upstate New York described how when the victim was "found his feet were tied together with his belt and a sheet was knotted around his neck and pillow slip had been stuffed into his mouth. The body was clad only in shorts." The paper added, "the face of the 200-pound 6-foot 7-inch man was bruised and blue indicating a severe beating."[79] Later reports would confirm that Murrett died from suffocation.

Murrett's murder provoked a large-scale investigation, involving local and state police in Mississippi, FBI crime labs, and even a local congressman. In September police arrested two men for the crime: eighteen-year-old Warren Koenig and twenty-three-year-old Lawrence Burns. Both men were on leave from Keesler Air Force Base near Biloxi, Mississippi, and both were from out of state—Koenig from Chicago and Burns from Cincinnati.

Surprisingly, the local press made little if anything of the queer context of the crime. While the *Clarion-Ledger* declared in a headline of large block letters, "Murrett Made Improper Advances," and reported how in Burns's trial "references to homosexuality and improper advances were made repeatedly," the newspaper was also dubious of such claims. Murrett met his killers at a "tavern known as the Wagon Wheel," which some *Clarion-Ledger* readers would have known as a gay gathering spot in the center of town.[80] As Burns and Koenig had no place to stay for the night, they agreed to join Murrett, who suggested renting a hotel room for the three of them. Describing Burns as the "victim of a homosexual act on the part of Murrett," the newspaper related the two men's testimony with unusual explicitness: "After registering at the hotel, they went to the room and all three got into a double bed. Shortly thereafter, they contended, Murrett began caressing and kissing Burns, and Koenig came to his companion's aid, 'rabbit punching' Murrett on the neck and beating him on the face and body."[81]

In rendering such an explicit image of the three men in bed together—an image that the newspapers often called a "lurid story"—press reports questioned how innocent the airmen were regarding Murrett's intentions. Burns's defense of justifiable homicide depended on the dubious claim that both Koenig and Burns were ignorant of Murrett's homosexuality when they first met.[82] The prosecution offered several witnesses who testified that at the Wagon Wheel, Murrett "appeared to be very drunk, and appeared to be 'queer.'"[83] Such details made clear to jurors and readers that the airmen knew what kind of person was taking them to the Heidelberg Hotel.

One notable moment in the trial and press coverage came during the cross-examination of the investigating detective, J. R. Luke. When asked if he had "heard reports that Murrett was a sex pervert," Luke replied that "some people made such remarks as a matter of opinion." Asked whether he investigated such rumors, the detective replied he did not, since he "wouldn't know where to start."[84] Such a claim was both a defense of the police department's investigation and a direct dismissal that homosexuality even existed in the capital of Mississippi. As one queer Mississippian recalled, before the 1960s there was "not a lot of crackdown" or "legal intervention" about homosexuality in Jackson. For many queers, as long as they lived their lives quietly and out of the public eye, they were of little concern.[85]

After five hours of deliberations, the jury returned a verdict of murder. Burns would be sentenced to life in prison. To avoid a trial, Koenig pleaded guilty and received a lesser sentence of twenty years. In referring to Koenig's troubled childhood and divorced parents, the judge said, "You haven't had the opportunity of a lot of boys your age. You were brought up in a home divided through no fault of your own."[86]

In December 1955, M. B. Pierce, the chief of detectives for the Jackson Police Department, was awarded a citation for his outstanding detective work in the Murrett case. In an article filled with effusive compliments about the Jackson police force, the *Clarion-Ledger* reported that "[f]ew cities of the nation can boast of a more efficient, hard-working police organization than Mississippi's capital city," concluding that the Murrett case was "by no means an isolated instance of local law enforcement efficiency but, on the contrary, is entirely typical of the vigilance and training which characterizes our fine department."[87]

The compliments, according to historian John Howard, reflected less an abiding concern for the murder of a queer man than the promotion of an image of Mississippi's capital as a center of law and order.[88] The Mississippian judicial system was notoriously corrupt, most acutely in the regular acquittals of white men in the violent lynchings of black citizens—when, on rare occasions, arrests for such crimes were even made. The very month that Koenig and Burns were arrested, two white men were acquitted of the lynching of Emmett Till, a fourteen-year-old African American who was visiting family in Mississippi from his native Chicago. Till had been beaten beyond recognition that August for the alleged offense of flirting with a white woman in a general store. After beating him and shooting him in the head, his killers tied his body to a seventy-pound cotton gin and threw it into the Tallahatchie River, where he was eventually found by a local fisherman. The case became a national tragedy and a flashpoint in the civil rights movement. When Till's body arrived back in Chicago, his mother refused to close the casket, wanting instead to "let the whole world see" what was done to her son.[89] The image of the teenager's bloated and beaten face, deformed beyond anything human, was published in the African American press across the country, serving as a powerful symbol of racist violence and constant failures of law and justice for African American citizens. Reports of the police investigation into Murrett's murder ran alongside stories of Till's lynching and the trial of his killers. Exploiting the successful arrests and conviction of Murrett's killers served as a striking contrast to the criticism of how the state handled Till's case.

While the press and the courts may have offered a mild accommodation of Murrett's homosexuality as the murder victim of two airmen from the north, it was done so in the sharpening spotlight on Mississippi's legal and judicial failures. This accommodation would not last long. As the civil rights movement gained momentum, queer men would increasingly be seen as a threat to the southern way of life.[90]

Stories of Prejudice and Suffering

Pervert Colonies, Homosexual Worlds, and the Birth of a New Minority

"POWDER PUFF LANE IS A CIVIC DISGRACE"

William Simpson worked as a flight steward for Eastern Air Lines in the 1950s. For nearly three decades, Eastern had offered passenger service along the East Coast and to the Midwest from its hub in Miami. The company's ads promoted its experience and dependability: "Those who know flying best . . . fly Eastern." In August 1954, Simpson was working a return flight from Detroit to Miami. A colleague, Dorothy Hoover, would later tell reporters that Simpson was "elated over an engagement" he had planned for his return to Miami. "He told me there was someone he wanted to have over," Hoover told the *Miami Daily News*, adding, "he didn't indicate whether it was a man or a girl." On the flight, Hoover recalled, "Simpson was acting kind of excited" and he was "humming and singing something that sounded like 'Life is but a dream . . .'"[1]

According to his landlady, a Mrs. Babcock, Simpson arrived home around nine in the evening. There he changed from his airline uniform into gray trousers, a white polo shirt, green socks, and brown loafers and left about an hour later. Simpson drove his cream-colored 1950 Chevrolet convertible north along Biscayne Boulevard. He was a "nice, quiet boy," Mrs. Babcock told reporters.

Just after midnight, twenty-one-year-old Dick Cline and his eighteen-year-old girlfriend, Joan Anchois, came across Simpson's body near Arch Creek in North Miami in an area known by locals as Lovers' Lane. He was lying in the middle of a sandy road in a "pool of blood." According to press reports, he had a gunshot wound on his left side and "severe lacerations on his hand and right index finger." His wallet was missing, and there were two sets of footprints leading away from the body, one made by shoes and the other by bare feet. Police would identify Simpson through his car registration. The vehicle was parked about five hundred feet from where his body was found. The front seat, according to reports, "was splattered with blood and a .22 caliber shell was found on the floor of the car." The *Miami Daily News* included a hand-drawn map of the crime scene, small "x" marks indicating where Simpson's body was found, where he was shot, and where his car was parked. But readers were undoubtedly confused by the map, since it contradicted the crime scene investigation. "Simpson was shot in the car," the *Daily News* reported about the police theory. "Then, they believe Simpson managed to get out of the car and stagger to the place where he was found. He is believed to have collapsed there and bled to death."[2]

A photograph of a younger Simpson dressed in an army uniform made the front page of *The Courier-Journal* in Simpson's hometown of Louisville, Kentucky. The newspaper reported that Simpson served in the military from 1945 to 1947 and had attended Kentucky College before moving to Miami in 1951. Not long after his move, Simpson took a steward position with Eastern Air Lines. "Relatives here," the article noted, "said Simpson had been in no trouble that they knew of."[3]

As the crime happened near a well-known area for sexual play for young straight couples, references and suspicions about Simpson's love life were pervasive in news reports. Simpson's roommate, Harold Shafer, who also worked as a steward for Eastern Air Lines, told the *Tampa Times* that Simpson "was not going steady with any girls although he had been engaged while in the Army." The article also noted that "Miss Hoover described him as handsome and 'a very refined, cultural, and pleasant man.'" This description would be echoed in a front-page article in *The Miami Herald*, which described Simpson as a "handsome Eastern airline steward" who was known for throwing "dinners for stewards and stewardesses." The article interviewed some of Simpson's coworkers, who said he dated frequently and was considered "a man with the ladies."[4]

Five days later, police arrested nineteen-year-old Charles Lawrence and twenty-year-old Lewis Richard Killen for the murder. The *Miami Daily News* reported that Lawrence had confessed to police that he "was standing at the corner of Biscayne Boulevard and 23rd Street about 10 p.m. Monday trying to hitch-hike a ride north on the Boulevard when he was picked up by Simpson." Simpson told Lawrence that he had a date but offered to drive him "where ever he wanted to go." Simpson drove near Arch Creek, according to Lawrence's statement to police, where the two talked about fishing. "Simpson attempted to make advances," the press reported from Lawrence's statement. While Lawrence "resisted the homosexual proposals," Simpson persisted and "even offered him money." At that point Lawrence pulled out a .22 caliber Italian Beretta automatic pistol. "I meant to fire through the windshield to scare him," he confessed. "But I guess I must have shot him." Lawrence fled the car and buried the pistol on a nearby street. After questioning Lawrence, detectives took him to the site of the murder and had him reenact the crime. A photograph of him smiling for the camera and pointing to the spot where he buried the pistol circulated in the Miami press.[5]

In contrast to Lawrence's claims of an innocent hitchhiking adventure turned into sexual solicitation and violence, Killen told police that the two "engaged in the practice of 'rolling' men for their money" by hitchhiking along Biscayne Boulevard, an area known for its queer cruising and socializing. Killen's explanation for why the two were at Lovers' Lane with Simpson would become central to the trial testimony in the coming months.[6]

Both Lawrence and Killen grew up in the residential area of North Miami. Press reports described Lawrence's family home as "a pleasant white, tree shaded bungalow." When reporters arrived at the house after his arrests, a neighbor informed them "Mr. and Mrs. Lawrence don't want to talk to anyone tonight."[7] Like the rest of the Miami area, North Miami had expanded in the postwar years. In the earlier decades of the twentieth century, Miami had been known for its liberal moral codes, which offered visitors a world of decadence and vice. In 1941, a columnist in *Time* magazine described Miami as "the last Gomorrah" and "the ultimate Babylon," underscoring an image of the city as one of unrestrained pleasures and indulgences, offering wealthy visitors a secluded and exotic realm outside social norms and customs.[8] According to historian Julio Capó, it was an image that Miami boosters, who playfully referred to the area as "fairyland" in those early decades, were eager to promote. Although such a term was meant to conjure the fantasy and escape one could find in Miami, its queer connotations were not that far off. Queer life was not uncommon on the nightclub stage or on the street, and was often accommodated by the police and city officials.

By the 1950s, Miami was changing from a decadent resort haven to an expanding city, fueled by the growing industries of aviation and manufacturing that transformed the city's landscape and population. While tourism was still a draw, it was not the only attraction to south Florida. Along with military families who settled in the area after the war, the city also attracted huge numbers of northerners, changing it from a town of transients and tourists to one of families and, increasingly, retirees. Gay men and lesbians were also settling in Miami, many of whom had been stationed there during the war. Between 1940 and 1960, the population of the greater Miami area more than doubled, reaching nearly half a million residents. North Miami attracted middle-class families who purchased newly constructed bungalows and concrete ranch-style homes, each surrounded by hibiscus and lemon trees on quarter-acre lots. The influx of families to the area was acutely evident in August 1954, when North Miami High School opened its doors for the first time, just days after Simpson's body was found near Lovers' Lane.[9]

The arrests and confession of Lawrence and Killen prompted a different image of Simpson in the press. Descriptions of him as a handsome and quiet boy were replaced by the image of a dangerous pervert. In turn, editors were quick to portray Lawrence and Killen as the real victims of the crime. *The Miami Herald* interviewed the wife of one of the assailants. Accompanied by a series of front-page photographs of Donna Killen sobbing through the interview, readers encountered a portrait of a distraught and pregnant newlywed (they had been married four months). She described how the two had met in high school, and that Killen was a "religious boy," was dedicated to the Bible, and avoided alcohol. She also related they needed money to pay off their car, a dire situation that led Killen to join Lawrence in the scheme to blackmail and rob queer men. "You can ask any kid from any school," she told reporters, "and they'll tell you if you want money just go down to Bayfront Park where 'such people' are. It's a standing joke." While she blamed Lawrence for drawing her husband into the plan, it was really Simpson, and homosexuals more generally, whom she pointed to as the reason her husband faced first-degree murder charges. Referring to the park area where gay men socialized, "'Why, oh, why,' she sobbed, 'don't they clean it up?'"[10]

In a *Miami Daily News* article headlined "Good Guys—Not Toughs," Glenn Kirchoff, a journalism intern at the newspaper who grew up in the same neighborhood as Lawrence and Killen, described them as "pretty good guys" who had "come from good homes and aren't considered toughs by any stretch of the imagination." But amid this confusion that such good guys could commit such a crime, Kirchoff, like Donna Killen, pointed readers to a likely cause for their deadly criminal behavior: "I do know that Lawrence had an intense hatred of homosexuals." Kirchoff went on to explain that this hatred started during Lawrence's high school experiences of hitchhiking.

"The homosexuals," he noted, "make a practice of offering rides to school boys," adding that "after one or two brushes with these persons, Lawrence apparently hated the sight of them." Kirchoff portrayed the two men as average boys, who liked sports and cars, just "like most young men." It was the financial constraints that might have propelled the two to rob homosexuals, Kirchoff suggested, claiming, "I find it hard to believe that they actually planned murder."[11]

In November the two men went on trial, both on the first-degree murder charge, one that carried the death penalty. The press would refer to the trial as the "lurid Simpson murder case." The assistant district attorney, Gene Williams, argued the "two youths killed Simpson during a robbery which was part of a plan in operation for several months to 'roll' sexual deviants in out-of-the-way places." While both Lawrence and Killen admitted they were targeting queer men in a scheme to blackmail and rob them, Lawrence maintained he accidentally shot Simpson "because I was afraid he would attack me sexually."

Killen offered the jury a detailed accounting of how the scheme worked. The *Miami Daily News* reported that "Killen, after an outburst of tears, admitted from the stand he and Lawrence got together early on the night of August 2 and worked out a scheme for 'getting money from perverts.'" In this plan, Lawrence "played the role of hitchhiker," robbing unsuspecting men in their cars. "I was to follow Lawrence," Killen testified, "after he had been picked up on the Biscayne Boulevard. After they stopped in a secluded place, I was to wait until they had enough time to begin an unnatural sex act," he told the jury. "Then, I was supposed to go up to the car where they were, scare Simpson by telling him I would report him to the police, and get whatever money he had." The article added that "both youths admitted they split $25 Simpson was carrying the night he was killed."[12]

As with press coverage of the arrests, Killen's wife, Donna, figured prominently in the trial coverage. "Dressed in a black skirt, a cotton maternity blouse, and low-heeled black shoes," the *Miami Daily News* reported, "the prospective mother looked like a small and frightened child as she sat beside her own mother on a bench in the courtroom." Readers learned that both Donna and her husband had been "active church members and leaders in youth work." The article also noted that she attended church service every Sunday and "prayed for God to give [her husband] strength to take whatever punishment they decide to give him." She gave Killen a Bible, which she said he was reading faithfully. Both men, she told reporters, "need courage and the Bible is giving it to them."[13]

Increasingly, the tragedy of Simpson's murder was a tragedy for the defendants and their families. In their closing arguments, defense attorneys implored the jury to "think of the parents and relatives" of the defendants. Killen's attorney "pointed to a front row lined with relatives of the accused and said, 'There is more at stake here than the lives of these two boys.'" There was no mention in the press of Simpson's family members attending the trial.

The district attorney must have been confident in his case, anchored as it was to the confessions of both killers, and their public testimony that their scheme to rob homosexuals turned deadly. According to one report, on three different occasions during the trial, Williams had rejected offers by the defendants to plead guilty to second-degree murder—a charge that carried life imprisonment. While the D.A. stuck by the charge of first-degree murder, the jury of twelve men was not at all convinced that Simpson's murder demanded such a harsh penalty. After four hours of deliberations, which ended around two thirty in the morning, the jury returned a verdict of manslaughter. Two days later the judge sentenced both men to the maximum of twenty years at Raiford State Prison.[14]

While the arrest and conviction of Lawrence and Killen was one story about Simpson's murder, another story had emerged in the press soon after the two were arrested. That story was not about the problems of youth crime and delinquency, as one might expect when two young men admit a premeditated scheme to entrap and rob other citizens. Instead, Simpson's murder provoked a panic in the press about a dire urban problem in Miami: the growing menace of the city's homosexual community. "Pervert Colony Uncovered in Simpson Slaying Probe," ran a headline in the *Miami Daily News* just days after Lawrence and Killen confessed to the killing, offering readers shocking revelations about the size and nature of the city's homosexual population. According to the article, the police investigation into Simpson's murder uncovered a "colony of some 500 male homosexuals" living in all parts of the city, particularly in the growing middle-class areas, a number that the newspaper described as "staggering." "I was not only surprised at the number of homosexuals turned up in the murder investigation," one detective told reporters, "I was amazed to find out that there were distinct classes, not only based on age groups, but also on the ages of the persons with whom they liked to consort and the groups based on types of perversion." Within this social structure, the article related, the colony had a "nominal head" or queen of the colony. Police initially believed that Simpson was the "queen," his murder understood as an attempt to depose him from his position by another homosexual.[15]

While such numbers lacked any actual data, in the ensuing weeks city officials and the the press offered the statistic as evidence of an immediate crisis that demanded action. On the same front page on which *The Miami Herald* ran the tearful interview with Donna Killen, the newspaper declared, "5,000 Here Perverts, Police Say," which fanned fears of a near epidemic of perversion in the city. The article noted that the city had twenty bars that catered to homosexuals, but the police reported that "we can't arrest them just on suspicion of being a pervert." Readers also learned that there had been several crimes in the same area as Simpson's murder, and along Bayfront Park. One case involved the beating and drowning of a man by a sailor he met at a local bar. "We have a very large number of young men," the police told reporters, "who don't consider it wrong to slug or rob a pervert."

The very next day the *Herald* increased the number by three thousand. "Official Urges Society to Face Pervert Problem," the paper declared. Readers learned that according to the head of Miami's homicide squad, Lieutenant Chester Eldredge, there were more than eight thousand "perverts" in the city. The population, Eldredge claimed, ranged from the "relatively harmless homosexual to the fierce sadist who horribly mutilates and tortures his victim." The article also informed readers, without data or expert commentary, that homosexuality was a combination of heredity and social environment, and it urged parents to "recognize the abnormal in their children," and to seek treatment for children who show "character deficiencies and bad tendencies."[16]

Such news stories appeared alongside exasperated editorials that called on police and political leaders to address this growing problem. "Let's do something about it," the editors of the *Miami Daily News* declared. "It is disgraceful that Miami learns of the existence of a 'colony' of homosexuals in the midst of one of its fine residential sections," the paper editorialized. The newspaper reminded readers that while Miami was for years "wide open for female impersonators whose acts have invited the assembly of perverts," such performances had been legislated against in recent years. "The problem of sexual perversion in Miami," the editors wrote, "is not a new one. But it is a continuing, growing one in spite of all attempts to enforce civic decency."[17]

The Miami Herald echoed such calls for civic improvement, editorializing that vast colonies of homosexuals would threaten the "wholesome growth of Greater Miami" and pointing to an almost accommodating position of the police toward such sexual perverts. In criticizing what the editors called "police approval" of homosexual meeting places, the *Herald* argued it was no wonder homosexuals "come here from all over the country to set up a residential concentration and meeting places." With a feminizing and supposedly derogatory attack directed at queer social hangouts, the editorial called upon city officials "to clean this place up and shut down 'Powder Puff Lane.'" The editorial concluded, "[G]ood people of Miami will insist upon it."[18]

Such editorializing and press reports about the homosexual population prompted police assaults on queer men across the region's different municipalities. One police raid targeted the beach near Twenty-Second Street where queer men socialized. Led by Miami Beach Police Chief Romeo Shepard, the raid, according to press reports, detained and arrested "men who act like girls," charging them with disorderly conduct. "Some of those arrested," the press noted, "were dressed in Bikini style bathing suits which amounted to little more than a strip of cloth fore and aft." Continuing a war-tinged rhetoric common in the press, articles described how Shepard had devised a "well formulated battle plan on pervert hangouts in Miami Beach," adding that "two suspects tried to swim away from the scene but were nabbed by lifeguards."

It was not only beaches that the police raided in the weeks after Simpson's murder. In an article headlined "Cops to Hunt Park Deviants," the Miami city manager offered a strong warning to queer men in the city. "We are going to run these people out of our city parks so that the general public can use the parks without hesitation," he told reporters. "We intend to eliminate the gathering of perverts at certain night spots in Miami," he continued, "and at any other places where they congregate."[19]

This fevered panic had been boiling all summer. Just weeks before Simpson's murder, a girl named Judith Ann Roberts was kidnapped from her grandparents' house in the middle of the night. The next day her body was found on a nearby beach. Blindfolded and with her hands tied behind her, the assailants had used her nightgown to strangle her to death. The police determined that she had been sexually assaulted. As was so often the case with such crimes of child murder and sexual assault in the era, Roberts's murder quickly sparked a media attack against queer men. *The Miami Herald* editorialized that the "police have erred in permitting perverts to assemble here—to corral them in places which are 'on limits' to them." Intoning the same hostile and derogatory rhetoric that it had used the weeks after Simpson's murder, the *Herald* complained, "Miami's 'powder puff lane' is a civic disgrace" and noted that "when large numbers of perverts are present in a community, the peril is multiplied."[20]

In response to the Roberts murder, police staked out many of the bars and beach areas where queer men socialized throughout the city. The press reported that detectives were gathering the names, addresses, and places of employment of all patrons at the bars; the intent, according to one detective, was "to make things hot for sex perverts in Miami," adding, "if we can discourage bars and night clubs from catering to this type of trade, perhaps these undesirables will leave."[21]

Weeks into the investigation, police arrested James Roberts, Judith's father, for the murder. At the time of his arrest he criticized the police investigation, telling reporters that the "sadistic" killer of his daughter would be found among the "perverts of Miami who are treated so tenderly" by the police.[22] Such comments would circulate through the wire service, appearing in front-page stories across the country, furthering a prewar image of the city that city leaders wished to dispel. Roberts was eventually released from custody. The killer of his daughter was never found, and the murder remains a cold case file.

It was within this frenzied atmosphere of sex panic that Lawrence and Killen devised and executed their scheme to entrap and rob queer men along Biscayne Boulevard. How many other men they were able to take advantage of was never reported in the press. The panic surrounding both murders was as much about fears of a growing population of sex deviants in the city as it was about changing the image of the city itself. In August 1954, Miami's mayor, Abe Aronovitz, publicly criticized his police chief, Walter Headley, in the press for "failing to stop perverts from gathering at certain Miami bars" and threatened to fire him if he didn't "get the police department in line," adding that the city was becoming known as a "gathering spot for rapists, child molesters, and all types of sexual deviants." The mayor's complaint would be reported around the state of Florida and beyond, underscoring a public relations concern that coupled municipal order with a toughness against homosexuals. "This city is spending hundreds of thousands of dollars for good publicity," he told reporters, "but the taxpayers' money is being wasted if we ourselves do not look at the cause of the bad publicity and try to remove it." For his part, Police Chief Headley countered that if he ran the homosexuals out of town, "some of Miami's first families would be leading the parade."[23]

In the same month, the *Miami Daily News* published a sensationalized three-part series about homosexuality by the well-known reporter Jack Roberts. The series offered readers little insight into the city's homosexual community, just as earlier reports had, instead focusing on the ways to control sex deviants through psychiatry and enhanced police efforts. "Miamians have learned," Roberts wrote, "that this community has become infected by a large colony of sexual deviants." He clarified, "The word 'infect' is used advisedly, since homosexuality is a social disease. It can be worse than drug addiction or alcoholism." In one article, Roberts interviewed Paul Kells, a "noted Miami psychiatrist." Readers were informed that not all homosexuals were child molesters, but that homosexuality was one form of psychopathic behavior. Readers also learned that not all men who act in effeminate ways are homosexuals, as a "normal" homosexual, Kells maintained, was "impossible to spot by physical characteristics." But it was the psychiatrist's claims about the origins of homosexuality that proved compelling for Roberts. "It's possible for anyone to become a homosexual, but people are not born to be such," Kells noted. For Roberts, this assertion pointed precisely to the problems of a growing population of homosexuals in the city, and the need to eliminate them. The idea of homosexual contamination beyond pervert colonies and queer social spaces was a strong fear underlying such concerns. "In a community where there are only a few homosexuals," Roberts wrote, "the chance for exposure to such practices is negligible." This point was echoed at the end of the interview, when Kells confirmed that "perverts tend to congregate in the same area of town."[24]

In another article in the series, Roberts compared Miami with Los Angeles, and considered how that California city handled "its 150,000 perverts." In Los Angeles, readers learned, the laws were stricter than they were in Miami, and the police were more vigilant in controlling homosexuals. "This thing is like a cancer," Thad Brown, deputy chief of detectives for Los Angeles, declared. "It keeps getting bigger and bigger each year. We process about 150 homosexuals a month who are caught in the act." The police in Los Angeles had a policy of harassment. "We keep a constant check on bars and restaurants where they hang out," Brown told Roberts. Such efforts were also put into context. Like the earlier reports about the numbers of homosexuals in Miami, Roberts speculated that there were between 6,000 and 8,000 homosexuals in the city, and calculated for readers what such numbers would mean. There was "one homosexual for every 100 hetero-sexual people" in Miami. By comparison, Roberts noted, in Los Angeles the ratio was about "four for every 100." The comparison was important because he saw in Los Angeles the problem of Miami's future. Even as his statistics were mere speculations, they were meant to fan fears and boost the need for stricter laws and more police surveillance.

At the heart of the series was a concern for the nation itself. Roberts warned his readers that without more diligence on the part of the police, the growing population of homosexuals in American cities heralded the country's downfall. "Historians are quick to point out," he wrote, "that moral degeneracy and the destruction of some of the greatest civilizations in the world were tied hand in hand." He added, "[T]he latter day emperors of Rome were perverts. Their deeds have been recorded for history but are too sordid to recount here." In a reference that would have been familiar to many of his readers, Roberts noted that "the top men of Hitler's Third Reich were perverts." The best approach to deal with the problem, Roberts pointed out throughout the series, was to eliminate the sex deviants in the city, either by intimidation, arrests, or institutionalization. This strategy was put in place directly by Miami Beach Police Chief Shepard, the man who led the beach raids in the weeks after Simpson's murder, who told Roberts, "I simply want them to get out of town."[25]

"SHADOWY WORLD OF INTRIGUE AND DECEPTION"

In his October 1955 syndicated column "Dream Street," published in the New York *Daily News*, writer Robert Sylvester complained about the in-creased crime on Manhattan's east side, a problem he linked to what he called the "Bird Circuit"—a collection of bars and restaurants where queer men socialized. "The midtown area," he bemoaned, "comprising some of the most valuable real estate in the city, after midnight now has much of the atmosphere of Eighth Avenue or 42nd St. west of Broadway." Sylvester detailed the dynamics of how queer hookups turned violent. "The small time hoodlum goes about his night's work easily," he wrote. "He frequents a bar which is a hangout for the queens. He allows himself to be 'picked up.' On the way to the homo's apartment he shoves his new 'friend' into a doorway, belts him around, and takes his money." As his dismissive rhetoric makes clear, Sylvester wasn't offering a warning for queer readers, but rather sounding an alarm for unsuspecting residents who were not queer. "It probably isn't important if a homo is roughed up by a hoodlum," he wrote; "the important thing is that when there are no available homos, any unprotected citizen makes a satisfactory substitute."[26]

Like the fevered panic in the Miami press a year earlier, Sylvester's column was another example of the growing concerns about the social worlds of queer men as a cause of crime and a menace to a city's inhabitants. "Prior to World War II," a New York City police detective told journalist Jess Stearn in the 1950s, it was common for homosexuals "to live together, surreptitiously, as man and wife. Now they no longer feel the necessity for being so secretive or so easily satisfied and can pick and choose more exciting relationships, cruising streets and bars until they find what they want. Where once they contented themselves with one partner, they are now constantly recruiting." For the detective, this openness and "recruiting" only encouraged other kinds of crimes. "Because of their social vulnerability, the great mass of uncounted homosexuals live in a gray, shadowy world of intrigue and deception," he noted; "their very homosexuality encourages crime, making them prime targets for all kinds of criminals—muggers, blackmailers, thieves, and petty grifters."[27]

For Stearn, such claims were as illuminating as they were disconcerting. In the late 1950s, he set out to write an "unbiased report" of the "everyday aspects of the homosexual's world," which, Stearn contended, was a "glittering make-believe world—at times tragic, sometimes ludicrous, even comical. Like any other world, it runs the gamut of human emotions, and no two emotions are the same." Published in 1961 and drawing its title from the Kinsey scale, *The Sixth Man* gives an eyewitness account of this homosexual world, from bars and gyms to private parties and parks. In the process Stearn interviewed queer informants, police detectives, and psychologists about homosexuality. "Was homosexuality becoming more prevalent, or was it just more open?" he asked in the introduction. More important, he asked, "Just how much impact did homosexuality have on the life of the city—and the nation? Was it really a mark of Western decadence or just something transitory washed up by the war?"

A former crime reporter, Stearn described how his professional experiences in the 1940s and 1950s prompted the idea for the book. Recalling various murders and assaults he covered for the New York *Daily News*, one in particular about a murder on Fire Island where "one homosexual killed another and the police explanation was simply 'jealousy,'" Stern gradually began to consider the underlying world of the victims and criminals of such stories. "My viewpoint began to change," he wrote, and the more he considered the social world of the victims, the more he came to realize "the homosexual was nearer to home than I had thought."[28]

Similar to an exposé of drug addicts or prostitution, Stearn's account offers an understanding of a marginal group viewed as a social problem. With a journalistic distance, Stearn explored the nature of homosexuality and the challenge it presented to Cold War society. "No longer are police surprised to pick up young killers and find they have backgrounds as male prostitutes," he wrote in a chapter that focused on police informants. "After a recent senseless killing in Manhattan's Hell's Kitchen," he related, "two teen-age slayers, known as the Umbrella Man and the Cape Man, boasted that their gang had been 'taking' homosexuals in the nearby Times Square area. 'It was almost,' the police official said acidly, 'as though it were a mark of distinction.'" In another chapter, we encounter a view of police entrapment from homosexual informants. "What do they expect after standing around posturing for a half hour," one queer informant complained, adding, "they should be the ones charged for loitering." Another complained about the surveillance in New York City subway stations: "'Who else,' a homosexual demanded, 'is spied on like this?'" Stearn also detailed how some queer men sometimes helped the police in their efforts to catch men who preyed on queer men. "Since it was essential to catch the crew in the act," he wrote, homosexuals "gladly volunteered as subway decoys."[29]

Stearn's narrative of queer life was not absent the era's cultural biases, seeing legitimate needs in protecting children from homosexuals and, more acutely, understanding the social problem of homosexuality as a problem of urban crime. In an interview with a transit police officer, he related how by "reducing homosexuality, they reduce crime more generally" in the subways. While on one hand *The Sixth Man* gives us insight into a complex social world of queer experiences that was well ahead of its time, the book also reminds us of how pervasive criminality was in any discussion of homosexuality during the Cold War.

The "homosexual world" was an increasing element of queer crime stories of the late 1950s, as newspapers detailed the bars, taverns, parks, and public meeting places within those crime stories. While William Simpson's murder in Miami illustrated how the press turned the murder of a queer man into a dire sex crime panic, such sensational accounts also illustrated a broader social landscape of queer experiences in the Cold War.

In the winter of 1957, the badly bruised and stabbed body of Louis Teboe was found by neighbors in the alley behind his apartment building on Pennsylvania Avenue, four blocks from the White House in Washington, D.C. Raised on the Winnebago Reservation along the eastern edge of Nebraska and Iowa, Teboe moved to Washington in 1952, when he was twenty-four, and worked as a payroll clerk for the Bureau of Indian Affairs. One press account noted, "Teboe was described by his superiors as a good worker who was well-liked in the Interior Department."[30]

A few days after the discovery, police arrested Gerald Lauderdale and James Swearingen, both eighteen, for the murder. A front-page article in *The Washington Post* defined the killing as a fight over a "money row" between the three men, with the defendants claiming that they had met Teboe at a tavern where he "promised them money."[31] Teboe took the two back to his apartment, but his roommate had company, and so they went to a nearby restaurant. According to reports, the staff refused service because

Teboe "was staggering."[32] It was on their return to Teboe's apartment that Lauderdale hit Teboe from behind and Swearingen, as one article reported, attacked him with "a stiletto-type knife," stabbing and cutting him several times, the fatal stab puncturing his heart.

Press reports noted that the men met Teboe at the Chicken Hut, a well-known bar popular with queer men on H Street near Lafayette Park. One regular to the bar recalled how the Chicken Hut was "the center of gay social life in the city in the late 40s and 50s."[33] The bar was a lively and crowded place, featuring a restaurant on the second floor with entertainment provided by "a short, bald man with glasses" who went by the name of Howard, but regulars called him "Miss Hattie." He entertained patrons with show tunes and "ballads with campy lyrics."[34]

While the press did not detail the queer nature of the Chicken Hut, many readers would have known its reputation. One report related that a waitress at the restaurant told police she overheard Lauderdale ask his friend, in reference to Teboe, "do you want to take this guy for a ride?"[35] Despite such evidence, the press offered a sympathetic image of the killers. "Thin, red-haired James Swearingen," *The Washington Post* related, "told the coroner's jury in a quavering voice that he fatally stabbed Louis J. Teboe in an alley behind Teboe's apartment last month."[36] In their police statement, the two men claimed they had no intention of hurting Teboe "until he started bothering" them. Readers also learned of Swearingen's remorse: "It's been tearing me apart since I've been in jail."[37]

At his trial, Swearingen claimed "that the stabbing was in self-defense," adding that Teboe "made an indecent proposal to him," and that when he rejected the sexual advances, Teboe "attacked him 'looking like a crazy man.'"[38] While little is mentioned of Teboe's race, the underlying image of a drunk and sex-crazed Native American simmers with racist and antiqueer sentiment.

The jury returned a verdict of second-degree murder. They believed the testimony that neither of the two young men intended to kill Teboe. The judge avoided the maximum penalty of life in prison, and instead sentenced both men to five to thirty years, stating that while the "evidence during their five-day trial indicated each was equally guilty," there was the "mitigating circumstances" of their ages.[39]

The same year Teboe was found murdered, social psychologist Earl Coon looked to the crime pages to analyze the social worlds of homosexuals in the journal *Archives of Criminal Psychodynamics*. The psychologist would need to "learn the argot of the deviant group, what streets, rest rooms, bars, hotels, etc., are favored for 'pick-ups,' he will learn the methods of procedure under various circumstances and in different localities. In short," Coon wrote, "he not only explores the dynamics of the individual, but also amasses a vast amount of information as to the social processes involved."[40]

Newspaper crime stories were a vital resource in defining such social processes for Coon. One 1956 article, for example, detailed how an army sergeant was shot in Rock Creek Park in Washington, D.C., after an afternoon of drinking, and "refused to tell police the name of his assailant or the circumstances to the shooting."[41] Coon speculated that "without knowing the circumstances, no one could be sure what had happened," but added, "it is obvious that if the circumstances had included the Sergeant's making homosexual advances to someone else, the shooting might then have occurred and the Sergeant would have been reluctant to tell who or why."[42]

In an article about another soldier, who was found dead in a hotel room "with a plastic pillow cover over his head," Coon speculated about the crime scene and the events that led to the murder. The circumstances, Coon wrote, "strongly suggest the soldier was bisexual who was taking advantage of being away from his wife to engage in homosexual pursuits." But Coon didn't stop there in his speculation, rendering a richer and more horrific scene of the crime. "It is possible that this soldier had picked up another man," he observed, "that sex relations had started between them in the hotel room, but that the unknown had gone into a homosexual panic. If the plastic pillow cover was immediately at hand on the bed, it may have been used as the closest means at hand—it might even have been slipped on in fun and the unknown might have impulsively seized the opportunity to kill as a result of paranoid projection." Coon concluded with a disturbing image where sodomy and murder intersect: "That there were no signs of a struggle suggest that they might have already been in physical contact with the unknown man in such a position as to be able to hold the soldier down for the time necessary to render him unconscious. A physical position such as might be used in sodomy would provide the opportunity."[43]

Vital to Coon's analysis was a link between spaces of queer socializing and the ways they fostered violent criminality. Examining an article about a man strangled by his younger companion in his apartment, Coon speculated that the killer "is typical of thousands of youths who can be found any night in bars in cities all over the country waiting to be 'picked up' by some homosexual," adding, "they don't consider themselves to be homosexual, they are interested only in the money they may gain." Although he acknowledged such realities of men targeting queer men for money, blackmail, or other sorts of gain, Coon again imagined that the killer most likely felt "guilt concerning his own homosexual desires and impulses" and that the brutality of the strangulation as well as the beating "was a form of projection connected with the need to repress these unacceptable desires. Whatever the exact constellation of emotional forces," he noted, "the beating which was intended to hurt became uncontrollable by him and he killed the man."[44]

Coon found in the physical geography a dangerous psychological uncertainty where queer socializing led to any manner of violent criminality or homosexual panics—or both. "It is only in the twilight zone between the law abiding and the criminal," he concluded, "that the homosexual may openly pursue new acquaintances."[45]

"FANTASTICALLY LARGE MINORITY OF HOMOSEXUALS"

Details of a queer social landscape evident in queer crime stories also reflected a more subversive shift that was taking hold in the 1950s: the radically new idea that homosexuals constituted a social minority. Since the late 1940s, popular magazines had been publishing articles that introduced the idea of a homosexual minority. A series of letters to the editor in the *Saturday Review of Literature* in 1949, for example, discussed the "Homosexual Minority." One letter complained to the editors that while the magazine engaged in a "frank and free discussion of current problems," it had failed to address the problems of homosexuals, which, like other minorities, "suffers from its position in society in somewhat the same way as the Jews and the Negroes." In recognizing that homosexuals are acutely aware of social prejudice and must hide their secret from others to avoid "active hostility directed against them personally," the writer argued that "most members of society would condemn them once their secret was betrayed." *Cosmopolitan* magazine ran a feature article on homosexuality entitled "The Unmentionable Minority." Popular novels also presented ideas of a homosexual minority. John Horne Burns's 1947 novel *The Gallery*, set in Allied-liberated Italy, situated homosexuality within a constellation of freedoms that had just been fought for in the war, most acutely the freedom from fear. In this way, the motivations behind the war itself buttressed a growing notion by some that homosexuals are "a minority that should be let alone."[46]

Such claims were anchored to a belief that homosexuals were a persecuted group who suffered from social prejudice and violence. In "Twilight for Greenwich Village," a 1949 essay published in *Negro Digest*, the writer Allan Morrison bemoaned the vigilante violence that was common in postwar New York. "Negroes have been beaten unconscious by gangs of white youths prowling the area," he wrote, "hell-bent on violence against Jews, Negroes, homosexuals, and Communists." That same year, a striking scene in Michael de Forrest's novel *The Gay Year* detailed the beating of the fairly flamboyant character Harold. "One of those gangs of boys," the narrator tells us, "that cruise the streets at night had jumped him and robbed him. Sometimes they waited to 'beat up the fairies,' sometimes 'a nigger with a wad of dough.' There were always three or four of them, and they usually half killed their victims. He had seen them roaming the Village late at night, strutting in and out of coffee wagons, lolling on the corners in front of bars, 'waitin' for the fairies to fly out' dragging on limp cigarettes set muggishly in their mouths. It was their sport and their 'crusade.'"[47]

In his groundbreaking 1951 book *The Homosexual in America*, Donald Webster Cory, the pen name of Edward Sagarin, defined what he called the "unrecognized minority." "In recent years the world has become extremely conscious of minority problems," Cory wrote; "upon industry, government, and indeed upon society as a whole, there is a constant pressure to recognize the rights of minorities." He added, "[I]t is my belief that another phase of the minority problem is demanding the attention of America. We who are homosexual constitute a minority that cannot accept the outlook, customs, and laws of the dominant group. We constitute a minority, and a unique one." Later he illustrated precisely the issues at stake in a striking condemnation of the public rhetoric of the times: "There is no Negro problem except that created by whites; no Jewish problem except that created by Gentiles. To which I add: and no homosexual problem except that created by the heterosexual society."[48]

Central to Cory's claims was an understanding of a unique social world of queer experiences. "One writer describes it as a submerged world, while another speaks of a society on the fringe of society. Both are correct, accurate, yet incomplete, for there is not one submerged world, one society on the fringe of society, but several, almost countless, different and disparate and dissimilar and almost disconnected, yet all having some relationship to one another." He continued by pointing readers to a geography of queer life. "The world of the street corner, or of a special and well-known path in the park, or the lonely and dark street on the breezy lake front, or the banks of a river in one of America's largest cities? Here they come, attracted by the burning desires, seeking release perhaps more than satisfaction, wondering with a driving curiosity what adventures are awaiting, fearful of the many dangers—medical, legal, extra-legal—yet coming with bravado, asserting to themselves that the dangers are quite fictitious and exaggerated." It is such dangers that hover over Cory's description of this gay world, despite the men's efforts to ignore them. "Thieves," he wrote, "not only in the night but even in the day are protected by the law that is indifferent to the fate of the outcast, but doubly protected by the stigma that attaches to the activity that may be the prelude to violence, a stigma that will hold in silence the tongues of the victim."[49]

A year after *The Homosexual in America* was published, the *Los Angeles Times* reported on a strange shooting and the subsequent arrests of several Mexican American youths by a plainclothes police officer in Edendale, a neighborhood north of downtown Los Angeles known for its leftist politics and cultural diversity. The newspaper described the youths arrested as "'park bandits' who have been preying upon lone men." One of the youths, William Rubio, was shot when he "jumped on Officer Ted Porter" as Porter left the Echo Park boathouse in the evening hours. While it is unclear in the article why the youths were preying on lone men, it was in the conclusion of the article that the queer undertones of the story were indicated: "Robbery detectives said gangs of youths have been attacking and robbing persons found alone in the park and that Officer Porter, in plainclothes, had been assigned to the park to prevent such crimes. Apparently, the detectives added, Rubio and his companions mistook Porter for a prospective victim."[50] The shooting of Rubio and the arrest of his friends incited local activists to the problem of police harassment of Latino men. The Civil Rights Congress, an organization dedicated to radical protest for African American civil rights and labor organizers, spoke out about the incident, critiquing the police action and claiming that such entrapment "can happen to anyone."

The shooting in Echo Park was a problem not only of "park bandits" but also of queer entrapment. Echo Park had a history of queer socializing and cruising since at least the 1930s. Along the southern edge of the Edendale neighborhood, where a number of gay men and lesbians lived, it was one of several city parks that "saw significant homosexual activity."[51] The police were not in the park to protect those "lone men" who were victimized by the youths. They were instead there to entrap and arrest queer men. Once arrested, Rubio's friends confessed that they had robbed queer men in the park earlier in the day, staking out the park bathroom for queer victims. The plainclothes policeman was set to entrap men in sexual solicitation and encountered Rubio, thinking he was a queer target. At the bathroom urinal, Rubio, thinking the police officer was a homosexual, resisted the man's aggressive efforts, shouting "Help!" in English and Spanish, calling his friends, who stood outside the bathroom. The fight that ensued resulted in the shooting and arrests. The incident prompted Harry Hay, a cofounder of the Mattachine Society, to take up the criticism of the police action as well. The Mattachine Society was the first postwar organization in the United States to promote the idea that homosexuals constituted a unique social minority, one that deserved civil rights. The Echo Park shooting was another example for Hay and other Mattachine members of how discrimination based on race and class was connected with the problems homosexuals faced as victims of social prejudice, criminal violence, and police harassment.[52]

Many Mattachine Society members were reticent to take a confrontational approach in their efforts at highlighting the problems of social prejudice. Instead, their intent was to show the positive efforts of homosexuals in society, demonstrating how homosexuals were average, normal citizens. Taking issue with such an approach, a few members formed *One*, a monthly publication that was mailed to subscribers across the country. "Members of the Mattachine Society wanted the emphasis to be on the contributions that homosexuals made to literature—to culture," Dale Jennings, *One*'s founding editor, recalled years later. "[T]he editors did not agree. We wanted to focus on gaining political rights."[53] For Jennings and his colleagues, the need for an independent publication to counter narratives of homosexual criminality and mental sickness in the popular press was crucial in building a wider consciousness about homosexuality as a minority identity. Launched in January 1953, the publication had more than two thousand subscribers within a few months.[54]

For Jennings and other editors of *One*, the crime pages offered compelling examples of the ways homosexuals were both targets and victims of social prejudice and violence. While editors educated readers on how newspapers sensationalized the dangers of sexual deviants, they also situated queer true crime stories within a broader constellation, transforming the individual tragedies into symptoms of an oppressive social and political system.

"Miami Hurricane" was how the editors referred to the police and media response to William Simpson's murder in 1954. The editors actively engaged the press about its reporting of the police raids and arrests that surrounded the frenzied panic following Simpson's killing. In Jack Roberts's three-part *Miami Daily News* series, he referred to "editors of a magazine for homosexuals," who "constantly crusade for a legitimate place in society." But such "crusades" were quickly dismissed, as Roberts, quoting an expert psychologist, wrote, "The most important thing to consider is where moral degeneracy can lead to."[55]

Such commentary was precisely what *One* editors wished to counter. They excerpted a number of articles from the local Miami press that reflected and amplified the hysteria surrounding Simpson's murder, creating a collage of quotes from city officials and editorials that brought the media hysteria into a new context of meaning for *One* readers. They also recounted a number of headlines that pointed to the obvious bias in the crime pages, including such scandals involving husbands killing their wives, a man killing his wife's lover, two women who were raped, and the curious incident of a stripper who "found Courts lenient when she snarled traffic by stripping near a highway in a skin colored Bikini." These stories, the editors pointed out, provoked little panic in the press.

One editors also educated readers in the ways the press was complicit in the vilification of homosexuals. The story of Simpson's murder, the editors wrote, "illustrates what trumped up hysteria can do in a few weeks to any city in the United States," adding, "corrupt politicians and opportunistic demagogues can endanger any community that permits itself to be herded into a pogrom." Describing how the press provoked the police assaults and made homosexuals in Miami "targets for such hate orgies," the editors concluded the "fantastically large minority of homosexuals is perhaps the top candidate for any new and large scale witch hunt in America."[56]

Jim Kepner, a journalist for *One*, would later recall that the press accounts of Simpson's murder and the subsequent attacks on queer men were "really formative events in our consciousness of how to deal with this subject politically." Kepner found in the political and press rhetoric a focused response "towards the idea that the chief purpose of *One* was to confront situations like that, to publicize them, and to demand justice."[57]

In its January 1956 issue, the magazine related a number of news accounts about the murder of a twelve-year-old shoeshine boy in Boston. In quoting from the *Boston Evening American*, which described how "detectives rounded up scores of known sex deviants and hoodlums in the hunt for the slayer," the editors noted that near the end of the article the chief of police declared that the police were "not overlooking the possibility that the victim might also have been knifed for a few bills." They also pointed to a report from the *Boston Daily Record* that related how witnesses described a seventeen-year-old "extortionist" who was "shaking down newsboys" as another possible motive for the attack on the shoeshine boy. Even as the article reported on the juvenile extortionist, *One* readers learned, the newspaper headline declared the murder a "sex death."

The sex panic swirling around the murder was fueled a few days later by a different child murder story, from Chicago, also published in the *Boston Evening American*, that the editors at *One* critiqued for similarly sensationalized coverage. The Boston newspaper reported on the death of three Chicago boys who "were slain by a sex maniac"—a claim it made without any arrests or leads in the case. Such rhetoric, the editors insisted, was "hysterically irresponsible." They pointed to the last paragraph of the story, which described how an "autopsy revealed that none of the victims had been molested sexually." *One* readers were warned: "much depends on which page or edition you read."[58]

One often targeted the homosexual panic defense with pointed critiques. The September 1958 New Orleans murder of Fernando Rios, a twenty-six-year-old tour guide from Mexico City, was one such crime. "Tulane Univ. student John S. Farrell, twenty, suggested to fellow student David Drennan, nineteen, and Albert Calvo, twenty, that they go down to the French Quarter and 'roll a queer,'" the editors informed readers in the March 1959 issue of *One*. The story of Rios's murder made sensational headlines for months in New Orleans. Found in an alley, Rios suffered a severe beating. "[B]oth his eyes were badly blackened" and he had "severe lacerations, bruises and factures on his skull, nose, and mouth," *One* readers learned.[59] Press coverage of the crime continually referred to the killers as students and Rios as a "Mexican tour guide," a distinction that furthered the prejudice toward the victim. It was Farrell who drew Rios into an alleyway in the French Quarter, having picked him up at a bar known for its queer patrons. Drennan and Calvo stayed off in the distance, waiting for Farrell's signal to rob Rios. At the trial, all three men admitted to the robbery scheme, and to taking Rios's wallet. But Farrell claimed the attack was prompted when Rios made an "improper advance." During the trial, Farrell's defense lawyer claimed that Farrell's actions were reasonable, as a man "may resist force with force," adding that all three defendants were just "kids who sometimes do foolish things." The three were ultimately acquitted after the jury deliberated for two hours and fifteen minutes. The *Times-Picayune* reported that despite the judge's order "that there be no demonstration, the packed courtroom rose almost *en masse* to applaud the verdict" as it was read out. The newspaper included a large photograph of the defendants, smiling and hugging their mothers after the verdict was announced.[60]

The effects of Rios's murder, like many such cases, were a direct assault on the social landscape of queer men in the city. The press fanned concerns about sex deviants in New Orleans bars and parks, prompting the city council and mayor's office to take action. News stories warned of "furtive characters" who loitered around schools and juvenile hangouts. One letter to the editor complained about the poor street lighting in the area where Rios was murdered, noting that years earlier the area was used by "whole families—couples and their children, women alone and men." But now, it is a "nightly hangout for characters and phantom-like creeps who flit around in semi-darkness." Even before the three defendants went to trial, the city proposed new laws to close bars "catering to sex deviants," and to prohibit any form of entertainment that would excite "'unnatural' sex desires or practices."[61]

"No one spoke on behalf of the dead man's besmirched character," *One* editors complained in commenting on the trial. "Rios having been a Mexican national," they noted in pointing to the racist undertones of the trial, "the defense appealed to jury prejudice by depicting the sinister influence of a foreign government in the trial." They added, "Farrell and Drennan were of choice, white 100 percent stock, good boys all around." The guilt of the defendants, the editors wrote, was transferred "to the consciences of twelve other men" of the jury. The article ended with a stern indictment of Farrell's all-too-common defense: "How many more times must the innocent die and the guilty go free before the unsubstantiated claim of an 'indecent proposal' ceases to be an alibi for robbery and murder?"[62]

The Philadelphia murder of nineteen-year-old Charles Ferro by twenty-year-old marine Charles Kernaghan, a native of Victoria, Virginia, a town of just 1,700 inhabitants in the southern part of the state, prompted an equally angry commentary in the March 1959 issue. "Most of the citizens of Victoria, Va., crowded into Philadelphia city hall court to see 'that justice was done for their boy,'" the editors wrote. The commentary described how Ferro invited the marine and a friend to his apartment where he "made immoral advances," prompting an argument, "whereupon Victoria's boy smashed Ferro's head with a rolling pin." After "hearing glowing character references from Victoria notables," the judge found Kernaghan not guilty of manslaughter. While *One* criticized the homosexual panic defense, the real criticism was aimed at the social attitudes that protected such dubious defenses. "The good citizens of Victoria, Va.," the article concluded, "trouped home, proudly feeling that justice had been done to their boy, and that they could sleep safely in their beds now that one more alleged queer was safely dead."[63]

At times the editors promoted expert psychological theories about homosexuality to counter the more dominant ideas that circulated in the popular press. The 1957 murder of Robert Bennett, a thirty-one-year-old bookkeeper in Memphis, was one example. Bennett was murdered by Ed Leonard. Drawing on press reports, *One* related how Leonard claimed he got annoyed when Bennett looked at him: "I got the opinion he was a queer. You can tell by the way a man looks. I don't want anyone to look at me like that. I got mad." On the outskirts of Memphis, Leonard shot and killed Bennett; he then hitchhiked to New Orleans. While in transit, he met up with Glen McMahon, whom he also shot and killed near a gas station. Leonard was arrested at the station and brought back to Memphis.

The psychiatrist quoted in the press claimed that "Leonard identified himself as feminine, that he was strongly motivated towards homosexuality, and that by killing a homosexual he was acting out a symbolic suicide— killing the homosexual in himself." Such a theory, which saw homosexual violence as a form of self-hatred, was not uncommon in the era. But for the *One* editors, the trial testimony offered a more compelling argument. "We don't know what causes homosexuality," the article noted, but, they added, "there is no curing it." The editors drew on the psychiatrist's claim that if Leonard had been allowed to express his homosexual desires freely rather than repress them, the brutal attack would most likely have been avoided. "Leonard could have been a free man," they argued, "and Bennett and McMahon still alive."

Many of the crime stories that *One* commented on were initially brought to their attention by readers of the magazine. The April 1960 issue, for example, contained a series of short articles from such disparate locales as Oklahoma City; Indianapolis; Houston; Baltimore; Detroit; Wooster, Ohio; and Wheeling, West Virginia. In this collection, readers learned about a variety of crimes, from violent assaults and arrests in bathrooms for disorderly conduct to police raids on private residences for "obscene photographs." As much as these various reports demonstrated the hysteria of antiqueer attacks, they also presented to readers a broad sense of queer experience across the country, from small towns to big cities alike. The catalog of queer crime stories that *One* republished and commented on almost monthly helped foster a growing awareness that individual assaults, robberies, and murders composed a collective experience of injury and abuse.

Such an awareness was keenly evident in the private homoerotic scrapbooks created by writer and artist Carl Van Vechten in the late 1950s and early 1960s. Van Vechten was an avid collector of books, classical and jazz music, and cultural ephemera. Between the 1930s and the 1950s he amassed a large archive of postcards, photographs, drag ball advertisements, and news and magazine clippings that documented a range of queer experiences of the era. The child of immigrants, Van Vechten grew up in Cedar Rapids, Iowa, and moved to New York City just after the turn of the twentieth century. Living in bohemian circles in New York and Paris, he worked as a dance and theater critic, and later as a writer and photographer. He embraced and embodied the ideals of the modernist art and literature of his day, and, more acutely, he had a talent for disrupting the lines between high and low art, investing the quotidian, the odd, and the marginal with artistic potential.

An early admirer and promoter of Harlem artists and writers in the 1920s, Van Vechten often brought groups of his mostly white bohemian friends on tours of Harlem nightlife, showing them the experience of dance halls and jazz clubs. In turn, he brought his friends from Harlem down to Greenwich Village to the salons and cafés of bohemia. Mabel Dodge, the wealthy patron of Village writers and artists, remembered one evening when Van Vechten brought an African American musician and a female dancer who performed at a party at her apartment, much to Dodge's dismay. "The man strummed a banjo," Dodge recounted, "and sang an embarrassing song while she cavorted and they both leered and rolled their suggestive eyes and made me feel first hot and then cold, for I never had been so near this kind of thing before."[64]

Van Vechten married twice; his second marriage, to the Russian actress Fania Marinoff, lasted fifty years, until his death in 1964. His homosexuality was an open secret throughout much of his life. While some have characterized him as a "cultural chameleon," it may be more accurate to define him as a montage of cosmopolitan modernity.[65] A white man who is best known for promoting black writers and artists, and a married man who enjoyed homosexual affairs throughout his life, Van Vechten used his own sexual and cultural crossings for aesthetic purposes. As one biographer described him, Van Vechten was "a modernist pioneer . . . and a prophet of a new cultural sensibility that promoted the primacy of the individual, sexual freedom, and racial tolerance and dared put the blues on par with Beethoven."[66]

By the 1930s, Van Vechten took up photography, creating studio portraits of the era's artists, writers, and socialites. He also began experimenting with homoerotic and male nude images of the many young men in his artistic circles during the 1930s and 1940s. These photographs, which fill many pages of his scrapbooks, show both the more flirtatious and often campy posing of erotica as well as the explicit images of men in sexual play, displaying with little shame or shyness their naked bodies and full erections for the pleasures of Van Vechten's lens.

During the Cold War and in the later years of his life, Van Vechten collected his homoerotic photographs and ephemera of queer life into collages composed on manila pages of several large scrapbooks, which one critic has called his "homemade sex books."[67] These collages document decades of queer experiences that were well outside the official archives of the day. They also injected the everyday newspaper articles and advertisements with a sexual undertone. In one, he composed a postcard of a French cyclist in his tight-fitting shorts with a headline from a magazine: "Want a *Lot* for a *Little*?" He played with headlines from supermarket advertisements, juxtaposing them with photographs of handsome men from the society page or athletes from the sports pages. He paired a photograph of a young tennis player from the sport pages, his beaming smile and tight polo shirt exuding a youthful, masculine energy, with the advertising headlines "The Best Man for the Job!" and "Some Like Action but Others Watch." On some pages, he pasted his own photographs of naked men, adding press headlines such as "Invitation Basket" or "Putting the Bite on 'Overhead!'"

Mixed with such collages, Van Vechten also pasted a large collection of queer crime articles. The inclusion of these articles, both large and small, suggests how crucial they were to the queer history that he was recording and preserving. While we may understand these scrapbooks as Van Vechten composing an unofficial history of queer life in midcentury America, the articles of men murdered and assaulted haunt this history as much as they illuminate it.

Like the crime stories in *One*, many of which were brought to the editors' attentions by subscribers around the country from local newspapers, many of the crime stories in Van Vechten's scrapbooks suggest that they were gathered from friends. Some included handwritten notations or underlining that point to the queer undertones of the story. One series of articles, for example, details the murder of Anthony Lankford in his "bachelor apartment" in Bucks County, Pennsylvania. The twenty-nine-year-old insurance executive was beaten, shot in the head, and had his throat slit with a broken glass at his home. In one article, someone, perhaps Van Vechten himself, underlined a crucial clue to the queer aspects of the crime: "Wolf had admitted meeting Lankford at a bar on Friday night . . . He said the two had several drinks and then went to Lankford's apartment." Van Vechten clustered these articles about Lankford's killing on the same page, detailing the assailant's testimony that he spent the day drinking heavily before he met Lankford at the bar. The assailant, a former sailor, claimed in court that Lankford had made an indecent advance that triggered his violent attack. "I don't remember inserting the glass into Lankford's neck, but I do remember pushing it," the article quoted him.[68]

We find in the scrapbooks both small crimes and sensational headlines. Van Vechten collected articles on the murder of the Nazi diplomat Walter Engelberg in his Brooklyn home in 1939; the Riverside Park stabbing of David Kammerer by the young Lucien Carr in 1944; and the gruesome 1945 murder and mutilation of Solon Burt Harger by Walter Dahl in the West Forty-Sixth Street Manhattan apartment the two men shared. The tabloid article about Harger's murder sits next to a *New York Times* article from 1937 with the headline "Dancer Found Slain in His Apartment," recounting the murder of Edward Dolan, the fifty-seven-year-old female impersonator who was murdered in his Lower East Side apartment. The juxtaposition of these two murders of dancers in their own apartments reflected how Van Vechten composed the crime story collages as constantly echoing each other across time and place, illuminating not just the particulars of the crime, but also how such crime stories are connected.

This juxtaposition created its own reading practices. On one page we encounter the murder of a "weirdly garbed man" found trussed in a Brooklyn rooming house, clad in "full-length jersey tights, bathing trunks, white sneakers, and a gray and yellow sweatshirt. On his head were two bathing caps, both pulled over his face, and a leather aviator's helmet that tied under his chin." Near this is pasted an article about twenty-one-year-old Brice Bowen, who was picked up by two sailors hitchhiking. At one point while driving around Philadelphia, one of the sailors "struck him a hard blow to the back of the head" and shoved him out of the car. Another article on the same page related the story of twenty-five-year-old Evan Stone, who was found "clad in only women's flimsy undergarment [*sic*]," his body discovered "hanging from a door hook in his downtown rooming house" in Des Moines, Iowa. Stone was described as "handsome," had many girlfriends, and "dated often."[69] As a patchwork of such queer true crime stories, the scrapbooks force us into a queer reading practice where the sexual subtext of every story and every sequence of stories becomes hard to ignore. As one historian has noted, Van Vechten "found homosexuality where homosexuality had been suppressed—the crime reports—and he found homosexuality where it was not supposed to be—the tennis court or the wrestling mat."[70]

This reading practice was acutely evident in the mysterious murder of Sanford Lewis Tillis, a twenty-six-year-old navy veteran and New York City set designer. Van Vechten clipped and pasted a *New York Times* article from 1952 reporting that Tillis's body was found in the ashes of his burning apartment on the Upper West Side of Manhattan. The article described how Tillis was "badly beaten, his hands and feet bound with an electric cord ripped from a bedroom light fixture." He was placed on an overturned sofa, and the apartment was set on fire. According to the article, Tillis was still alive when the apartment was set ablaze. Tillis's father told reporters his "son dated young women, but did not have a 'steady girl.'" Tillis's murder would be republished in newspapers in Baltimore, St. Louis, and Cincinnati. *The Brooklyn Eagle* included a photograph of the burned-out apartment, noting that the "handsome and mustached Tillis" was a "quiet man who seldom had visitors."[71] Situated among more explicit accounts of queer true crimes, the subtext of Tillis's brutal murder becomes apparent.

The crimes that fill Van Vechten's scrapbooks come together to tell a story about the marginal in society. In mixing the public ephemera of the newspapers with his own private photographs, drawings of naked men, and published accounts of queer crimes, Van Vechten's scrapbooks illustrate how these crime stories blurred the lines between personal desires and public life, and between crime story and queer experience. While the campy collages in the scrapbooks show what one Van Vechten biographer calls a playful and ironic sensibility about his homosexuality, the queer true crime newspaper clippings of assault, strangulation, and mutilation reflect a darker and insensitive reality.[72]

On his death in 1964, Van Vechten donated the scrapbooks to Yale University, directing they be sealed for thirty years. It was a prediction that such work would be better understood and appreciated well beyond the Cold War moralities. In composing these scrapbooks amid the fears, harassment, and homophobic rhetoric of the 1950s, Van Vechten saw in the crime articles both a collective history of queer experience and a documentation of suffering that needed to be preserved.

Politics of Violence

In the summer of 1962, the police department in Mansfield, Ohio, began a surveillance operation of the men's public restroom in a town park. The operation was an advancement in such surveillance because it employed a 16 mm film camera to capture men's sexual and social interactions. No longer did the authorities need plainclothes officers to sit in bathroom stalls and entrap would-be felons into a sexual solicitation. Instead, an officer wedged himself into a small cut-out space behind a two-way mirror and, with movie camera in hand, captured grainy, static images of the cruising and sexual activities of men moving between urinals and sinks and lingering outside the stall walls. As the unsuspecting men exited the underground bathroom, the cameraman would signal via walkie-talkie to officers outside, who would arrest them. The film footage, unsteady in its documentation and limited in its view of the bathroom from a single vantage point, provided dubious evidence of exactly what the men were engaged in. Increasingly the police were arresting men for simply being in the bathroom.

The public toilet surveillance was prompted by an all-too-familiar sex crime panic. Eighteen-year-old Jarrell Howell had confessed to the brutal murder of two girls under the age of ten. Howell told police he stomped on their bodies and threw them into the river. The girls, according to Howell, refused him oral sex, something he had learned from men in the public bathroom.[1]

That August, the front page of the *Mansfield News Journal* reported on "the most spectacular investigation of homosexual depravity ever undertaken," adding that the men's restroom in Mansfield's Central Park was "long suspected as a meeting place for male sex deviants." The article noted that seventeen men had been arrested and charged with sodomy, though that number would increase to more than thirty. The newspaper listed the names and addresses of the men arrested in the raid, noting that many of them were married and had children. One man told police he didn't know why he "committed such acts, except that he sometimes got 'an urge,'" adding, "he would despise himself at the conclusion of a depraved act, had consulted a minister and made other attempts to straighten himself out, but to no avail."[2]

With this film, the state of Ohio was able to convict over thirty-five men on charges of sodomy, with a mandatory one-year prison term. Many of the men convicted were sent for a period of time to the Lima State Mental Hospital, where homosexuals were labeled psychopaths and subject to shock therapy and heavily addictive medications. Other men, whom the police caught but did not have enough evidence to convict, were placed on lists of "sex deviants" and subjected to random police questioning.[3]

Four decades later, contemporary artist William E. Jones, who grew up in Mansfield but had never heard of the police raids and arrests, found the surveillance footage in a neighbor's garage. He turned the film into *Tearoom* (2007), an art installation that was part of the Whitney Museum Biennial. *Tearoom*, a gay colloquialism used in the 1950s and 1960s to describe a public restroom where men found sexual partners, gives us the grainy 16 mm film in a relatively unedited version of the original. "The images of all these men meeting and having sex had a great sense of pathos," Jones related in an interview, "because I knew that these men had been prosecuted and sent to jail." He added, "I did attempt to put the footage into some form that looked like art. I made a version like that, and it was simply too much." Instead, we confront *Tearoom* as it was meant to be—a grainy film of men's encounters in a public restroom used as police evidence.[4]

But while the film may not have changed, the viewing of it has—or at least the understanding of these men has. Today, we can't look at these men through the policeman's gaze and simply see their criminality. Instead, it is a kind of witnessing that Jones's *Tearoom* offers us. We witness not only the men who were subjected to arrests within a sex panic fueled by the press and the police; we also witness a moment where the police, armed with the weapon of the film camera, literally framed an image of queer criminality, and used that spectacle with great force against the men who left that bathroom in that summer of 1962. Today, it is difficult to see the men in *Tearoom* as anything but victims.

Like the police camera, queer true crime stories from the decades before Stonewall illustrate a story of queer criminality framed by the editors and journalists of the times. But like Jones's *Tearoom*, it is hard to read these stories in the same way they were intended when originally published. This changed consciousness attests to the dramatic shifts that have happened in the decades since the emergence of gay liberation and the continued fight against the criminalization of queer citizens.

And yet, as I did the research for this book, I was often confronted with the reality that these stories are not that far from us. We know that life for many queer citizens is dramatically different today than it was in the early decades of the twentieth century. Through activist efforts over the past half century, we have witnessed dramatic legal changes and political gains, most acutely with the decriminalization of sodomy, repeals of state-proscribed discrimination, and a network of community and national organizations that support and advocate for LGBTQ rights. But alongside these gains, arguments about the nature of homosexuality and the rights of queer citizens continue to play out in our political contests and media debates, often through a moralizing religious framework. Queer people continue to be portrayed as a public issue, despite some gains in our private freedoms.

We see this in how anti-LGBTQ violence has continued in the years since Stonewall with alarming and brutal frequency. A recent report by the

National Coalition of Anti-Violence Programs entitled "A Crisis of Hate" has found a drastic spike in reports during 2017 of violent attacks against LGBTQ persons, constituting an 86 percent increase from the previous year.[5] While all racial and sexual categories reported sharp increases that year, a majority of the violent attacks were on transgender persons of color—though such crimes are less likely to make headlines. We witness it in the continued use of gay conversion therapy, which replays post–World War II arguments that homosexuality is a condition that can be (and should be) cured. We can also see this in arguments that bemoan LGBTQ influence in mass culture, the press, or education, arguments that owe much to those earlier sex panics, promoted for political gain at the expense of making queer people scapegoats. While the rhetoric today may be different, the efforts to criminalize and marginalize queer people has not disappeared.

In researching and writing this book, I was often haunted by the stories I uncovered. This haunting had as much to do with the gruesome ways these men were tortured and murdered as with difficult detective work required to uncover these stories. Newspapers did not catalog "gay murders" in the decades before Stonewall. Even searching the word "homosexual" wouldn't get me too far in the print or digital databases. Eventually, I focused on particular search terms such as "man found slain in hotel" or "man found beaten in park" or "sailor found murdered." I would sift through pages and pages of articles searching for the sensational headlines and the suggestive, quieter ones. I was seeking clues of the crime's queer subtext (such as the relationship between killer and victim; location of the murder; how the two met; what, if anything, was revealed in the confession of the assailant). From these leads, I searched the names of the victims or killers, which usually generated additional articles detailing the crime scene, the search for the assailants, arrest reports, and subsequent court trials and sentencing. I also searched the newspapers from the victims' hometowns, trying to piece together as much as I could about the men who were murdered. This whole process required a constant curiosity about these awful and brutal crimes.

I was struck, although not surprised, by how difficult it was to recover this history of abuse and murder and to witness these crimes today. The stories filled my waking and dreaming life with grotesque and poignant details I found hard to shake.

"People are trapped in history and history is trapped in them," James Baldwin wrote in the 1950s with respect to racism—a useful idea for the history of queerness as well. Baldwin, in order to recognize how history has trapped us, has shaped how we see the world and others in it, helps us imagine a different reality in the present. In this sense, the history of queer true crime is also a history of social movements and the radical resistance against the criminalization of queer lives. Protesting against the many ways that queer people were criminalized was at the heart of the early gay rights movements of the late 1960s and 1970s. But unlike the approach of the Mattachine Society a decade earlier, these later protests were more directed and combative, reflecting the urgency of the times. As historian Martin Duberman points out, amid the antiwar and black power movements, which both promoted confrontational protests, queer radicals saw in those earlier homophile tactics a reserved and old-fashioned approach to social change.[6] What happened at the Stonewall bar in June 1969, when patrons dared to push back against the violence of a police raid, was as much about the political consciousness of the era as it was a reaction to the forces that had criminalized queer people for decades.

Another tactic in this resistance was the establishment and growth of queer newspapers and magazines that represented LGBTQ experiences and history against the prejudiced stories found in the mainstream press. After the brutal police raids on the gay bar Black Cat in Los Angeles in 1967, a protest that foreshadowed the Stonewall resistance two years later, local activists started *The Los Angeles Advocate*, a newsletter that would grow into a national magazine in the early 1970s. While *The Advocate* would retreat from its early political focus, local community newspapers in many big cities offered readers a sense of queer historical and cultural awareness, as well as a political consciousness about the shared struggles against prejudice and injustice.[7] The resonances of these efforts of protest and publication would echo for years, reshaping the rhetoric and history of the criminalization of queer citizens in the law and the press.

We can hear this echo in the spring of 1972, when members of the newly organized Gay Activists Alliance (GAA) were attacked in a New York City hotel as they protested at the annual banquet of the Inner Circle, a group of political newspaper writers and editors. Just as the main course was being served in the New York Hilton ballroom, six activists entered throwing flyers into the air and condemning what they called "media oppression." The incident was sparked by an editorial in the New York *Daily News* that celebrated a recent Supreme Court decision allowing state governments to refuse employment to homosexuals. "Fairies, nances, swishes, fags, lezzes— call 'em what you please—should of course be permitted to earn honest living in nonsensitive jobs," the editors declared, adding, "but government should have full freedom to bar them from jobs in which their peculiarities would make them security or other risks."[8]

As the activists were forced out of the banquet hall, some guests decided to follow them. One of the guests was Michael Maye, a former Golden Gloves boxer and the president of the New York City Uniformed Firefighters Association. According to an eyewitness, Maye insulted and then severely beat twenty-one-year-old Morty Manford, one of the activists. Other firemen followed GAA members out of the hotel and down into the streets, threatening violence.

On the stand months later, Maye claimed he was simply trying to help a fellow firefighter and had no intention of injuring Manford. One reporter noted that Maye told the judge, "Look at the size of me! If I stomped on anybody, you think that fellow'd be walking around?" Other firefighters testified to Maye's innocence. The judge would eventually charge Maye with harassment, a misdemeanor that carried a penalty of up to fifteen days in jail. "A simple harassment charge, in view of the assault which took place at the Hilton, is ludicrous," the president of the GAA told reporters. "[I]t's another example of how gay women and men have no rights in our society."[9]

The same year that the Inner Circle was zapped by queer protesters, psychologist George Weinberg published *Society and the Healthy Homosex-*

ual, which defined a new disorder he termed "homophobia." The condition was "an attitude held by many non-homosexuals and perhaps a majority of homosexuals in countries where there is discrimination against homosexuals." For Weinberg, homophobia took many forms, including a "dread of being in close quarters" with homosexuals, a "self-loathing" by homosexuals themselves, as well as a general social prejudice against sexual minorities. In reversing the idea that homosexuals were sick, neurotic, and mentally ill, Weinberg's theory of homophobia pointed instead to the larger social attitudes about homosexuality as the real problem. "I would never consider a patient healthy unless he had overcome his prejudice against homosexuality," Weinberg claimed. He was one of many psychiatrists at the time who resisted the dominant theories about the origins and nature of homosexuality that had been pervasive since the end of World War II. In 1973, after a prolonged series of heated internal debates, the American Psychiatric Association removed homosexuality from its list of psychological disorders.[10]

We can hear this echo in another event of 1973: the tragic fire at the Up Stairs Lounge in New Orleans that killed thirty-two people. The victims were burned beyond recognition. The city coroner relied on jewelry and hotel room keys to identify some of the victims. The lounge was more than a bar. It served as a community space and a meeting place for the New Orleans chapter of the Metropolitan Community Church, which was founded in Los Angeles in 1968 specifically for the gay and lesbian community. The gay newspaper *The Advocate* called the arson a "Holocaust in New Orleans" and criticized the mainstream press's prejudiced reporting of the fire, which characterized the place as a "homosexual hangout" frequented by "thieves." *The Advocate* also reported on the homophobic attitudes found in the city toward the tragedy, including several bigoted jokes that circulated on local radio stations.[11] As writer Robert Fieseler reminds us, while the tragedy disappeared from the news almost as quickly as the fire consumed the place, its emotional and political impact on the local queer community would be felt for years to come.[12] It remained the largest mass murder of sexual minorities in modern U.S. history until the 2016 Pulse nightclub shooting in Orlando, Florida, which killed forty-nine people.

And we can hear this echo most clearly in the caustic 1977 campaign in Miami–Dade County by the self-described religious right group "Save Our Children" in its successful efforts to repeal a homosexual rights ordinance. Led by former beauty queen Anita Bryant and her husband, the campaign would spread fears about the immoral and violent threats homosexuals posed to the children and good citizens of Miami, just two decades after the city was enthralled by ferreting out "pervert colonies" in the wake of William Simpson's murder. Bryant's rhetoric fueled attacks on queer men, including random shootings at patrons outside gay bars and a number of beatings and robberies of gay men targeted and lured from such bars.[13]

The force of the campaign reached far beyond Miami when Robert Hillsborough was murdered in San Francisco in the summer of 1977. The *San Francisco Examiner* reported that Hillsborough and his roommate were attacked outside their apartment by "four well-dressed youths who, according to witnesses, were shouting 'faggot, faggot.'" While his roommate was able to flee, the assailants stabbed Hillsborough several times, with one man shouting, "Here's one for Anita." The newspaper ran a front-page article on Hillsborough, in which his mother described her son as a "quiet, meticulous man who loved classical music and who built beautiful wooden model ships," adding that he "abhorred violence." In an unprecedented move, San Francisco Mayor George Moscone ordered the flag outside city hall to be flown at half-staff in the days after Hillsborough's death.[14] Reports of Hillsborough's killing made news across the country. One pride parade organizer told reporters in San Francisco that Hillsborough's "brutal slaying dramatically illustrates how desperate the need is for us to challenge the hate-mongering of those who exploit people's differences for personal gain."[15]

A year later, Mayor Moscone and city supervisor Harvey Milk were murdered by fellow supervisor Dan White, a former Vietnam paratrooper, policeman, and firefighter. Milk was the first openly gay politician in the city's history. "I know that when a person is assassinated after they have achieved victory, there are several tendencies," Milk stated in a private recording he made after his election victory in the event of his murder. "One is to have some people go crazy in the streets, angry and frustrated, and the other is to have a big show and splash, a great service. Naturally, I want neither."

People did take to the streets "angry and frustrated" in the summer of 1979, when a jury found Milk's assassin guilty of manslaughter, ignoring the district attorney's indictment for murder. Police and firemen wore "Free Dan White" T-shirts in the months leading up to his trial. City Supervisor Harry Britt, described by some newspapers as an "avowed homosexual" and Milk's appointed successor, told reporters, "We are sick of the Dan Whites of this world and the violence they are allowed to perpetrate on us."

More than four thousand demonstrators marched to protest the verdict. Their rage quickly turned violent as they set squad cars on fire and resisted the police with anything they could. The journalist Randy Shilts wrote of the night in his biography of Milk, *The Mayor of Castro Street*:

> Nearly three hours after the first rock had shattered the City Hall doors, a wide wedge of officers appeared, the flames of the burning police cars casting ominous shadows on their helmets. They marched sternly into the pandemonium, beating their baton on the pavement before them like a Roman legion out to make their final conquest. Minutes after walking into the crowd, small groups broke away from the wedge to take on knots of rioters. With the formation destroyed, Civic Center plaza became a mélange of skirmishes between gays and police. Police were surprised and enraged at the depth of resistance they encountered. Gays beat back police with branches torn from trees, chrome ripped from city buses, and slabs of asphalt torn from the street.[16]

The verdict and the anger prompted the formation of the Community United Against Violence in San Francisco the following year, the first organization of its kind to address anti-LGBTQ violence. Similar organizations would emerge around the country, transforming private injuries into vital public and political issues. These groups focused on support for victims, accurate reporting of crimes, and public advocacy for increased visibility of such crimes in the press. Such media activism was vital to the political movements that emerged in the 1980s and 1990s, which focused on the new legal category of "hate crimes."[17]

Amid these shifts in the politics of violence, assailants continued to claim homosexual panic as a defense for murder and assault. Long stripped of its origins as a condition of repressed homosexual desires, the gay panic defense, as it became known, furthered the belief that any "reasonable man" would react with brutal violence against another man's sexual solicitation or flirtation. High-profile murders in the late twentieth century, such as that of Matthew Shepard in 1998, repeated the defense with varying degrees of courtroom success. A University of Wyoming undergraduate, Shepard was beaten, tied to a fence, and left to die in the middle of a field outside Laramie by two young men he met at a bar. His death sparked national outrage, and the crime was told and retold in press accounts, books, movies, and plays. His killers argued gay panic, although later recanted such claims, admitting the murder was a robbery gone too far. As Shepard was a wealthy, out-of-state college student and his killers were local working-class men, the story of the crime replayed a number of narratives about masculinity, sexuality, and class, all set against the backdrop of the rural western landscape of cowboy country. Although some states are beginning to ban gay panic defense, it still remains a viable courtroom tactic in much of the United States.[18]

The history of queer true crime stories reminds us how queer people have been shaped by competing and often contradictory social forces from political and legal rhetoric, social prejudices, religious beliefs, medical theories, gender expectations, and the unseen hand of history. Depending on one's race and class, these realities can be more acute for some queer citizens than for others. We can draw from this history larger insights about the nature of injustice and the injuries that queer people have endured. We can also consider the social movements that emerged in response to the criminalization of queer people. But there is another personal and intimate thread in this history about the men who suffered unimaginable violence in their search for sexual adventure and community. It's their stories, however incomplete and mysterious they may have appeared on the crime pages, that I hope we continue to recover and witness in the years to come.

Acknowledgments

I will be forever grateful to my husband, Greg Salvatori, who patiently supported and encouraged me through the years of research and writing. I
can't imagine this book being completed without him. And I can't imagine
a good photograph of myself without his beautiful eyes behind the camera.
It is Greg, to whom I dedicate this book, who always finds a way to put me
in the best light. And I hope I do the same for him.

My extraordinary agent, Deirdre Mullane, believed in this project almost from the moment the proposal arrived in her inbox. Her enthusiasm
and comments, as well as her countless hours with the proposal and manuscript, were crucial to shaping what this book has become.

It has been a great pleasure to work with the smart and talented people at Counterpoint. Executive editor Dan Smetanka understood and cared
about this book from our first phone conversation. He is the ideal editor
who can balance between encouragement, questioning, and good humor.
The often unsung hero of any book is the copy editor, and Trent Duffy was
no exception. He made the book more precise in prose and meaning, and for
that I am forever grateful. I'm also grateful for Donna Cheng's lovely cover

design and Jordan Koluch's book design, and how Jordan kept the editing process amazingly on track. Katie Boland answered so many of my questions with patience, and educated me on the ins and outs of book events. My publicist, Becky Kraemer, shaped the public life of the book with expertise and loving care.

The origins of this project were planted several years ago in my dissertation at New York University. Philip Brian Harper, Lisa Duggan, Andrew Ross, and Carolyn Dinshaw helped me frame the central research questions and ideas of the dissertation. Support for the dissertation came from a James D. Woods III Fellowship from the Center for Lesbian and Gay Studies at the City University of New York, and a Dean's Dissertation Fellowship from the Graduate School of Arts and Sciences at New York University.

Without the dedicated work of so many anonymous librarians and archivists across the country who labored to preserve thousands of old newspapers and then create a digital database of them, this book would not have been possible. Staff at the Bobst Library at New York University and the New York Public Library provided valuable assistance at various stages of my research. Timothy Young at the Beinecke Rare Book and Manuscript Library at Yale University offered crucial insights about the Van Vechten scrapbooks.

I am grateful to my many students at New York University and Princeton who have helped me think about the nature of creative nonfiction storytelling, and the meanings of crime stories as historical documents.

There have been so many friends and colleagues who have generously listened to me talk, obsess, and stress about the research and writing over the years: Scott Gerace, Patrick McCreery, Janet Burstein, Kate Caulkin, Carley Moore, Matt Longabucco, Kathleen Fitzpatrick, Chad Heap, Frances Guerin, Matthew Roy, Henry Castrillon, Jen Meyer, Emily Sweeney, Patrick Guédon, Mary Lou Longworth, Ifeona Fulani, Chris Packard, Peter Nickowitz, Lidia Salvatori, Allen Ellenzweig, John Howard, Amanda Herold-Marme, Cree Lefavour, Bridget Brown, Erin McMurray, Sean McNeal, Mary Helen Kolisnyk, Melissa Haley, Donette Francis, Cyndi

Mitchell, Bob Mills, Martin Dines, Suzanne Menghraj, Nina D'Alessandro, and P. G. Kain.

And finally, my parents, Jack and Gloria, who sacrificed much to provide me with opportunities they never had, supported the choices I have made over the years, and shaped the person I have become.

Notes

Introduction

1. Lyle Leverich, *Tom: The Unknown Tennessee Williams* (New York: Crown, 1995), 476–77.
2. Ibid., 478–79.
3. Heather Love, *Feeling Backward: Loss and the Politics of Queer History* (Cambridge: Harvard University Press, 2007), 1–2.
4. "Man Slain, Sailor Hunted," *New York Times*, 18 October 1942, 38; "Slain Man Identified," *New York Times*, 19 October 1942, 21.
5. "Sailor Sought in Death of Summit Man," Bridgewater (NJ) *Courier-News*, 19 October 1942, 1; "Sailor Is Sought After Slaying," New Brunswick *Central New Jersey Home News*, 19 October 1942, 2.
6. "Sailor Is Sought After Slaying," 2; "Sailor Sought in Death of Summit Man," 1; "Sailor Sought in N.Y. in Man's Fatal Beating," Wilmington (DE) *Morning News*, 19 October 1942, 10.
7. Karen Halttunen, *Murder Most Foul: The Killer and the American Gothic Imagination* (Cambridge: Harvard University Press, 1998), 3.
8. Sara Knox, *Murder: A Tale of Modern American Life* (Durham, NC: Duke University Press, 1998), 17.
9. Simon Cole, *Suspect Identities: A History of Fingerprinting and Criminal Identification* (Cambridge: Harvard University Press, 2001), 109.
10. Jonathan Finn, *Capturing the Criminal Image: From Mug Shot to Surveillance Society* (Minneapolis: University of Minnesota Press, 2009), 13.
11. Joey Mogul, Andrea Ritchie, and Kay Whitlock, *Queer (In)Justice: The Criminalization of LGBT People in the United States* (Boston: Beacon Press, 2011), 14–15.

12. Robert Beachy, *Gay Berlin: Birthplace of a Modern Identity* (New York: Alfred A. Knopf, 2014), xii.

13. Bryne Fone, *Homophobia: A History* (New York: Metropolitan/Henry Holt, 2000), 349, 351.

14. Jennifer Terry, *An American Obsession: Science, Medicine, and Homosexuality in Modern Society* (Chicago: University of Chicago Press, 1999), 119.

15. George Chauncey, *Gay New York: Gender, Urban Culture, and the Making of the Gay Male World, 1890–1940* (New York: Basic Books, 1994), 144–45.

Chapter 1. When the Men Came Home

1. "Mystery in Murder of Wealthy Briton," New York *Daily News*, 4 November 1920, 3.

2. "Seek Swarthy Man as Waters Slayer," *New York Times*, 6 November 1920, 8.

3. "Waters Murder Recalls Career of Baroness Blanc," *St. Louis Post-Dispatch*, 11 November 1920, 20; "Murdered in Hotel Room," *New York Tribune*, 4 November 1920, 1, 9.

4. "Murdered in Hotel Room," 1, 9.

5. "Mystery in Murder of Wealthy Briton," 4.

6. "Silk Underwear Clew to Slayer," *Washington Post*, 5 November 1920, 1.

7. "Waters Murder Recalls Career of Baroness Blanc," 20.

8. "Baroness Blanc's Ex-Husband Slain in Hotel in N.Y.," Philadelphia *Evening Public Ledger*, 4 November 1920, 1.

9. "Mystery in Murder of Wealthy Briton," 3; "Silk Underwear Clew to Slayer," 1.

10. "Clubman's Slayer Traced by Police to Gamblers Lair," New York *Daily News*, 6 November 1920, 4.

11. "Man Murdered by Three Holdup Men in Central Park," New York *Daily News*, 24 November 1920, 22.

12. "Man Is Murdered in Central Park by Highwaymen," *New York Tribune*, 24 November 1920, 3.

13. "Hold 4 in 2 Murders: Solve Waters Case," *New York Times*, 5 December 1920, 1.

14. "Confesses to Killing Waters," *Boston Globe*, 5 December 1920, 2.

15. "Hold 4 in 2 Murders: Solve Waters Case," 1.

16. "No Spectators Allowed at Trial of Reidy," New York *Daily News*, 7 April 1921, 6; "Waters Slayer on Trial," *New York Times*, 2 April 1921, 21; "Acquit Wisconsin Sailor of Slaying," Madison *Wisconsin State Journal*, 10 April 1921, 10.

17. "Benner Is Convicted in Slaying of Barber," *New York Herald*, 30 April 1921, 4.

18. Eric Burns, *1920: The Year That Made the Decade Roar* (New York: Pegasus, 2015), 192.

19. Frederick Lewis Allen, *Only Yesterday: An Informal History of the 1920s* (New York: John Wiley, 1931), 30.

20. Ibid., 95.

21. Quoted in Burns, *1920*, 200.

22. "Mr. Harding Begins Well," *New York Times*, 4 November 1920, 12.

23. "Now Let's Go Back to Work," New York *Daily News*, 3 November 1920, 9.

24. Allen, *Only Yesterday*, 45.

25. David Goldberg, *Discontented America: The United States in the 1920s* (Baltimore: Johns Hopkins University Press, 1999), 41.

26. Ibid.

27. Beverly Gage, *The Day Wall Street Exploded: A Story of America in Its First Age of Terror* (New York: Oxford University Press, 2009), 159.

28. Goldberg, *Discontented America*, 43.

29. "2 Mysterious Murders Solved," New York *Daily News*, 6 December 1920, 4.

30. "Ex-Sailor Charged with Aiding in Rice Murder," *New York Tribune*, 9 December 1920, 21.

31. "Paint Newport a Vice Hotbed," *The Washington Herald*, 21 January 1920, 2.

32. George Chauncey, "Christian Brotherhood or Sexual Perversion? Homosexual Identities and the Construction of Sexual Boundaries in the World War One Era," *Journal of Social History* 19, no. 2 (1985): 190.

33. Lawrence Murphy, *Perverts by Official Order: The Campaign Against Homosexuals by the United States Navy* (New York: Haworth, 1988), 210.

34. Margo Canaday, *The Straight State: Sexuality and Citizenship in Twentieth-Century America* (Princeton, NJ: Princeton University Press, 2009), 72.

35. "Charges 'Vile Practice' in Prosecuting Seamen," *New York Times*, 20 January 1920, 2.

36. Murphy, *Perverts by Official Order*, 256.

37. Ibid., 133.

38. Jennifer Terry, *An American Obsession: Science, Medicine, and Homosexuality in Modern Society* (Chicago: University of Chicago Press, 1999), 119.

39. Chauncey, "Christian Brotherhood or Sexual Perversion?" 195.

40. Lawrence Murphy, "Cleaning Up Newport: The U.S. Navy's Persecution of Homosexuals After World War I," *Journal of American Culture* 7 (1984): 64.

41. George Chauncey, *Gay New York: Gender, Urban Culture, and the Making of the Gay Male World, 1890–1940* (New York: Basic Books, 1994), 148.

42. "Declare Newport 'Clean,'" *New York Times*, 5 March 1920, 4.

43. Murphy, *Perverts by Official Order*, 267.

44. "Ex-Soldier Killed in Hotel Room," *New York Times*, 15 August 1919, 8.

45. "Identify Victim of Murder at Hotel M'Alpin," New York *Daily News*, 16 August 1919, 4.

46. "Oregon Soldier Murdered in East," Portland *Oregon Daily Journal*, 16 August 1919, 1.

47. "Young Rabbi, Beaten Dies Unconscious," *New York Times*, 7 April 1923, 6.

48. "California Police Will Come After Richardson," *Arizona Republic*, 25 April 1923, 1.

49. "Admits Murder of Rabbi," *Los Angeles Times*, 24 April 1923, 11.

50. "Rabbi Slayer Arrives Here, Admits Guilt," *San Francisco Chronicle*, 4 May 1923, 5.

51. "Murder Charge in Lafee Case Dropped," *San Francisco Chronicle*, 30 June 1923, 14.

52. "Sailor May Be Victim of Murder," *Los Angeles Times*, 11 June 1926, 10.

53. "Trio Face Hanging," *Los Angeles Times*, 16 June 1926, 14.

54. Richard Noll, *American Madness: The Rise and Fall of Dementia Praecox* (Cambridge: Harvard University Press, 2011), 191.

55. Milton Engel, "Psychoanalysis and Psychosis: The Contribution of Edward Kempf," *Journal of American Academy of Psychoanalysis* 18 (1990): 175–76.

56. Ibid., 147.

57. Edward Kempf, *Psychopathology* (St. Louis: C. V. Mosby, 1920): 477.

58. Ibid., 478.

59. Gerald N. Grob, "Origins of the DSM-I: A Study in Appearance and Reality," *American Journal of Psychiatry* 148, no. 4 (1991): 426.

60. Terry, *An American Obsession*, 108.
61. Kempf, *Psychopathology*, 480.
62. Ibid., 479.
63. Ibid., 514.
64. Ibid., 725–27.
65. Canaday, *The Straight State*, 63.
66. Allen, *Only Yesterday*, 60.
67. "Village Raid Nets 4 Women and 9 Men," *New York Times*, 5 February 1923, 17.
68. Chauncey, *Gay New York*, 147.
69. Ibid., 172–73.
70. "Policeman Takes Stand," *New York Times*, 18 January 1927, 27; "Policeman Is Convicted," *New York Times*, 19 January 1927, 10.
71. "Actor Dies from Blows of Central Park Officer," *New York Amsterdam News*, 1 September 1926, 1; "Roosevelt Frees Cop Who Slew Man," *New York Amsterdam News*, 24 April 1929, 1.
72. "Third Sex Plague Spreads Anew!" *Brevities*, 2 November 1931, 1.
73. "Decorator Slain; Companion Sought," *New York Times*, 11 September 1931, 2.
74. "Norwalk Fugitive Is Found a Suicide," *New York Times*, 12 September 1931, 2.
75. "Aarhus Released in Murder Probe," *Boston Globe*, 12 September 1931, 1.
76. "Man Sought for Norwalk Murder Ends Life," *Hartford Courant*, 12 September 1931, 3.
77. "Ambulance Chasing Blamed on Excessive Overcrowding of Legal Profession in State," *Brooklyn Eagle*, 2 March 1928, 14.
78. "Wealthy Mill Man Beaten Up," *Boston Globe*, 15 April 1926, 1.
79. "Attack on Gibbs Proves Mystery," *Boston Globe*, 16 April 1926, 5.
80. Chauncey, *Gay New York*, 324.
81. Niles Blair, *Strange Brother* (1931; repr., New York: Arno Press, 1975), 256.
82. Ibid., 267.

Chapter 2. War on the Sex Criminal

1. "Theatre Man Slain in Paterson Home," *New York Times*, 11 September 1933, 12; "Find Theatre Man Slain After All-Night Party," New York *Daily News*, 11 September 1933, 3; "Shead Battered to Death with Electronic Iron," New York *Daily News*, 12 September 1933, 44.
2. "Norman Man Slain in East," *Daily Oklahoman*, 11 September 1933, 1; "Murder Victim," *Indianapolis Star*, 13 September 1933, 2.
3. "Two Men Hunted in Brutal Killing of Theatre Head," New Brunswick *Central New Jersey Home News*, 11 September 1933, 1.
4. For more on the hotel's history, see www.junghotel.com/history (accessed October 1, 2017).
5. "Hitch-Hiker, Woman in Black Sought in Hotel Death Puzzle," New Orleans *Times-Picayune*, 20 September 1933, 1.
6. Ibid.
7. "Search for Sheffield Clark's Killer Spreads Through South," *The Tennessean*, 20 September 1933, 2.

8. "Killer of 2 Slew So He Could Show Girl a Good Time," New York *Daily News*, 22 September 1933, 3; "Trio Charged in Clark Murder," Shreveport *Times*, 22 September 1933, 1.

9. "Killed 2 in Week, Jobless Man Says," *New York Times*, 21 September 1933, 2.

10. "Killer of 2 Slew So He Could Show Girl a Good Time," 3.

11. "Singing Job Quest Ends in Killings," *Los Angeles Times*, 22 September 1933, 18.

12. "Hotel Murderer Caught in East Describes Crime," New Orleans *Times-Picayune*, 21 September 1933, 2.

13. "Neu Cheerfully Relates Details of Hotel Slaying; Expects 'to Pay,'" New Orleans *Times-Picayune*, 29 September 1933, 12.

14. Ibid., 1.

15. Ibid., 12.

16. "Hotel Murderer Caught in East Describes Crime," 2.

17. "Neu Cheerfully Relates Details of Hotel Slaying," 12.

18. "Neu to Begin Fight to Escape Gallows Today; State Rests," New Orleans *Times-Picayune*, 14 December 1933, 1.

19. "Quick Crime Solution," New Orleans *Times-Picayune*, 21 September 1933, 8.

20. "Jury Completed for Trial of Neu in Hotel Murder," New Orleans *Times-Picayune*, 13 December 1933, 3.

21. Karen Halttunen, *Murder Most Foul: The Killer and the American Gothic Imagination* (Cambridge: Harvard University Press, 1998), 221.

22. "Many Witnesses Say Neu Unsound," *Atlanta Constitution*, 15 December 1933, 13.

23. "Neu Found Guilty of Murder with Capital Penalty," New Orleans *Times-Picayune*, 16 December 1933, 2.

24. "Neu Sings as Jury Returns Verdict of Death for Murder," New Orleans *Times-Picayune*, 16 December 1933, 1.

25. "Debonair Night Club Entertainer Is Hanged Today," *Corsicana* (TX) *Semi-Weekly Light*, 5 February 1935, 19; "Sings and Dances Before He's Hanged at Southern Prison," *Chicago Tribune*, 2 February 1935, 10.

26. H.M. Kallen, "Is Minding Behaving?" *New Republic*, 1 February 1922, 285.

27. E. Boyd Barrett, "'Psychology' or Science," *New Republic*, 16 November 1927, 343.

28. "Tall Blond Sailor Sought for Quiz in Triple Tragedy," *Los Angeles Times*, 27 April 1935, 1.

29. William J. Mann, *Behind the Screen: How Gays and Lesbians Shaped Hollywood, 1910–1969* (New York: Viking, 2001), 141.

30. "Sensation Near in Hollywood Crime Mystery," *Chicago Tribune*, 28 April 1935, 5; "Bare Bizarre Trial in Movie Slaying," New York *Daily News*, 27 April 1935, 3; "Ivar's Past Searched for Murder Motive," *Boston Globe*, 20 April 1935, 6.

31. "Sailor Nabbed for Quiz over Film Killings," New York *Daily News*, 28 April 1935, 3; "Sensation Near in Hollywood Crime Mystery," *Chicago Tribune*, 28 April 1935, 5.

32. "Debt Blamed for Killing," *Los Angeles Times*, 1 May 1935, 20.

33. "Want to Hang, Walter's Plea," *Boston Globe*, 19 June 1936, 1.

34. "Girl Slaying Confessed," *Los Angeles Times*, 19 June 1936, 3.

35. "Strangler of Girl Sex Pervert, Says Father at Hearing," *Klamath* (OR) *News*, 2 July 1936, 6.

36. Philip Jenkins, *Moral Panic: Changing Concepts of the Child Molester in Modern America* (New Haven, CT: Yale University Press, 1998), 64.

37. Estelle Freedman, "'Uncontrolled Desires': The Response to the Sexual Psychopath, 1920–1960," *Journal of American History* 74 (1987): 87.

38. Ibid., 89.

39. Ibid., 92.

40. Jenkins, *Moral Panic*, 49.

41. Douglas M. Charles, *Hoover's War on Gays: Exposing the FBI's "Sex Deviates" Program* (Lawrence: University Press of Kansas, 2015), 26–27.

42. "Salient Facts About Lynching," *Pittsburgh Courier*, 23 January 1937, 13.

43. "What Is There to Lose?" *Saturday Evening Post*, 18 September 1937, 26; Jenkins, *Moral Panic*, 58.

44. Marjorie Van de Water, "Sex Crimes," *Pittsburgh Press*, 30 September 1937, 16; Marjorie Van de Water, "Sex Crimes," in Van Vechten Scrapbooks, Carl Van Vechten Collection, box 4, vol. 13, Beinecke Rare Books and Manuscripts Library, Yale University, New Haven, CT.

45. J. Edgar Hoover, "War on the Sex Criminal!" *Los Angeles Times*, September 26, 1937, K2.

46. Kenneth Ackerman, *Young J. Edgar: Hoover, the Red Scare, and the Assault on Civil Liberties* (New York: Carroll and Graf, 2007), 404.

47. Matthew Cecil, *Hoover's FBI and the Fourth Estate: The Campaign to Control the Press and the Bureau's Image* (Lawrence: University Press of Kansas, 2014), 60.

48. "Sex and the News," *Green Bay* (WI) *Press-Gazette*, 24 August 1937, 6.

49. "Subway Mob Tries to Lynch Man as Shout of 'Sex Maniac,'" *Washington Post*, 29 August 1937, 1; "Mob Grabs 'Sex Maniac,'" *Oakland Tribune*, 28 August 1937, 23.

50. "Crowd Attacks Accused Man," *Reno Gazette-Journal*, 28 August 1937, 5; "Subway Mob Tries to Lynch Man as Shout of 'Sex Maniac,'" 1; "1,000 Attack Alleged Masher in the Subway," *New York Herald Tribune*, 29 August 1937, 7; "Mob Grabs 'Sex Maniac,'" 23.

51. Mann, *Behind the Screen*, 207.

52. William J. Mann, *Wisecracker: The Life and Times of William Haines, Hollywood's First Openly Gay Star* (New York: Viking, 1998), 263–64.

53. Ibid., 264.

54. "Mob Beats Ex-Actor," *Los Angeles Times*, 3 June 1936, 1.

55. "Haines, Ex-Film Star, Is Beaten by a Mob," *New York Times*, 3 June 1936, 3.

56. "Haines and His Companions Are Beaten by Mob," Staunton (VA) *News Leader*, 3 June 1936, 1.

57. "Kluxers Beat Up Ex-Star," *New York Mirror*, 3 June 1936, 3.

58. Mann, *Wisecracker*, 273; "Haines Cites Mob Attack," *Los Angeles Times*, 5 June 1936, A1.

59. "Fellow Convict Slays Slayer of Franks Boy," *Chicago Tribune*, 29 January 1936, 1.

60. Ibid.

61. "Officials See Loeb as Victim of Death Plot," *Lansing* (MI) *State Journal*, 1 February 1936, 1.

62. "Richard Loeb Killed in Chicago Gaol Brawl," *North China Herald and Supreme Court and Consular Gazette*, 5 February 1936, 239.

63. "Razor Battle in Prison's Bath Described by Slayer of Loeb," *Washington Post*, 30 January 1936, 1; "Loeb Knifed to Death by Fellow Prisoner," *Washington Post*, 29 January 1936, 1; "Prison Mate Ends Life of Killer Loeb," *Los Angeles Times*, 29 January 1936, 1.

64. "'Thrill' Killer Is Slain in Prison Fight," *Pottstown* (PA) *Mercury*, 29 January 1936, 2.

65. "Loeb's Violent Death Stirs Illinois Prison," *Manitowoc* (WI) *Herald Times*, 29 January 1936, 1.

66. "Original Thrill Slayer Slashed to Death in Prison," *Corsicana Semi-Weekly Light*, 31 January 1936, 9.

67. "Inquest in Loeb Case Bares Sordid Prison Secret," *Alton* (IL) *Evening Telegraph*, 29 January 1936, 2.

68. "Day's Lurid Story Ends Loeb Trial," New York *Daily News*, 4 June 1936, 2.

69. "Felon Describes Slaying of Richard Loeb; Pleads Against Murder Charges," *Petaluma* (CA) *Argus-Courier*, 3 June 1936, 1.

70. "Day's Lurid Story Ends Loeb Trial," 2.

71. "Jury Acquits Razor Slayer of Young Loeb," *Chicago Tribune*, 5 June 1936, 1.

72. Paula Fass, "Making and Remaking an Event: The Leopold and Loeb Case in American Culture," *Journal of American History* 80, no. 3 (1993): 919.

73. "Decadent Criminals," Salem (OR) *Daily Capital Journal*, 2 June 1924, 4.

74. Mark Lynn Anderson, *Twilight of the Idols: Hollywood and the Human Sciences in 1920s America* (Berkeley: University of California Press, 2011), 62.

75. Simon Baatz, *For the Thrill of It: Leopold, Loeb, and the Murder That Shocked Chicago* (New York: HarperCollins, 2008), 309.

76. David Churchill, "The Queer Histories of a Crime: Representations and Narratives of Leopold and Loeb," *Journal of the History of Sexuality* 18, no. 2 (2009): 301.

77. "Slayers 'King' and 'Slave,'" *Chicago Tribune*, 28 July 1924, 1.

78. "Last of Loeb," *Time*, 10 February 1936, 15.

79. "Demand State Prison Cleanup to End Scandal," *Chicago Tribune*, 31 January 1936, 1.

80. "Luxury in Prison," *Hartford Courant*, 6 February 1936, 14.

81. In 1938 Illinois passed a sexual psychopath law. One of only a handful of states to enact such a law in the 1930s, Illinois consolidated a number of legal actions directed toward sexual deviants following Loeb's murder. See William Eskridge Jr., *Gay Law: Challenges to the Apartheid of the Closet* (Cambridge: Harvard University Press, 1999).

82. Churchill, "The Queer Histories of a Crime," 313.

83. "World's Worst," *Time*, 5 February 1934, 15 (italics added).

84. Joseph Fishman, *Sex in Prison: Revealing Sex Conditions in American Prisons* (New York: Padell, 1934), 121.

85. Ibid., 81.

86. Regina Kunzel, *Criminal Intimacy: Prison and the Uneven History of Modern American Sexuality* (Chicago: University of Chicago Press, 2008), 81.

87. Andrew Giambrone, "LGBTQ People Suffered Traumatic Treatments at St. Elizabeths Hospital for the Mentally Ill," *Washington City Paper* (online), 31 May 2018, www.washingtoncitypaper.com/news/article/21007233/independent-scholars-uncover-the-traumatic-treatments-lgbtq-people-suffered-at-st-elizabeths (accessed 9 September 2018).

88. Richard Wilson, "End Prisons, Treat Crime as Disease, Expert Urges," *Minneapolis Star*, 4 October 1937, 2.

89. Ibid., 1.

Chapter 3. Behind the Headlines

1. "Better Things: Rogers Peet and Co.," www.ivy-style.com/better-things-rogers-peet-co .html (accessed 8 August 2018).

2. "Store Executive Slain and Robbed in 42nd Street Subway," *New York Times*, 15 May 1936, 1.

3. "Arrests in Slaying of Eckert Are Laid to Lunchroom Row," *New York Times*, 29 May 1936, 1.

4. Ibid.

5. "Store Executive Slain and Robbed in 42nd Street Subway," 1.

6. "Clothing Firm Official Slain by Tube Thug," New York *Daily News*, 15 May 1936, 2.

7. "14 Arrested in Subway Murder," Hazleton (PA) *Plain Speaker*, 15 May 1936, 1.

8. "Fourteen Suspects Held After Edgar Eckert Killed," *Owensboro* (KY) *Messenger*, 16 May 1936, 7; "Victim of Subway Murder Mystery," *Coschocton* (OH) *Tribune*, 21 May 1936, 15.

9. "Arrests in Slaying of Eckert Are Laid to Lunchroom Row," 1.

10. "Two Are Seized in Subway Killing; Traced from Pawnshop to Boston," *New York Times*, 28 May 1936, 1.

11. George Chauncey, *Gay New York: Gender, Urban Culture, and the Making of the Gay Male World, 1890–1940* (New York: Basic Books, 1994), 197.

12. Ibid., 192.

13. Herbert Huncke, "Excerpts from *Guilty of Everything*," in *The Herbert Huncke Reader*, ed. Benjamin Schafer (New York: William Morrow, 1997), 240.

14. George Henry, *Sex Variants: A Study of Homosexual Patterns* (New York: Harper and Brothers, 1941), 378.

15. Tennessee Williams, *Memoirs* (New York: New Directions, 2006), 53.

16. Chauncey, *Gay New York*, 197.

17. "Decorator Slain in His Hotel Room," *New York Times*, 5 November 1936, 56.

18. "New Yorker Found Garroted in Hotel; Police Hunt 2 Guests in Death Probe," Rochester (NY) *Democrat and Chronicle*, 5 November 1936, 1.

19. "2 Held as Slayers in Garroting Case," *New York Times*, 8 November 1936, 12.

20. "Pair Pleads Guilty to Hotel Murder," Rochester *Democrat and Chronicle*, 19 March 1937, 2.

21. "Handyman Confesses New Year's Eve Killing of N.J. Senator's Aide," *Philadelphia Inquirer*, 3 February 1940, 2.

22. Ibid.

23. "Hatry Gets Life Term for Murder," *Philadelphia Inquirer*, 11 June 1940, 19.

24. Margot Canaday, *The Straight State: Sexuality and Citizenship in Twentieth-Century America* (Princeton, NJ: Princeton University Press, 2009), 96.

25. George Henry, M.D., and Alfred Gross, "Social Factors in the Case Histories of One Hundred Underprivileged Homosexuals," *Mental Hygiene* 22, no. 4 (1938): 605.

26. Ibid., 606.

27. Ibid., 605.

28. Ibid., 607.

29. Ibid.

30. Charles McCabe, "Riverside Drive, 1932," *San Francisco Chronicle*, 7 April 1978, quoted

in Gary David Comstock, *Violence Against Lesbians and Gay Men* (New York: Columbia University Press, 1991), 19.

31. Chauncey, *Gay New York*, 60.

32. Mathilde Roza, *Following Strangers: The Life and Literary Works of Robert M. Coates* (Columbia: University of South Carolina Press, 2011), 31.

33. Ibid., 149.

34. Robert M. Coates, "One Night at Coney," in *The American Mercury Reader*, ed. Lawrence Spivak and Charles Angoff (Garden City, NY: Blue Ribbon Books, 1944), 192.

35. Ibid., 195.

36. Ibid.

37. "Female Impersonator Slain in New York," *Baltimore Sun*, 28 May 1937, 4; "Dancer Found Slain in His Apartment," *New York Times*, 28 May 1937, 3.

38. "Publisher Slain, Autopsy Shows," *New York Times*, 27 November 1937, 34.

39. "Slugger Sought for Murder of Thriller Editor," *Washington Post*, 27 November 1937, 3.

40. "Salvation Army Captain Slain," New York *Daily News*, 21 June 1942, 3; "Stabbing Fatal to Salvation Army Official," *Detroit Free Press*, 21 June 1942, 10; "Quiz 6 British Sailors in N.Y. Hotel Slaying," *Chicago Tribune*, 21 June 1942, 11.

41. "Hammer Fingerprints Hunted in Byrne's Death Mystery," *Los Angeles Times*, 25 June 1939, 3; "Hammer Killing Prints Checked," *Los Angeles Times*, 26 June 1939, 12; "Elderly Dog Fancier Murdered by Welcomed Guest, Jury Told," *Los Angeles Times*, 29 June 1939, 22.

42. "Cowboy Held as Murderer," *Los Angeles Times*, 4 February 1943, 2; "Fate of Cowboy Rests with Jury," *Los Angeles Times*, 30 March 1943, 2; "Cowboy Found Guilty in Slaying of Army Man," *Los Angeles Times*, 31 March 1943, A3.

43. Raymond Chandler, *Farewell, My Lovely* (1940; repr., New York: Vintage Crime, 1992), 47.

44. Ibid., 71.

45. Ibid., 197.

46. F.A. McHenry, "A Note on Homosexuality, Crime, and the Newspapers," *Journal of Criminal Psychopathology* 2 (1941): 533.

47. Ibid.

48. Ibid., 537.

49. Ibid., 535.

50. Ibid., 536–37.

51. Ibid., 545.

52. "Nazi Consulate Aide Here Beaten to Death in Home," *New York Times*, 7 December 1939, 1.

53. "Bludgeon Slayer of Nazi Consulate Secretary Sought," Alexandria (LA) *Weekly Town Talk*, 9 December 1939, 1.

54. "Rally Here Scores Reich and Soviet," *New York Times*, 14 December 1939, 1.

55. "22,000 Nazis Hold Rally in Garden; Police Check Foes," *New York Times*, 21 February 1939; "Europe's Hatreds," New York *Daily News*, 22 February 1939, 25.

56. "Police Brand Slain German a Nazi Spy," *Washington Post*, 8 December 1939, 1; "FBI Acts in Slaying of Nazi Aide Here; Spy Angle Traced," *New York Times*, 8 December 1939, 1.

57. "Link Slain Nazi to Ring of '200 Spies,'" *New York Mirror*, 10 December 1939, 3.
58. "FBI Acts in Slaying of Nazi Aide Here," 1.
59. "Police Brand Slain German a Nazi Spy," 1.
60. "Case of Bedroom Slipper," *Time*, 18 December 1939, 12.
61. McHenry, "A Note on Homosexuality, Crime, and the Newspapers," 541.
62. "Boxer Confesses N.Y. Nazi Murder," *San Francisco Examiner*, 20 December 1939, 5.
63. "Killer Kehler," *Time*, 1 January 1940, 10.
64. Ibid.
65. Robert Beachy, *Gay Berlin: Birthplace of a Modern Identity* (New York: Alfred A. Knopf, 2014), 244–45.
66. "Blood Purge," *Time*, 9 July 1934, 16ff. In an earlier article, *Time* characterized Röhm as a "queer sub-commander" and printed a photo of him in military uniform, arms crossed, Hitler-style mustache and hair cut with the caption "Queer Capt. Roehm." See *Time*, 20 March 1933. For press coverage of the 1934 purge, see "Hitler Crushes Revolt by Nazi Radicals," *New York Times*, 1 July 1934, 1; "Civil War Feared in Reich as Hitler Crushes Revolt, Killing Chief Nazi Enemies," *Washington Post*, 1 July 1934, 1. For a history of the purge and the subsequent attacks on homosexuals in Germany, see Richard Plant, *The Pink Triangle: The Nazi War Against Homosexuals* (New York: Henry Holt, 1986).
67. Beachy, *Gay Berlin*, 245.
68. "Killer Confesses," *New York World-Telegram*, 19 December 1939, 4.
69. "Killer Kehler," 10.
70. "Seek Nazi Killer in Broadway Haunts," *New York Mirror*, 9 December 1939, 3.
71. "Boxer Admits He Slew Nazi Consul's Aide," *Brooklyn Eagle*, 19 December 1939, 6.
72. "Will Justice Triumph?" New York *Daily News*, 21 January 1940, 8–9.
73. McHenry, "A Note on Homosexuality, Crime, and the Newspapers," 542.
74. "Brokerage Employe [sic] Is Found Unconscious," *New York Times*, 2 December 1938, 3.
75. "Engelberg Slayer Convicted by Jury," *New York Times*, 12 March 1940, 9.
76. Ibid.
77. McHenry, "A Note on Homosexuality, Crime, and the Newspapers," 542.
78. Ibid., 548.

Chapter 4. Terror in the Streets

1. "Columbia Student Kills Friend and Sinks Body in Hudson River," *New York Times*, 17 August 1944, 1.
2. Ted Morgan, *Literary Outlaw: The Life and Times of William S. Burroughs* (New York: Henry Holt, 1988), 85.
3. Ibid., 86.
4. Ibid., 89.
5. Ibid.
6. "Columbia Student Kills Friend and Sinks Body," 13.
7. "Lucien Carr Pleads Guilty of Manslaughter," *St. Louis Post-Dispatch*, 15 September 1944, 1.
8. "Confessed Slayer of School Teacher Sentenced Today," *Wilkes-Barre* (PA) *Times Leader*, 6 October 1944, 29; "Murder Laid to Sophomore," *Baltimore Sun*, 25 August 1944, 1; "Student Held in New York Murder," New Philadelphia (OH) *Daily Times*, 18 August 1944, 4.

9. "Admits Killing of Alleged Pervert," Hazleton (PA) *Plain Speaker*, 15 September 1944, 22.

10. Dorothy Ricker, "Should Girl Forgive Boy After Improper Advances?" *Denton* (TX) *Record-Chronicle*, 6 April 1958, 11.

11. "Indict Georgia Youth for Talking on Phone," *New York Amsterdam News*, 16 June 1945, 12B.

12. "Columbia Student Kills Friend and Sinks Body," 13.

13. "Student Is Silent on Slaying Friend," *New York Times*, 18 August 1944, 14.

14. "Student Accused as 'Honor' Slayer," New York *Daily News*, 17 August 1944, 4; "Student Is Silent on Slaying Friend," 14; "Student Is Held Without Bail in Slaying of Man," *New York Herald Tribune*, 18 August 1944, 10.

15. "Columbia Student Kills Friend and Sinks Body," 1.

16. "Student Is Held Without Bail," 10.

17. Ibid.

18. "Police Avoid Questioning in Carr Case," *St. Louis Star and Times*, 21 August 1944, 3.

19. George Chauncey, *Gay New York: Gender, Urban Culture, and the Making of the Gay Male World, 1890–1940* (New York: Basic Books, 1995), 182.

20. Charles Ford and Parker Tyler, *The Young and Evil* (1933; repr., Salem, MA: Ayer Company, 1993).

21. "Hudson Yields Body, Youth Held," *New York Mirror*, 17 August 1944, 5; "Student Accused as 'Honor' Slayer," 4.

22. "Student Accused as 'Honor' Slayer," 4.

23. "Guilty Plea Made by Carr in Slaying," *New York Times*, 16 September 1944, 15; Morgan, *Literary Outlaw*, 108.

24. "Student Is Held in Death of Man Found in River," *New York Herald Tribune*, 17 August 1944, 15.

25. "Witness in Slaying Case Freed," *New York Times*, 31 August 1944, 19.

26. Ellis Amburn, *Subterranean Kerouac: The Hidden Life of Jack Kerouac* (New York: St. Martin's, 1998), 86.

27. Ibid., 54.

28. Ibid., 86.

29. Ibid., 54.

30. Gore Vidal, *Palimpsest* (New York: Random House, 1995), 233.

31. Amburn, *Subterranean Kerouac*, 194.

32. Ibid., 89.

33. Jack Kerouac, *Vanity of Duluoz: An Adventurous Education, 1935–1946* (1968; repr., London: Penguin, 1994), 230.

34. Ibid., 237.

35. Ibid., 250.

36. "Student Slayer Sent to the Reformatory," *New York Times*, 7 October 1944, 15.

37. Ibid.

38. Allen Ginsberg, *The Book of Martyrdom and Artifice: First Journals and Poems, 1937–1952*, ed. Juanita Liebermann-Plimpton and Bill Morgan (New York: Da Capo, 2006), 63.

39. Ibid.

40. William Burroughs and Jack Kerouac, *And the Hippos Were Boiled in Their Tanks* (London: Penguin, 2008), 170.

41. Ibid., 199 (quoted in "Afterword").
42. "A Strange Case," *Columbia Spectator*, 18 August 1944, 2.
43. "2 Cowboys Confess Killing Sailor in Hotel," *Brooklyn Eagle*, 17 October 1940, 12.
44. "2 Cowboys Held Here in Steward's Killing," *New York Times*, 18 October 1940, 23.
45. "Man Found Slain in Cambridge Home; House Ransacked," *Boston Globe*, 18 June 1945, 1.
46. "Jury Acts Monday in Murphy Murder, Four Youths Held," *Boston Globe*, 22 June 1945, 1.
47. Ibid.
48. "Room-mate Is Held in Dancer Slaying," *New York Times*, 7 October 1945, 37.
49. Eric Payne, "How Murder Struck Dance Team," *Philadelphia Inquirer*, 11 November 1945, 123.
50. David Krajicek, "Ballroom Dancer Killed by Roommate in NYC Apartment in 1945; Body Parts Scattered in City Waters," New York *Daily News*, 17 December 2017 (online).
51. "Room-mate Is Held in Dancer Slaying," 37.
52. Ibid.
53. "Salesman Ends Torso Mystery; Slew His Chum," New York *Daily News*, 7 October 1945, 45.
54. "Broadway Beau Held in Murder," Minneapolis *Star Tribune*, 7 October 1945, 7.
55. "Dancer Killing Admitted Roommate," *St. Louis Star and Times*, 8 October 1945, 5.
56. Payne, "How Murder Struck Dance Team," 123.
57. "Slayer Gets 10–20 Years," *New York Times*, 17 May 1946, 13.
58. Krajicek, "Ballroom Dancer Killed by Roommate."
59. Alfred Monahan, "Wakefield Man Slain in N.Y.," *Boston Globe*, 31 March 1947, 1.
60. "Queens Man Held in Homicide Case," *New York Times*, 31 March 1947, 40.
61. "Convict Decapitated Leaving Mess Hall of Texas Prison Farm," *Chicago Daily Tribune*, 14 December 1948, 1; "Texas Convict Decapitated; Sexual Attacks Are Blamed," *Miami* (OK) *Daily News Record*, 14 December 1948, 1; "Murdered Convict Was Homosexual," *Hope* (AR) *Star*, 14 December 1948, 1.
62. "Murdered Convict Was Homosexual," 1.
63. Quoted in George Chauncey Jr., "The Postwar Sex Crime Panic," in *True Stories from the American Past*, ed. William Graebner (New York: McGraw-Hill, 1993), 171.
64. Estelle Freedman, "'Uncontrolled Desire': The Response to the Sexual Psychopath, 1920–1960," *Journal of American History* 74 (June 1987): 96–97.
65. Ibid., 177.
66. Quoted in Chauncey, "The Postwar Sex Crime Panic," 162.
67. Quoted in David Johnson, *The Lavender Scare: The Cold War Persecution of Gays and Lesbians in Federal Government* (Chicago: University of Chicago Press, 2004), 56.
68. "Sex Crimes," *Washington Post*, 27 August 1947, 10.
69. Johnson, *Lavender Scare*, 58.
70. Ibid., 59.
71. "The Hoodlum," *Washington Post*, 11 March 1951, B7; "Crime Stalks Streets," *Philadelphia Inquirer*, 11 March 1951, 194; "The Terror That Stalks Our Streets," *Chicago Tribune*, 25 February 1951, 154.
72. Howard Whitman, *Terror in the Streets* (New York: Bantam, 1951), 311.
73. Ibid., 316.
74. Ibid., 116.

75. Ibid., 117–18.

76. "Beats Man and Then Tosses Him Out of 14th Floor Hotel Window," *Chicago Tribune*, 29 December 1948, 6; "Admits Murder of Longview Teacher," Centralia (WA) *Daily Chronicle*, 18 April 1952, 1.

77. "Officer Tells Confession in Priest Slaying," *Chicago Tribune*, 24 August 1953, B4; "Youth Admits Slaying Priest," Lubbock (TX) *Evening Journal*, 24 August 1953, 1; "Detective Says Hoosier Admits Killing Priest," Louisville (KY) *Courier-Journal*, 24 August 1953, 1; "Escapee Confesses Murder of Priest," *Arizona Republic*, 24 August 1953, 1.

78. "Hester Declares Parts of His Murder Trial Testimony Untrue," Lubbock (TX) *Morning Avalanche*, 3 May 1949, 19.

79. "Police Search for Killer of NYU Student," *New York Amsterdam News*, 14 May 1949, 17.

80. "Ex-GI Admits Sordid 'Act' Led to Death," *New York Amsterdam News*, 18 June 1949, 17.

81. "Thompson Denies He Intended to Kill," *Richmond News Leader*, 4 June 1952.

82. "Thompson, 23, Gets 60 Years in Death Case," *Richmond News Leader*, 5 June 1952.

83. "Indictment Lays Murder to Three Young Soldiers," *Washington Post*, 11 September 1956, 3.

84. "Cruel Blueprint for Death Bared," Baltimore *Afro-American*, 18 August 1956, 1.

85. "N.Y. Police Arrest Man in Fifth Ave. Exec's Murder," *Newsday*, 26 March 1953, 1.

86. "Advances Lead to Murder; Jobless Garment Worker Admits Village Slaying," Baltimore *Afro-American*, 4 April 1953, 3.

87. "Young S.C. Negro Arrested in Slaying of N.Y. Employment Agency Executive," Greenwood (SC) *Index-Journal*, 26 March 1953, 1.

88. Robert Loughran, "'Stop Me!' Hammer Killer Pleads in Threatening to Kill Again in Phone Calls," Harrisburg (IL) *Daily Register*, 7 August 1952, 1.

89. "Hammer Killer Tells Cops, 'I'm Glad He's Dead,'" *Chicago Tribune*, 18 August 1952, 23.

90. "Chicago Hammer Killer Scares Murder Suspect in Jail Cell," *Tucson Daily Citizen*, 18 August 1952, 6.

91. Whitman, *Terror in the Streets*, 123.

92. Ibid.

93. Ibid.

94. Ben Karpman, "Mediate Psychotherapy and the Acute Homosexual Panic (Kempf's Disease)," *Journal of Nervous and Mental Disease* 98, no. 493 (1943): 98.

95. "Fifty Years of Psychiatric Nomenclature: Reflections on the 1943 War Department Technical Bulletin, Medical 203," *Journal of Clinical Psychology* 65, no. 7 (2000): 937.

96. William C. Menninger, M.D., *Psychiatry in a Troubled World: Yesterday's War and Today's Challenge* (New York: Macmillan, 1948), xiii.

97. Gary David Comstock, "Dismantling the Homosexual Panic Defense," *Law and Sexuality Review* 2, no. 81 (1992): 83.

98. American Psychiatric Association, *Mental Disorders, Diagnostic and Statistical Manual* (Washington, D.C.: American Psychiatric Association Mental Hospital Service, 1952), 121.

99. Burton Glick, "Homosexual Panic: Clinical and Theoretical Considerations," *Journal of Nervous and Mental Disease* 129, no. 20 (1959): 20.

100. Ibid., 25.

101. Comstock, "Dismantling the Homosexual Panic Defense," 83.

102. Cynthia Lee, *Murder and Reasonable Man: Passion and Fear in the Criminal Courtroom* (New York: New York University Press, 2007), 72.

103. Richard Brooks, *The Brick Foxhole* (New York: Harper and Row, 1945), 87.

104. Ibid., 88.

105. Ibid., 89.

106. Ibid., 165.

107. Ibid., 163.

108. James Baldwin, "Preservation of Innocence," *Zero* 1, no. 2 (1949): 21.

Chapter 5. The Homosexual Next Door

1. "Death Leap Blamed on Ex-Husband," *Washington Post*, 2 August 1948, 1.

2. "Police Think They Know Who Killed Hotel Victim," *Washington Post*, 9 December 1948, 1.

3. Ibid.

4. "Bartender Held, Ring Recovered in Hotel Murder," *Washington Evening Star*, 9 December 1948, 1.

5. "GI Student Held for Grand Jury in Slaying of Man Hotel Guest," *Washington Post*, 10 December 1948, 1.

6. "Grand Jury Indicts Perez for Murder," *Washington Post*, 4 January 1949, B1.

7. "Admits Slaying in Washington," *Green Bay* (WI) *Press-Gazette*, 9 December 1948, 27; "Milwaukee School Dean Held on Morals Charge," *Green Bay Press-Gazette*, 9 December 1948, 27; "Bartender Who Hoped to Be a Cop Kills Man," *Sheboygan* (WI) *Press*, 9 December 1948, 1; "Suspect Admits Killing Painter in Hotel Ring Theft," *Belvidere* (IL) *Daily Republican*, 9 December 1948, 1.

8. "Perez Gets 15-Yr. Term for Murder in Hotel," *Washington Post*, 14 May 1949, B1.

9. "Perez Pleads Guilty to Second Degree Murder," *Green Bay Press-Gazette*, 14 April 1949, 10.

10. "Bartender Facing 15 Years to Life in Ambassador Hotel," *Washington Post*, 14 April 1949, B1.

11. James H. Jones, *Alfred Kinsey: A Public/Private Life* (New York: W. W. Norton, 1997), 574.

12. Ibid.

13. Jeffrey Escoffier, *American Homo: Community and Perversity* (Berkeley: University of California Press, 1998), 83.

14. Charles Kaiser, *The Gay Metropolis: 1940–1996* (New York: Houghton Mifflin, 1997), 54–56.

15. Jennifer Terry, *An American Obsession: Science, Medicine, and Homosexuality in Modern Society* (Chicago: University of Chicago Press, 1999), 323.

16. Quoted in John D'Emilio, *Sexual Politics, Sexual Communities: The Making of a Homosexual Minority in the United States, 1940–1970* (Chicago: University of Chicago Press, 1983), 36.

17. David Allyn, "Private Acts/Public Policy: Alfred Kinsey, the American Law Institute and the Privatization of American Sexual Morality," *Journal of American Studies* 30, no. 3 (1996): 406.

18. Kaiser, *The Gay Metropolis*, 60.

19. Gore Vidal, *The City and the Pillar* (New York: E. P. Dutton, 1948), 303–7.

20. Kaiser, *The Gay Metropolis*, 61.

21. Gore Vidal, "Preface," *The City and the Pillar and Seven Other Stories* (New York: Random House, 1995), xvii.
22. "Romanski, Vidal, Rosmond," *New York Times*, 11 January 1948, BR22; "Taboos Cast Aside in Gore Vidal's Novel," *Chicago Tribune*, 25 January 1948, F8; "Some of the Recent Fiction," *Cincinnati Enquirer*, 17 January 1948, 5; "Intermediate Sex," *Hartford Courant*, 1 February 1948, SM14; "*The City and the Pillar* by Gore Vidal," *Washington Post*, 11 January 1948, B7.
23. "Navy Lieutenant Strangled Here," *New York Times*, 26 February 1948, 14.
24. Ibid.
25. "'Torture Knot' Takes Life of Former Iowan," *Iowa City Press-Citizen*, 26 February 1948, 1.
26. "Hunt Murderer of Minnesotan," Huron (SD) *Huronite and the Daily Plainsman*, 27 February 1948, 2.
27. "Witness Saw Caller Enter Room, Wore Sailor's Denims," *Washington Post*, 27 February 1948, 1.
28. "Navy's Man's Death Laid to 2 Thugs," *New York Times*, 27 February 1948, 44.
29. "N.Y. Police Baffled on Haeberle Slaying," *Washington Post*, 10 March 1948, B1.
30. "Torture Robbery Linked to Slaying," *New York Times*, 26 February 1948, 14.
31. "Tied with Bedsheet, State Employe [sic] Slain," *New York Times*, 6 September 1948, 26.
32. "Murder Case Against GI Heard," *New York Times*, 10 September 1948, 48.
33. "Youth Confesses Slaying Executive in Waldorf Suite," *New York Times*, 6 November 1948, 1.
34. Ibid., 1, 7.
35. Allen Bérubé, *Coming Out Under Fire: The History of Gay Men and Women in World War Two* (New York: Free Press, 1990), 115.
36. George Chauncey, *Gay New York: Gender, Urban Culture, and the Making of the Gay Male World, 1890–1940* (New York: Basic Books, 1994), 350.
37. "Waldorf's Suspect's Ma Here to Help Him," New York *Daily News*, 8 November 1948, 3.
38. "Youth Confesses Slaying Executive in Waldorf Suite," 1.
39. "Hunt for Ex of Waldorf Suspect Wed When 15," New York *Daily News*, 12 November 1948, 4.
40. "Michigan Youth Denies Waldorf Murder Charge," *Detroit Free Press*, 7 November 1948, 1.
41. Ibid. "Hunt for Ex of Waldorf Suspect Wed When 15," 4; "Waldorf's Suspect's Ma Here to Help Him," 3; "Youth Denies Guilt in Waldorf Death," *New York Times*, 7 November 1948, 55.
42. "Waldorf's Suspect's Ma Here to Help Him," 3; "Youth Denies Guilt in Waldorf Death," 55.
43. "Murder Charged to Ralph Barrows," Montreal *Gazette*, 17 September 1949, 3; "Youth Denies Guilt in Waldorf Death," 55.
44. "Youth on Trial Today in Murder at Waldorf," New York *Daily News*, 6 January 1950, 28; "Youth Goes to Trial in N.Y. Slaying," *Detroit Free Press*, 7 January 1950, 3.
45. "'Hopeless,' Waldorf Slayer Gets 20 Years," New York *Daily News*, 2 March 1950, 8.
46. Jess Stearn, *The Sixth Man* (New York: Doubleday, 1961), 14.
47. Patricia Highsmith, *The Talented Mr. Ripley* (1955; repr., New York: Vintage, 1992), 34; "Corner's Verdict," *Washington Post*, 18 December 1955, E7; "A Report on Criminals at Large," *New York Times*, 25 December 1955, BR11.
48. Bérubé, *Coming Out Under Fire*, 263.

49. Ibid., 262.

50. "Police Sound Alert for Back Bay Killer," *Portsmouth* (NH) *Herald*, 10 December 1953, 10.

51. "Sailor Admits Bludgeoning Boland to Death," *Boston Globe*, 13 December 1953, C1; "Michigan Sailor Indicted by Jury," *Lansing* (MI) *State Journal*, 15 December 1953, 2.

52. "Jury Indicts Hoover in Mahoney Murder," Shreveport *Times*, 18 March 1949, 1.

53. "Beaten, Garroted Body Discovered," *Monroe* (LA) *News-Star*, 22 February 1949, 1.

54. "Jury Indicts Hoover in Mahoney Murder," 1.

55. "Millionaire Dined with New Suspect," *Kingsport* (TN) *News*, 1 March 1949, 1.

56. "Hoover Suffers Attack During Orleans Trial," Shreveport *Times*, 26 October 1952, 1.

57. Ibid.

58. Ibid.

59. "Ex-'Czar' of Soccer is Fatally Beaten," *New York Times*, 22 September 1953, 38.

60. "Hunt Friend in Slaying of Attorney; Two Men Shared Apartment Until Two Weeks Ago," *Philadelphia Inquirer*, 22 September 1953, 1.

61. "Seek Convict in Murder of Schroeder," *Philadelphia Inquirer*, 10 October 1953, 1.

62. Marc Stein, *City of Sisterly and Brotherly Loves: Lesbian and Gay Philadelphia, 1945–1972* (Chicago: University of Chicago Press, 2000), 119.

63. "Sailor Accused in Slaying of Noted Soccer Official in '53," n.d., in Van Vechten Scrapbooks, Carl Van Vechten Collection, box 3, vol. 9, Beinecke Rare Books and Manuscripts Library, Yale University, New Haven, CT.

64. "Prosecution Demands Wetling Be Sentenced to Death for Murder," *Philadelphia Inquirer*, 24 September 1957, 31; "State Rest Case at Wetling Trial in 1953 Slaying," *Philadelphia Inquirer*, 25 September 1957, 43; "Ex-Sailor Acquitted in Schroeder Slaying," *Philadelphia Inquirer*, 26 September 1957, 27.

65. "Detective School Owner Slays Former Partner," *Los Angeles Times*, 7 October 1958, 5.

66. "Former Sailor Freed in W. Phila. Slaying Shot, Killed in West," *Philadelphia Inquirer*, 17 October 1958, 20.

67. "Man's Body Is Found in Locked Apartment," *Washington Post*, 28 November 1956, A3.

68. Untitled article, *Washington Post*, 30 November 1956, A3.

69. Alfred E. Lewis, "Marine Says He Strangled Host," *Washington Post*, 1 December 1956, A3.

70. Jerry Landaner, "Marine Held for Trial at Inquest," *Washington Post*, 15 December 1956, A3.

71. "Marine Says He Strangled Nashuan in His Apartment," *Nashua* (NH) *Telegraph*, 1 December 1956, 1.

72. "'I Grabbed Him,' Marine Testifies," *Washington Post*, 8 May 1957, A14.

73. "Murder Suspect Weeps over Story of Childhood," *Washington Post*, 2 May 1957, A3.

74. *Jim B. Edmonds v. United States of America*, Open Jurist, openjurist.org/273/f2d/108/edmonds-v-united-states (accessed 15 May 2016).

75. Ibid.

76. "Marine Edmonds Guilty of Strangling Ex-Nashua Student," *Boston Globe*, 27 November 1958, 37.

77. John Howard, *Men Like That: A Southern Queer History* (Chicago: University of Chicago Press, 1999), 129.

78. "Hotel Slayers Still Hunted," Jackson (MS) *Clarion-Ledger*, 26 July 1955, 1.

79. "Silver Creek Man Robbed, Murdered in Jackson, Miss.," Canandaigua (NY) *Daily Messenger*, 26 July 1955, 8.
80. Howard, *Men Like That*, 129.
81. "Koenig Faces Murder Trial," Jackson *Clarion-Ledger*, 11 December 1955, 11.
82. Howard, *Men Like That*, 139.
83. Ed Goins, "Witnesses Deny Planning to Rob John R. Murrett," Jackson *Clarion-Ledger*, 1 December 1955, 1.
84. Ed Goins, "Says Murrett Made Improper Advances," Jackson *Clarion-Ledger*, 30 November 1955, 1.
85. Howard, *Men Like That*, 142.
86. "Koenig Sentenced to Twenty Years," Jackson *Clarion-Ledger*, 13 December 1955, 1.
87. "National Recognition for Local Police Department," Jackson *Clarion-Ledger*, 9 November 1955, 14.
88. Howard, *Men Like That*, 141.
89. Quoted in Dora Apel, *The Imagery of Lynching: Black Men, White Women, and the Mob* (New Brunswick, NJ: Rutgers University Press, 2004), 179.
90. Howard, *Men Like That*, 140.

Chapter 6. Stories of Prejudice and Suffering

1. "EAL Man Is Slain on 'Lovers' Lane,'" *Miami Daily News*, 3 August 1954, 1.
2. Ibid., 2; "Man Hunted in Slaying of Air Steward," *Washington Post*, 5 August 1954, 3.
3. "Ex-Louisvillian, Airline Steward, Found Slain on Outskirts of Miami," Louisville (KY) *Courier-Journal*, 4 August 1954, 15.
4. "Miami Police Press Hunt for Steward's Killer," *Tampa Times*, 4 August 1954, 7, quoted in Fred Fejes, "Murder, Perversion, and Moral Panic: The 1954 Media Campaign Against Miami's Homosexuals and the Discourse of Civic Betterment," *Journal of the History of Sexuality* 9, no. 3 (2000): 328.
5. "Youth, 19, Confesses Killing Air Steward," *Miami Daily News*, 8 August 1954, 1.
6. "Jury Deliberates Murder Charge in Simpson Slaying," *Miami Daily News*, 7 November 1954, 6.
7. "Youth, 19, Confesses Killing Air Steward," *Miami Daily News*, 8 August 1954, 1.
8. Quoted in Julio Capó Jr., *Welcome to Fairyland: Queer Miami Before 1940* (Chapel Hill: University of North Carolina Press, 2017), 1.
9. Ibid., 279.
10. Quoted in Fejes, "Murder, Perversion, and Moral Panic," 329.
11. "Why Boys Killed Steward Pondered by Schoolmate," *Miami Daily News*, 9 August 1954, 9.
12. "Jury Deliberates Murder Charges in Simpson Slaying," *Miami Daily News*, 7 November 1954, 6.
13. "Young Wife Courageous at Mate's Death Trial," *Miami Daily News*, 5 November 1954, 8.
14. "2 in Simpson Case Could Get 20 Years," *Miami Daily News*, 8 November 1954, 6; "Killers of Steward Get 20-Year Terms," *Miami Daily News*, 10 November 1954, 13.
15. "Pervert Colony Uncovered in Simpson Slaying Probe," *Miami Daily News*, 9 August 1954, 9.
16. Quoted in Fejes, "Murder, Perversion, and Moral Panic," 331.

17. "Let's Do Something About It," *Miami Daily News*, 10 August 1954, 14.

18. Quoted in Fejes, "Murder, Perversion, and Moral Panic," 333.

19. "Six Suspected Perverts Held in Beach Raid," *Miami Daily News*, 13 August 1954, 6; "Cops to Hunt Park Deviants," *Miami Daily News*, 3 September 1954, 2.

20. Quoted in Fejes, "Murder, Perversion, and Moral Panic," 326.

21. Ibid., 321.

22. Ibid., 327.

23. Jack Roberts, "'Coddling' of Perverts Endangers Evans' Post," *Miami Daily News*, 26 August 1954, 7.

24. Jack Roberts, "A Disease 'Worse Than Alcohol,'" *Miami Daily News*, 13 August 1954, 9.

25. Jack Roberts, "How L.A. Handles Its 150,000 Perverts," *Miami Daily News*, 15 August 1954, 1; Jack Roberts, "Great Civilizations Plagued by Deviants," *Miami Daily News*, 16 August 1954, 10.

26. Robert Sylvester, "Dream Street," New York *Daily News*, 11 October 1955, 81.

27. Jess Stearn, *The Sixth Man* (New York: Doubleday, 1961), 22.

28. Ibid., 22.

29. Ibid., 153.

30. "Pair Sought for Probe in Slaying," *Beatrice* (NE) *Daily Sun*, 15 December 1957, 10; "Iowan Stabbed to Death in Washington; Hunt Pair," *Quad-City Times* (Davenport, IA), 15 December 1957, 3.

31. Alfred Lewis and Albon Haily, "Youths Lay Slaying to Money Row," *Washington Post*, 4 January 1958, A1.

32. Ibid.

33. David K. Johnson, *The Lavender Scare: The Cold War Persecution of Gays and Lesbians in the Federal Government* (Chicago: University of Chicago Press, 2004), 163.

34. Ibid.

35. "Officers Tell of Trying to Stop Teboe Stabbing," *Washington Post*, 23 April 1958, B9.

36. Connie Foeley, "Inquest Holds 2 in Teboe Death," *Washington Post*, 8 January 1958, B1.

37. Ibid.

38. "Killing Suspect Accuses Victim," *Washington Post*, 25 April 1958, B8.

39. "Youths Get 5–30 Years for Slaying," *Washington Post*, 30 May 1958, B16.

40. Earl O. Coon, "Homosexuality in the News," *Archives of Criminal Psychodynamics* 2 (1957): 844.

41. "Soldier Shot in Park; Mum About Attack," *Washington Post*, 9 April 1956, 3.

42. Coon, "Homosexuality in the News," 856.

43. Ibid., 855.

44. Ibid., 860.

45. Ibid., 862.

46. Martin Cutler, "Homosexual Minority," *Saturday Review of Literature*, 4 June 1949, 5; Allen Bérubé, *Coming Out Under Fire: The History of Gay Men and Women in World War Two* (New York: Free Press, 1990), 251.

47. Allan Morrison, "Twilight for Greenwich Village," *Negro Digest*, January 1949, 28; Michael de Forrest, *The Gay Year* (New York: Woodford Press, 1949), 112.

48. Donald Webster Cory, *The Homosexual in America: A Subjective Approach* (New York: Greenberg, 1951), 4, 228.

49. Ibid., 116.

50. "Five Quizzed in Echo Park Gang Holdups," *Los Angeles Times*, 29 January 1952, 2.

51. Daniel Hurewitz, *Bohemian Los Angeles: And the Making of Modern Politics* (Los Angeles: University of California Press, 2006), 52.

52. Ibid., 258–60.

53. Quoted in Fejes, "Murder, Perversion, and Moral Panic," 322.

54. John D'Emilio, *Sexual Politics, Sexual Communities: The Making of a Homosexual Minority in the United States, 1940–1970* (Chicago: University of Chicago Press, 1983), 73.

55. Roberts, "Great Civilizations Plagued by Deviants," 10.

56. Dal McIntire, "Miami Hurricane," *One*, December 1958, 7.

57. Quoted in Fejes, "Murder, Perversion, and Moral Panic," 323.

58. Dal McIntire, "Fourth Estate," *One*, 1 January 1956, 15.

59. Dal McIntire, "Tangents: News and Views," *One*, 1 March 1959, 13.

60. "Jury Acquits 3 Students Tried in Slaying of Guide," New Orleans *Times-Picayune*, 14 January 1959, 1.

61. "Views of the Readers," New Orleans *Times-Picayune*, 30 November 1958, 6, quoted in Clayton Delery, *Out for Queer Blood: The Murder of Fernando Rios and the Failure of New Orleans Justice* (Jefferson, NC: Exposit, 2017), 79–80.

62. Dal McIntire, "Tangents," *One*, March 1959, 13–15.

63. Dal McIntire, "Tangents," *One*, February 1959, 12.

64. Quoted in Christine Stansell, *American Moderns: Bohemian New York and the Creation of the New Century* (New York: Metropolitan/Henry Holt, 2000), 103.

65. Kristen MacLeod, "The 'Librarian's Dream-Prince': Carl Van Vechten and America's Modernist Cultural Archives Industry," *Libraries and the Cultural Record* 46, no. 4 (2011): 361.

66. Edward White, *The Tastemaker: Carl Van Vechten and the Birth of Modern America* (New York: Farrar, Straus and Giroux, 2014), 9.

67. Jonathan Weinberg, "'Boy Crazy': Carl Van Vechten's Queer Collection," *Yale Journal of Criticism* 7, no. 2 (1994): 44.

68. "Suspect Is Denied Bail in Broken-Bottle Killing," n.d., in Van Vechten Scrapbooks, Carl Van Vechten Collection, box 3, vol. 9, Beinecke Rare Books and Manuscripts Library, Yale University, New Haven, CT.

69. "Man Found Hanged in Girl's Lingerie, Slain Then Suspended from Door Hook in Des Moines," n.d., in Van Vechten Scrapbooks, box 3, vol. 10.

70. Weinberg, "'Boy Crazy,'" 31.

71. "Find TV Actor Slain in His Blazing Home," *Brooklyn Eagle*, 10 October 1952, 1.

72. White, *The Tastemaker*, 294.

Conclusion

1. Donn Gaynor, "Hidden Movie Camera Used by Police to Trap Sexual Deviants at Park Hangout; 17 Arrests Climax Probe," *Mansfield* (OH) *News Journal*, 22 August 1962; republished in William E. Jones, *Tearoom* (Los Angeles: Second Cannons Publications,

2008), 4. Jones produced and published a limited-edition pamphlet that compiled historical documents about the trial, the arrests, and the use of film in surveillance work in the
1960s.

2. Jones, *Tearoom*, 4.

3. Ibid., 40.

4. Quoted in Dietmar Schwärzler, "More Than One Way to Watch a Movie!" in *Smell It!*
(Vienna: Kunsthalle Exnergasse, 2009), 74–79 (also available on williamejones.com).

5. Emily Waters and Sue Yacka-Bible, "A Crisis of Hate: A Report on Lesbian, Gay, Bisexual,
Transgender, and Queer Hate Violence Homicides in 2017," National Coalition of Anti-
Violence Programs, January 2018, available at avp.org/wp-content/uploads/2018/01/a-crisis
-of-hate-january-release.pdf.

6. Martin Duberman, *Stonewall* (New York: Plume, 1994), 170.

7. Jim Downs, *Stand by Me: The Forgotten History of Gay Liberation* (New York: Basic Books,
2016), 117.

8. "Any Old Job for Homos?" New York *Daily News*, 5 April 1972, 30.

9. Calvin Trillin, "A Few Observations on the Zapping of the Inner Circle," *New Yorker*, 15
July 1972, 69; Michael Kramer, "Fireman's Brawl," *New York*, 22 May 1972, 6; William
Proctor and Paul Meskil, "Maye Hit with a Rap in Gay Tiff," New York *Daily News*, 23
May 1972, 120.

10. Daniel Wickberg, "Homophobia: On the Cultural History of an Idea," *Critical Inquiry* 27
(2000): 47; Herb Kutchins and Stuart Kirk, *Making Us Crazy: DSM—The Psychiatric Bible
and the Creation of Mental Disorders* (New York: Free Press, 1997), 67.

11. Downs, *Stand by Me*, 30.

12. Robert W. Fieseler, *Tinderbox: The Untold Story of the Up Stairs Lounge Fire and the Rise of
Gay Liberation* (New York: Liveright/W. W. Norton, 2018), xxix.

13. Gary David Comstock, *Violence Against Lesbians and Gay Men* (New York: Columbia University Press, 1991), 26.

14. Larry Kramer, "Slain Gay's Mom Tells of Good Life," *San Francisco Examiner*, 27 June
1977, 1.

15. "Gay Supporters Stage Marches Across U.S.," *Tampa Tribune*, 27 June 1977, 41.

16. Randy Shilts, *The Mayor of Castro Street: The Life and Times of Harvey Milk* (New York:
St. Martins/Griffin, 1988), 98.

17. Valerie Jennes and Kendal Broad, *Hate Crimes: New Social Movements and the Politics of
Violence* (New York: Aldine De Gruyter, 1997), 4.

18. Joann Wypijewski, "A Boy's Life: For Matthew Shepard's Killer, What Does It Take to Pass
as a Man?" *Harper's*, September 1999; Tom Dart, "After Decades of 'Gay Panic Defense' in
Court, U.S. States Slowly Begin to Ban Tactic," *The Guardian*, 12 May 2018, available at
www.theguardian.com/us-news/2018/may/12/gay-panic-defence-tactic-ban-court.

Index

© Greg Salvatori

JAMES POLCHIN, PhD, has taught at the Princeton Writing Program, the Parsons School of Design, the New School for Public Engagement, and the Creative Nonfiction Foundation. A clinical professor at New York University, he lives in New York City with his husband, the photographer Greg Salvatori. *Indecent Advances* is his first book. You can follow him at @jamespolchin.

Printed in the United States
by Baker & Taylor Publisher Services